DATE DUE

THE COMPLETE
CANADIAN
ELDERCARE
GUIDE

THE COMPLETE CANADIAN ELDERCARE GUIDE

Expert Solutions to Help You Make the Best Decisions for Your Loved Ones

C AROLINE T APP - M C D OUGALL

John Wiley & Sons, Canada, Ltd.

John Wiley & Sons Canada Ltd
6045 Freemont Boulevard
Mississauga, Ontario
L5R 4J3

National Library of Canada Cataloguing in Publication

Tapp-McDougall, Caroline, 1956–
    The complete Canadian eldercare guide : expert solutions
to help you make the best decisions for your loved ones / Caroline
Tapp-McDougall.

Includes index.
ISBN 0-470-83449-8

    1. Aging parents—Care—Canada. 2. Aged—Services for—Canada.
3. Caregivers—Canada. I. Title.

HV1475.A3T35 2004   362.6'0971   C2004-901561-3

Production Credits
Cover & interior text design: Interrobang Graphic Design Inc.
Cover photo: Masterfile Corporation
Printer: Tri-Graphic Printing Ltd.

Printed in Canada
10 9 8 7 6 5 4 3 2 1

Contents

WARNING—
Faint of Heart Read No Further

Regardless of one's reason for becoming a caregiver, the respon-sibility entails a significant commitment that can be intense and time consuming. Meeting care demands often necessitates life adjustments and may affect the time a caregiver can spend with family and friends, paid employment and household responsibilities.

Source: "Canada's Caregivers" (a Statistics Canada study— www.hc-sc.gc.ca/seniors-aines/pubs/unsorted/survey.htm)

Within hours of my mother's stroke, I became the "older daughter," making decisions, evaluating rehabilitation choices, and rushing between hospital and long-term-care facilities despite my hopeless inexperience. As I look back, that was the simple part. Daily life après stroke was the challenge. Like it or not, over the next few months, my mother's quality of life and medical care became primarily my responsibility. Mom's life changed, and so, unfortunately, had mine, my brother's, and my family's.

The Family Stretch

Caring was not something I could opt out of. It wasn't a matter of choice. Through it all, my family had to compromise, stretch, and flex. Things at home became disorganized, Mom's triumphs were often not at all what we'd imagined, and the financial impact and time away from work were significant.

Our next year consisted of stroke rehab treatments and equip-ment issues, crisis planning, and the final eye-opening realization that Mom would never speak, walk, or use her entire right side again. Her house and car became expensive albatrosses, the hospi-tal and Tim Hortons our second home. Adult diapers, nursing routines, the comfort of wheelchair seating cushions, and "pressure relief" became dinner-table talk.

Live and Learn

Today, I'm a veteran coper. It's a squeeze of time and effort. We've made the two-hour return trip to Mom's home town more times than I'm willing to keep track of—rain, snow, or shine. Summer evenings on the nursing-home lawn and awkward trips to the toilet in Wal-Mart are routine. I can even chuckle a bit at a few of the funny incidents along the way. Gradually, I've been able to reduce my loss of income and the extra expenses, and let go of the turmoil of daily care. My brother and I have learned to manage the drill from afar and lose the daily guilt of not being there. And we're blessed to have her good friend Don very involved in her care and leisure activities.

The lessons I've learned along the way from others have given me strength. When I'm there, Mom and I have a special routine. We laugh. We try to communicate without words. We sing. I visit as often as I can and call her whenever I remember (usually at dinner time). We go out when I feel strong enough to push and lift. This life is not at all what any of us planned. But that's how it is and we're making it work.

We're in This Together

We family caregivers are a unique and growing bunch. Some days it feels like we belong to a special club, where the membership criterion is an aging parent. We glance knowingly at each other beside walkers and wheelchairs like we used to behind strollers. We help with our parents' hats, mitts, and coats, we worry about safety, and we talk to each other about how to care.

To all of us, I dedicate this book. Join me in learning to come to terms with your parents' aging and to balance your life with theirs. Make your health a priority so you can stay the course. Be strong enough to plan and research well. Shed the adult-child attitude, be ready to take advice, and ask for help and say no when it's too much. Forget the obligation and lose the guilt. This is a labour of love.

Find pleasure and joy in small things. Look for energy in your parents' occasional smiles and signs of gratitude. Keep your chin up and take pride in preparing for and doing the best job you can.

—*Caroline*

Introduction

Eldercare and its inherent superhero responsibilities are the new facts of life for aging Canadians and the invincible baby boomers. Today, as adult sons and daughters with high-maintenance careers, as spouses with ailing partners or relatives, we find ourselves juggling work, life, and care responsibility. We are, as the saying goes, "sandwiched" between the care needs of others and our still-dependent children.

Research shows that families are, for the most part, unprepared for the eldercare challenges that lie ahead. Many move directly into "care in crisis" mode, make plans on the fly, and regret not making decisions about aging issues in advance.

Workplace health, wellness, and productivity issues are huge. Today, employers and governments identify productivity, absenteeism, presenteeism, and retention as key factors for their aging work forces with the statistics pointing to eldercare as one of the biggest hurdles to overcome.

Of note:

- More than 3.5 million Canadians are currently over the age of 65. By the year 2020, that number will more than double.[1]

- For 70% of Canadians age 30 to 60, caregiving for aging parents is now a reality with eldercare being shared across families.[2]

- More than 70% of informal caregivers are women, most often wives (24%) or adult daughters (29%).[3]

---

[1] Roy Romanow, *Building on Values: The Future of Health Care in Canada*, November 2002.

[2] Romanow, *Building on Values*.

[3] Romanow, *Building on Values*.

- Spouse caregivers are less likely to have backup support than others.[4]

- Half of the informal caregivers in Canada are more than 60 years old and 36% are older than 70.[5]

Making Tough Decisions

Are you at work or at home? Whether it's "roll up your sleeves" daily care or long-distance hands-off management, each family's eldercare situation is as diverse as the individuals involved. The common factor, though, is that for most of us daily life with our parents gets hard to manage. Tough choices must be made, finances must be brought out of the closet, and guilt and emotions will hit an all-time high.

Wimps beware…this is no time to bury your head. Mother doesn't always know best—especially now! To dig yourself out you need to take charge, listen up, and get the help that's worth its weight in gold. But look before you leap. This book will help you do that. It contains simple, best-practice gems from health professionals and family caregivers "in the know." You'll be able to revive yourself with tips to preserve work-life balance and find some really time-sensitive alternatives that'll put you back in the driver's seat. At your fingertips is useful information that will make eldercare less stressful and, if you're lucky, more rewarding. Along the way, you may even learn how to cope with your "hard to handle" brother, forgetful father, or critical sister-in-law.

Caregiver Hint: Heads up! If you read nothing else, check out these caregiving sanity savers that are sure to help you through the week. They're even worth posting on the fridge for daily reminders.

Ten Eldercare Survival Tips

Improving your caregiving stamina will take more than a little work on your abs. Being "fit to care" requires a healthy mind and body and a good old-fashioned dose of a "can-do" attitude. Make

---

[4] Roy Romanow, *Building on Values*.

[5] Romanow, *Building on Values*.

it easier on yourself. Think positive and make things happen...at your pace. Be upfront, be creative, and have reasonable expectations for yourself. Gain control of your caregiving experience. Stay fresh, eat well, and get physically active.

By building your physical and emotional strength, you'll be strong and clearheaded enough to battle negative thoughts and take charge of potentially overwhelming caregiving situations.

1. **Play the hand you're dealt.** The circumstances you find yourself in may not be exactly what you hoped for. Accept the fact that your parent needs you and decide whether you intend to be there for him or her. Don't carry around the emotional baggage with thoughts like "I wish it wasn't like this!" or "How did I get stuck in this?" Come to terms with your situation, be clear regarding your objectives, and set out to make the best of it.

2. **Think positive.** Never underestimate the power of a positive outlook. From it will come the determination and strength to triumph over daily challenges. If you weren't born with it, taking this rosy view of life takes practice. Listen to yourself to catch your negative comments. Even in an awful situation, try to take a "glass half full" rather than the "glass half empty" approach, especially with those around you. Things won't seem so desperate, and your community of family and friends will rally to give you the help you need when you look on the brighter side. A positive attitude pays dividends—everywhere.

3. **Make things happen.** Despite what you may sometimes think, you are not totally at the mercy of your circumstances. Refuse to let your present situation control you or wreak havoc with the rest of your life. You can initiate changes for the better. You can make things happen to take the pressure off. Seek solutions, logically and realistically.

4. **Set goals.** Be realistic and clear about what needs to be done and what you can manage. Setting goals in conjunction with your parents and health professionals is a great way to start. Goal setting facilitates clear communication and helps prioritize limited time and resources.

5. **Prioritize.** You can't be all things to all people. Work and life must be kept in balance. Decide what's important to you and how much time you're prepared to spend on each area of your life (in both the short and long term). Tradeoffs are part of the picture. Keep in mind that the more time you spend with Mom, the less time you'll have to spend with your kids or at work—don't be surprised if you don't get that promotion at work. If you've thought it through and have made those choices, you won't be surprised or disappointed with the outcomes. Recognize and choose whether your role is to achieve short-term stability in your parents' life or to accept a new longer-term and more significant caregiving role.

6. **Ask for help.** This is a team effort—recognize and respect other members of your home-care or caregiving team. Don't try to do it all yourself. Conversely, keep your eye on other family members (spouse, brother, sister) who might be burning out themselves. Sharing care responsibilities reduces the load on each caregiver and makes it easier. Even if it's sharing the visiting times at the nursing home, be creative and involve others whenever possible.

My Story: Don't Try to Go It Alone

After feeling guilty for months that Mom was alone on Saturday nights at the nursing home, I had a pleasant surprise when I dropped in one evening. Some of Mom's neighbourhood friends, older newlyweds for whom my mother had been matchmaker, were coming in to see her most weekends. No one was more thankful than I to see them happily visiting and sharing a few laughs. My lesson: Don't try to go it alone. Recognize that your parents' friends are often more than willing to chip in and visit.

---

7. **Overcome your fear.** Sudden or sustained responsibilities can be draining. New demands often require ramping up with new skills. There'll be lots of questions, and not so many clear answers. While it's only natural to feel trepidation, try not to get overwhelmed. It's like having a new baby. Some things sort

of come naturally—think about it, changing an adult diaper is not a new experience, it's just a larger effort. Be organized. Keep your head clear, even if it involves going for a walk on your own to regroup. Take it one step at a time. Recognize and respect your parents' right to live at risk.

8. **Be good to yourself.** Uncertainty or self-doubt and the stress of caring for someone else takes its toll. You're over the top when you start to make mistakes, yell at people, and feel that you have no time to yourself. Avoid this vicious circle. Treat yourself well (including taking respite, fitness, and wellness breaks), and you will have the inner strength to better care for others.

9. **Watch what you eat and respect your body.** Ensuring your body is up to the task begins with what you eat. Foods that you choose will dramatically affect your energy levels as well as prevent illness and disease. Remember:

   - Eat three balanced meals a day.
   - Eat five servings of fruits and vegetables a day.
   - Drink 8 to 10 glasses of water a day.
   - Sneak exercise into your busy schedule.

   A hint: If you can't fit in a full exercise workout, find ways to keep in shape as you go. Get an at-home exercise video and work with your parent to stay limber. Walk across the parking lot to the store rather than parking in the front row. Take the stairs.

   Keep your weight in check; it takes a lot of energy to move excess pounds around. It also makes it harder to handle the physical parts of caregiving. Be sensible with alcohol. If you find yourself using it as a relaxer or to avoid facing reality, chat with your doctor. As for smoking or breathing second-hand smoke, don't!

10. **Live for today.** Yesterday's gone and tomorrow may never come. Learn to live in the present. Take a calm look at what you can do to make life better for yourself, your family, and the person you are caring for, today. Don't zap your energy fretting about your parents' loss of strength, independence, or vitality. Put your energy into finding ways to enjoy today.

Reality Check

This quick questionnaire will help you determine the type of care and support your elderly parent may need. Answer "yes" or "no" to the following questions to get a sense of where you and your parents stand.

1. Does your parent suffer from moments of memory loss which at times jeopardizes his or her safety?

   ❏ YES

   ❏ NO

2. Is your loved one less able to maintain the home (do you notice the lack of cleanliness is becoming worse)?

   ❏ YES

   ❏ NO

3. Is your parent often alone?

   ❏ YES

   ❏ NO

4. Is your parent affected by a worsening illness or disability that's making it more difficult to manage independently?

   ❏ YES

   ❏ NO

5. Is your parent facing a life-threatening illness yet plans to live for the remaining days of his or her life at home?

   ❏ YES

   ❏ NO

6. Do you, as a caregiver, find yourself exhausted and feeling like you have no time to yourself?

   ❏ YES

   ❏ NO

If you answered "yes" to one or more questions from numbers 1 to 4, you may require Adult/Elder Care services.

If you answered "yes" to question number 5, Palliative Care programs can help.

If you answered "yes" to question number 6, Respite or Caregiver/ Family Care will be helpful.

Read on to learn more about meeting your parents' needs while maintaining your work-life balance.

CHAPTER 1

Coming to Terms with Our Parents' Aging

Accepting the fact that our parents are getting older and experiencing deteriorating health is often a difficult thing to do. When a particular event, such as a fall, occurs, it can be a rude awakening. As kids we thought they would live forever and as adults we're used to Mom and Dad being such an active part of our lives. Roles reverse and suddenly they seem more vulnerable and we're in charge.

As Mom and Dad grow older, the normal parent-child relationship begins to flip. Our parents, whom we have depended on for so many years, may now start to want help and expect to rely on us both physically and perhaps emotionally. This feels, for many of us, very awkward. As we become spokespeople for our parents' needs and requests, we'll have to learn new skills and perhaps develop the patience of Job. Many of us recognize personality traits that we once admired getting in our way as our parents begin to be more dependent. The rules change. The balance between decisively acting on their behalf and attempting to honor their independence—while watching and waiting—is delicate.

> "The secret of staying young is live honestly, eat slowly and lie about your age."
> —*Lucille Ball*

Talk Honestly

Getting to the truth is often hard but experts tell us that, despite the fact that parents often want privacy or think they can shield their kids from worrying, families need to speak openly. It's vital to encourage your elders to be clear and honest about their needs. If they want help with finances or errands or doctors' visits, they should say so. Stating needs openly helps ease your anxiety about how you can help, limits bad feelings and confusion, and assists in managing their expectations of you. Set your limitations and be clear. Are you the primary caregiver or are others there to help? Caregiving can be a collaboration that sees both parties achieving their goals in a win-win situation without hard feelings and burnout.

Admit It, Embrace It

The next step is to identify yourself with the term "caregiver." It's a term that is becoming increasingly visible in the media and with medical professionals, but it's one we're not used to using when it comes to ourselves.

Many people, especially kids or spouses, see themselves as just fulfilling their family responsibilities and don't think of themselves as caregivers—calling this a job or giving it a label may for many, especially older spouses, be seen as a sign of asking for help or a label of helplessness, inadequacy, or failure.

Think about what you're doing and how you are explaining your actions. One recent definition that I came across sums it up well: "A caregiver is a person who informally cares for and supports a family member, friend, neighbour, or individual who is frail, ill, or disabled, and who lives at home or in a care facility." Is this you?

How Does Canada Care?

According to Statistics Canada, the typical provider of care in the home is
- female
- aged 40 to 64
- an immediate family member
- working full-time
- balancing other activities, such as raising a family
- likely to be caring for an elderly parent or spouse

Be Alert to "The Signs"

Watch for clues that your parents need more care than they are willing to admit to. A new or worsening condition is an obvious indication but, often, other signs can be more subtle. For example, a house slowly falling into disrepair may indicate that your parents are less mobile and not physically capable of looking after the house. Or they may be suffering a decline in their mental abilities or their vision and just don't realize what needs to be done. Food spoiling in the fridge may mean that they are not eating proper meals. Lack of attention to personal care is high on the list of warning signals.

> "And in the end, it's not the years in your life that count, it's the life in your years."
> —Abraham Lincoln

Outside help may be needed if one parent who provides care for the other (e.g., your mother acting as informal caregiver for your father) begins to complain or show signs of physical or mental exhaustion. You may hear about this from the doctor or family friends rather than from your mother or father. Why? Many parents try to tough it out on their own for fear of being separated or making things worse for themselves. Admitting defeat or weakness perhaps makes them afraid that you will step in and make sudden changes.

Look Beyond Your Immediate Family

The latest topic at church functions, water cooler breaks, and fundraising soirées seems to be eldercare. Just as a few years ago when childcare and nannies, Montessori and French immersion were the talk of the town, today it's what's up with our aging relatives. Try this test next time you're with a group of five or more people. Ask who knows someone who's having trouble with their parents. Odds are, you'll hear a story and if you're lucky, learn something new. To pick up the most helpful advice on the fly...

- Watch and learn from other families in the same life phase. Look around at how your friends are managing with elderly parents or relatives. Note resources they use and strategies that seem to work.

- Ask friends about the role they play in their parents' lives and how they cope with concerns and sources of stress.

- Be frank about what kind of issues you may be concerned about. There's nothing to be embarrassed about here.

- Your parents' family doctor should be a resource. Find other health providers, such as social workers or other therapists attached to the local hospital, or professionals at community health centres. Independent home-care organizations—both not-for-profit and private—can also provide advice and, often, hands-on help.

Are They Managing?

Over time, case managers suggest that with an "I can cope on my own attitude" several things will happen in an eldercare situation:

- Available services to which a loved one is entitled will be overlooked.

- There is a much greater risk of accidents or falls in the home.

- Regular appointments become hard to keep and may be forgotten.

- Things that required attention around the home are left unnoticed.

- Personal hygiene—bathing, laundry, and oral health—may be compromised.

- Abuse or dominance by the surviving spouse may come into play.

- Medical management and detection of illness or new frailties may be left unchecked.

- Depression or exhaustion could go untreated.

Know When It's Too Much for You

Don't forget you are important too. No doubt you are channelling much of your time and energy into providing the best possible care, support, and advice, but keep in mind that your health is a priority. If you become ill, who will provide the care, guidance, and assistance you've been giving? Caregiving can be exhausting, so be sure to focus on ways to stay healthy, both physically and emotionally. Proper nutrition, exercise, and adequate sleep are vital to your well-being, as is the help and support provided by family, friends, self-help groups, and community services.

CHAPTER 2

Plan Ahead—Not on the Fly!

When the time comes, a lucky few of us will find instructions for care in a sealed envelope just waiting to be opened. The reality is, most of us enter the caregiving world with few guidelines as to what our parents and loved ones really want and what choices are available. Needs change, opinions differ, but it makes good sense to get some groundwork done ahead of time to lighten your load in the future. Also, this is your golden opportunity to gracefully ask some of those not-so-popular questions that your parents will probably be reluctant to answer.

The 75/25 Rule of Thumb

"You know you're getting old when all the names in your black book have M.D. after them."
—Arnold Palmer

More than 75% of what life delivers is predictable, plannable, and hence somewhat manageable (this is what I've distilled from my daughter's four-year business degree). Simply put, I govern myself as if there is about a 25% chance of a sudden not-so-nice surprise at any given time.

Using this principle, I believe that by applying some "proactive smarts" in our role as the adult children of aging parents, we have the ability to avoid most crises and manage change.

Caregiver Hint: Planning makes perfect—not always in the case of eldercare but it certainly makes a significant difference in minimizing disasters and costly lost time.

> ### fast fact
>
> Research suggests that 40% of seniors have at least one disability that affects their activities of daily living. Therefore, there is every chance that your parents will need some care and support as they age.

Does What They Want Match What They Need?

As circumstances evolve and people age, the amount and type of support they might need begins to change. Knowing how much, or how little, help can be expected and available will help you to feel and be better prepared.

Here's a scenario many of you are familiar with. It's 2:30 p.m. on a Tuesday and you've been urgently called away from the office. Your mother has fallen again. This time she was out in the garden and crashed to the ground. You rush to the local hospital to meet the ambulance and find that, while she's not seriously injured, she has scraped her hands, knees, and face badly, and both of your parents are shaken.

This is the third crisis and most alarming upset within a few months. What can you do for your parents' safety? What kind—or level—of help do they need? Can you prevent things from getting worse, or is this type of incident something you'll all have to live with if your parents want to remain living at home?

Aging delivers different things to different people. For some there are sudden not-so-nice surprises. For others there's a more gradual, somewhat predictable process over time. Sometimes what our elders want is not what we think they need. Our perception and their reality don't match. But before you worry and argue yourself silly, know that individuals (read "our parents") have the right to live at risk at least until they're deemed to be a danger to themselves and/or others.

Needless to say, as the adult child of an aging relative, you'll often be faced with plenty of difficult decisions at all the wrong times in your life. Take comfort in the fact that in many cases, there's simply nothing that you can do to change things today. Just like the parents of teenagers, as the adult children of aging parents you're sometimes destined to shake your head, close your mouth, and just watch and wait.

Caregiver Hint: Try asking now so that you'll be able to understand what your loved one will or would want. My take is that a bit of awkwardness now will save no small amount of guesswork, angst, and hard feelings in the long run.

The Right to Live at Risk

Let's face it, your parents' health will decline and they'll probably face a crisis or life-altering event, such as the death of a partner or a serious illness. With ongoing changes in their physical and mental health, you and/or your siblings may need to accept more responsibility. Know, however, that your parents have the "right to live at risk."

This means that unless they are mentally incapable or causing harm to others, they can make their own decisions concerning their housing, legal issues, care, and finances. While you may be concerned and have some great ideas for possible solutions, be aware that ultimately and legally, it is your parents' decision as to if, how, and when they would like care.

As caregivers, we have to be careful not to pass judgment on, or interfere with, some of the choices our parents may make. This is a very difficult notion to grasp because of the value differences between baby boomers and their parents. For example, baby boomers may be willing to pay for needed care, while an older generation may think it should be provided by the government, free of charge. Boomers have grown up in an environment of constant and rapid change and innovation, and have learned to live with the pace. For the most part, our older parents are happier living at a slower, less hectic pace and are resentful of the changes happening to them physically, financially, and socially.

Aging parents may also consider themselves very private and independent, so having someone care for them in their house may be a foreign notion to them. If your parents are capable and recognize their limitations and strengths, the best you can do is help them with their decisions and then be prepared to accept their choices, even if you do not always agree. Remember, it is their choice to "live at risk."

The ability to be independent generally changes over time, and the type of assistance your parents will need can likely be predicted in what professionals have called "stages of care." In order to help in the most appropriate way possible, it's wise to understand and appreciate what stage they are at in their day-to-day life.

The Impact of Providing Care

Beware: Family caregivers are known to struggle with these four issues during the time that they are providing care.

1. Deteriorating health—sometimes resulting in long-term health problems—44.7%

2. Social isolation—39.5 %

3. Emotional detachment—36.9%

4. Financial repercussions—28.9 %

Source: WeCare Home Health

---

fast fact

Financial concerns are top of mind. A recent survey found that 78% of people worry that they won't be able to afford care for themselves or their parents beyond what the government provides.

Source: VHA Home Health Care

The Four Stages of Care

Health is the key determinant in establishing levels of care. The accompanying table may be useful in helping you determine what stage your relative is at and offers some suggestions for the type of care he or she may need. (Thanks to Barbara Carter of Papillon Consulting for this information, which originally appeared in *Solutions Magazine*.) Here are some things to consider.

Stage 1: Active Lifestyle

Stage 1 is fairly clear-cut when it comes to your role. The good news: while your parents are fit, healthy, and independent, they do not need or want your help. That doesn't mean you shouldn't call and visit regularly or start helping out with the yard work. They are still able to care for themselves. Perhaps the pace at which they're going is not quite as swift, but they can manage day-to-day housing, shopping, and financial tasks. Be mindful that a critical event, such as stroke or the death of a spouse, however, could change the care situation overnight. The more help you can provide with the major physical tasks around the house, the less risk there is of falls or accidents. Try to "fall-proof" the house as a preventive measure. (See the chapter on household safety.)

Stage 2: Stable Lifestyle and Stage 3: Limited Lifestyle

The middle stages are the areas where adult children have the most difficulty. Here, we find ourselves second-guessing, looking for help and support and trying to juggle to ensure that our parents receive whatever they need on an uncertain schedule. Often we shift between the job of caregiver and being a son or daughter and back again. The lines of responsibility are fuzzy.

In stage 2 (stable lifestyle), your elder may be in their late 70s or early 80s, and perhaps has recently lost a spouse and is living alone. He or she seems to be managing, but you notice that you're starting to get calls at work just to talk, and regular requests to help with things outside the home like driving him or her to appointments or grocery shopping and helping with finances (these have been coined "instrumental aids to daily living" by researchers at McMaster University).

At this stage you might want to start considering what's called "homemaking" support, which includes laundry, meal preparation, chores, and running errands. Many of our parents will continue to live fulfilling independent lives and not move beyond the stage 2 level of care. Make sure you are cautious, attentive, and aware of next steps, as you need to be prepared for change at any time.

In stage 3 (limited lifestyle), your elder may be in their mid to late 80s and have just experienced a serious medical setback such as a fall, a minor stroke, or a diagnosis of early Alzheimer's. You may find that your elder needs your attention and may be more forgetful. During this stage, the care delivery is of a more personal nature. Activities of daily living involve more hands-on care and include such things as dressing, toileting, and helping with medications. While many children will willingly help with household tasks, they may not be as comfortable with personal or medical care. Often this type of care is delivered by the spouse or health professionals.

Stage 4: Restricted Lifestyle

In stage 4, nursing home or long-term care is likely what's needed. Some families choose to provide this care in the home with private nursing or round-the-clock family care, but this is often not sustainable for an extended period. At times, ill relatives are cared for in hospital or, if their situation is chronic but stable, in a long-term care facility. (At this point, the elder is likely very frail and may be mentally incapable and in need of full-time, day-and-night care.) In Canada, long-term care is regulated through federal and provincial programs and is offered in both private and not-for-profit settings. If you are the primary person responsible for care, you would now have advocacy and power of attorney in your role.

The Four Stages of Care				
	Stage 1	Stage 2	Stage 3	Stage 4
Independence	Very independent	Somewhat independent	Somewhat dependent	Totally dependent
Lifestyle	Active	Stable	Limited	Restricted
Health	Good	Fair	Frail	Poor
Housing	Own home/ apartment	Own home/ with help	Seniors or retirement housing	Hospital

	Stage 1	Stage 2	Stage 3	Stage 4
Triggers to Move to Next Stage	Calling you at work; lonely; restricted mobility; life-altering event	More forgetful; serious medical diagnosis; lonely; unable to be alone and safe	Unable to walk, talk; serious medical condition; unable to eat, bathe independently; loss of support system	
Caregiver	Self	Spouse/family/ close friends or neighbours; home-care worker; visiting nurses; care agencies	Physiotherapist (PT); occupational therapist (OT)	PT, OT, plus nurses, doctors
Care Delivery	Rare/Weekly/as needed	A few hours daily	24 hours a day	
Care Activities	None	**Help needed with:** laundry; transportation; home maintenance; meal preparations; shopping; household chores; mobility inside and outside home	**Stage 2 plus help with:** dressing; personal hygiene; toileting; eating; medication use	Total patient care medical in long-term care environment palliative hospice
		Other help: Helping with money management; arranging community services; completing forms; providing financial assistance; dealing with serious memory problems; dealing with mood swings due to mental changes; help in a crisis		

Developing a Care Plan

Virtually everyone we meet today has an older person in their life they worry about. To best serve that individual's needs, you must develop a care plan. *A care plan is essentially a comprehensive list—a list that includes every type of care your loved one will require and also looks at all those other things associated with caregiving.* This involves first establishing the level of care that is needed, then determining the resources available, and then considering your own willingness to accept the caregiver role.

Don't waste precious time. One of the first steps you need to take is to sit down and make a comprehensive list of the needs, wants, and present and future wishes of everyone involved. This should include the person being cared for, other members of the immediate family (i.e., spouse, children, etc.), and yourself. When the list is finished, you'll find that you have a good idea of exactly where you're at. (See the workbook page in the appendix for some helpful hints.)

Begin with an Assessment

Ideally the best method to determine what, if any, care is needed is to have a medical assessment done by a care professional, such as a physician, health nurse, occupational therapist, or local home-care agency. They can identify where your parent needs the most help and give you some guidance as to what to do next. This may include accessing the various care services in your area, including home care.

Ask yourself whether you are physically, mentally, and financially able to give the care to your parent directly, or are you more comfortable arranging for the care to be delivered.

Implementing care can be difficult and may even be met by resistance from your parents, for a number of reasons. However, if care is needed, implementing it in stages may not only be the most efficient, it may also be the path of least resistance.

So that you can benchmark the current situation, ask yourself how your parent's personal care needs are currently being managed on a daily basis.

	Yes	No
Is the person		
• independent	___	___
• in need of minimal assistance	___	___
• in need of maximum assistance	___	___
• improved	___	___
• improving	___	___
• declined	___	___
• declining	___	___

Care Indicators: Activity Levels and Other Clues

Assessing care needs is a hard and subjective task, as your parent or elder is often in denial. Examining activity levels and watching out for common clues is a good place to start. Some of the first clues that an older person may need care include

- feelings of loneliness
- deteriorating health
- poor eating habits
- calling you at work
- forgetfulness
- declining mobility
- life-altering events (e.g., death of a spouse, illness, etc.)

You will need to look at how a person is able to handle activities such as dressing, eating (handling utensils, swallowing, etc.), bathing (turning on taps, sitting and standing unsupported), toileting, personal hygiene and grooming (teeth, hair, face, hands, nail care), and transfers (getting in and out of bed, going from room to room, etc.). As your elder does these things, is he or she sure and timely or slow and confused? Can you leave the person alone during any or all of the above tasks? Will your elder eat on his or her own? Can he or she manage Meals on Wheels? Answer the telephone? Answer the door?

Take a Reality Check

An occupational therapist can help you to determine care levels and equipment that are needed. He or she can also help point you in the direction of government support programs and home-care agencies in your area.

The occupational therapist or case manager will help you identify areas that are difficult or situations that could put your parent at risk. Depending on what you or your parent feels is important, they will check

- physical abilities: for example, strength, coordination, and balance

- mental abilities: for example, memory, organization skills, and ways of coping

- support available to you from family, school, work, and community

- physical setup of your elder's house and community

- specific activities you want to do to improve your elder's abilities

Once you and your occupational therapist identify the problem(s), you may work with your elder to

- learn new ways of doing things: for example, dress or cook using one arm, remember things when memory is poor

- do activities to help maintain or improve abilities: for example, increase strength and confidence

- adapt the material or equipment: for example, the use of properly fitted wheelchairs, special bath equipment, and toilet seats

- make changes to the environment: for example, change the layout of the home or office to make it more accessible or prevent further injury

• develop new skills, abilities, and interests

Caregiver Hint: Consider meeting with an occupational therapist or care manager, or interviewing local nursing agencies to understand costs and options before you're up to your ears in it.

After overarching guidelines have been established that will set the "standards for care," it's time to move on to daily details that can ensure consistency, safety, and quality of life.

Involving Mom and Dad: Opening Discussions with Parents

This ain't your standard business meeting (or is it?). With our rush-every-where, try-to-be-efficient worlds, we tend to forget that our parents may not be schedulable within a Palm Pilot window.

It may seem at first as if scheduling a meeting with your parents is a bit unfriendly, but this is every bit as important as any of the business meetings you arrange every day. In addition, discussions with parents can pick up on a few tried and true business principles, if we don't get carried away. A list or an agenda can help you to stay organized. If your parents haven't been in business themselves you might not want to appear too stiff or businesslike. However, a meeting no matter how informal must be scheduled. This planning step does require a beginning, a plan, and a defined path toward certain goals, but be prepared to move slowly and gently. You may be far ahead of them in foreseeing what the future holds. Remember, you might need to be patient and give them time to catch up to you or understand where things are headed.

Consider this: Your elders may be scared. What lies ahead is often a frighteningly difficult, unpleasant journey that most of us would prefer to avoid if the truth were known.

Suggestion: Be gentle and supportive as you help to move things forward.

After your parents reach a certain age, most doctors' visits will result in more tests, diagnosis, and treatment of one condition or another and, if statistics are to be believed, the prescription of yet another medication with its inherent side effects. (According to Dr. Chris Frank, Queen's

University, Department of Medicine, Department of Geriatrics, the average senior takes 11 medications each day.) Combine this with the need to travel outside on a winter day, wait in a crowded doctor's office, and spend more money at the drug store, and it's no surprise that Mom and Dad aren't any more excited than you are about doctor's visits.

Home and Community

Following an assessment by an occupational therapist or a geriatric care or nursing manager, make a list of essential tasks that need to be performed, including meal preparation, laundry, housekeeping (daily and janitorial, such as window cleaning, spring cleaning), outdoor maintenance (garbage removal, lawn care, raking leaves, snow removal, cleaning eavestroughs, shrub trimming), banking, shopping (groceries and personal), and general maintenance.

Consider labour-saving or assistive devices to maximize independence and safety. If you or your parents can afford it or your insurance or health plan will provide the service, you might want to arrange for regular homemaking services. Lawn and garden care, snow removal, Meals on Wheels, delivery of frozen food entrées, as well as home shopping or delivery services can help to keep people in their own homes for as long as possible.

When planning is in this phase, it's important to recognize the changing needs of our parents and the modifications that are needed quite regularly with the passage of time. If your parents are unable to manage alone, this part of the book is for you.

Assessing Their Environment

Review the space needed for special equipment and the compatibility of existing equipment in your home—for example, a special bed, lift system, or bathroom safety devices. Predict potential changes in your parents' health conditions and needs to help you decide whether it's best to renovate, compromise, or move.

Look for hazards that will increase the potential for falls or fires. What is their ability to escape from the home in an emergency? Be sure they know how to access 911 or police, fire, and ambulance and have the instructions prominently displayed in the home. Do they hear, smell, and see well enough to ensure their own safety in an emergency? Assure yourself that they are fully capable of understanding and are aware of emergency procedures. Make sure they are not going to be at an above-average risk of senior fraud or neighbourhood robberies because of their frailty. Do they have any difficulties related to mental illness that might compromise their safety?

Consider an environmental safety assessment or the use of personal-alert systems and communication devices.

Safe Mobility Matters

Usually, sooner rather than later, Mom or Dad will need a cane, crutches, walker, scooter, or wheelchair. Suddenly, you're the techie who's in charge of buying, lugging, fixing, cleaning, and making this all work for them.

Review accessibility: door width, counter heights, flooring, stairs, hand rails, light switch heights, closet and clothing access, taps, pathways and hallways, and lighting. Will your home and theirs need a ramp, a stair lift, or an elevator? Do the pathways and hallways need to be cleared of obstructions? If they begin using power equipment (a scooter or power wheelchair), you'll need to figure out what is required for "home and away" access, and plan for storage and lifting, transportation, and battery recharges. Also, you'll need to think about whether it's safe for them to "drive" the equipment.

Can the same equipment be used safely inside and outside the home? Is the equipment compatible with your family vehicle? Do you need a van with a special lift for easy wheelchair access? How will you transfer your parent from the house, nursing home, or hospital into the car, taxi, or bus?

Is there convenient access to buildings where they'll be going for medical appointments and shopping? Will you or your parent be able to drive and park with a handicap-parking permit? Check to make sure stairs will not be barriers to shopping areas or

> **My Story: Ho! Ho! Ho!**
>
> Our first Christmas post-stroke with Mom was quite the event. I was determined and so was Mom to celebrate the same way. It took four guys to carry (read drag) my more-than-willing mother up the 10 steep front stairs to our house. Once inside, she was restricted to one floor and treated to the indignity of a commode with a curtain in a private corner of my newly renovated kitchen. None of this seemed to bother her, but my daughters lost their appetite for dinner and one of my house guests ended up with a sore back. Thankfully nothing went wrong, but it was an accident waiting to happen. Would I do it again? No! Luckily, she's now invited for Christmas at my brother and his wife's more accessible cottage.

My Story: Mama Needs Power?
After my mother had a stroke that paralyzed her entire right side, my younger brother was gung-ho to get her a souped-up power wheelchair. It broke his heart to see her struggling to learn how to wheel a manual chair. The rehab team agreed to a trial. Using her reprogrammed left hand, her first act was to charge quickly straight into the wall. Once redirected, she joyfully headed straight for a fellow patient with a walker. Not only was mobility an issue, but sadly, her level of cognition wasn't sufficient to handle the complexities of power driving. The occupational therapist was right. It took Mom a while to learn to wheel but today, she's as fast as can be in the manual chair. Her upper body is good, and she's perfectly safe wheeling around the nursing home independently.

doctors' and dentists' offices. Often wheelchair access is available through certain doors but they may be hidden or difficult to find at a glance. Is there an accessible washroom? Where? Will the equipment fit in the doctor's examining room or the store's changing room?

Cultural and Religious Expectations

As you work through the decisions about the level and type of care your parent needs, take into account his or her background, beliefs, nationality, and heritage. While many elders have integrated into life in Canada over the years, there are many others who retain close ties to their original culture. With family and church support, it is possible to maintain traditions that are important to them, whether it's in the area of communication, language, diet, festivities, or lifestyle.

On the positive side, research on the impact of religious participation by aging members of our population has shown that for those involved in their religion, there are quality of life indicators, enhanced social network connections, and lower levels of depression. It seems that local church congregations provide much-needed outreach to vulnerable citizens in their community; chaplaincy services in hospitals and nursing homes fulfill the same function.

Caregiver Hint: Religious participation doesn't cost much and is widely available.

Did You Know...

Dr. Harold Koenig, a Duke University psychiatrist, found that religious elderly patients cost the health system less money than those who were less observant. In addition, religious patients reported spending just six days in hospital during the previous year, compared to 12 days among the less religious.

Resources

You should review your parents' and your own financial situation. Are funds required and available to purchase or rent equipment? To make necessary renovations? For transportation or vehicle modifications?

"You know you are getting older when size 12 is much smaller than it used to be."
—*Anonymous*

If appropriate, investigate funding agencies such as Extended Health Insurance from private insurers or health plan benefits, Department of Veterans' Affairs, local social services agencies, Assistive Devices Program, or diagnosis-specific agencies (e.g., the Multiple Sclerosis Society). Local Rotary or Kiwanis Clubs will often provide financial support for equipment or special services for those without sufficient personal resources.

More Support Needed?

Governments and health experts have a seemingly endless number of definitions of home care…but all it really means to the typical Canadian is getting the help and support to be able to care for loved ones themselves.

This help includes both medical and support services. Generally speaking, services provided by "professionals"—nurses, doctors, physiotherapists, and occupational therapists—don't cost clients, while "softer" services, such as homemaking, may come with a fee attached, or, in the case of Ontario, with a service limit.

For the most part, home-care programs are administered by provincial and territorial health or social service departments or local community or regional health boards. Services may be delivered directly by home-care-program staff or by contracted agencies (for-profit or not-for-profit), or by a mix of both. In spite of all the seemingly available services, one of the things caregivers say they need most is assistance in navigating the maze of home-care services now available.

Home care is a provincial responsibility. It is not enshrined in Medicare. Therefore, each province has put together a crazy quilt of services and programs they call "Home Care."

Caregiver Hint: *Solutions Magazine*, Canada's family guide to home health care and wellness (www.solutionsmagazine.ca), is a great source of information and contacts, with the usual proviso of being aware of the source of the information. If you're using the Internet, start with reliable sites sponsored by governments or agencies and follow their links.

Home Care: Know the Terrain

Each province has its own way of delivering health services, with specific rules and regulations. In Ontario, for example, there are 43 Community Care Access Centres (CCACs) across the province. These are government-funded, not-for-profit organizations serving as a local point of access for in-home health care, information and referral services, and access to long-term placement. Similar organizations exist in other provinces.

Regardless of where you live, eligibility for home-care help will likely be dependent on certain criteria, such as having a valid health card number, being unable to access out-patient services, or needing one of the professional or personal support services for a condition that can be appropriately treated at home and having a home environment suitable for implementing these services.

It is important to understand what home care is and what it provides. Home care has been described as a basket of services that help people receive care at home when they are ill, disabled, recovering from illness or surgery, or dying. Home care enables people with poor or deteriorating health to live at home, with the goal of preventing, delaying, or substituting for long-term care or acute-care facility-based nursing care.

Whether you need to have someone keep your elder company so that you get a break, need daily assistance, or if your parent requires complex nursing care, you are entitled to ask for home care. In some cases, you might have the option of paying for additional hours of care if your elder needs more than your government agency is able to provide.

Learn What You Can

Knowledge is an empowering tool. Learn as much as you can about your elder's medical condition or care needs. Ask questions and share ideas with family members and health professionals. You'll find a wealth of information about caregiving in libraries, caregiver magazines, established medical organizations, and on the Internet. Very often caregivers have neither the knowledge nor patience to go on-line. If you're not comfortable with the computer, ask a friend or relative to do some research on the 'Net for you. Caution: Keep in mind that Internet sites are not regulated in any way, so check the source and timeliness of the information.

Hold Team Meetings

If you are fortunate enough to have developed a support network of family and friends, now is a good time to have a team meeting. If possible, the care recipient should be included in the decision-making. Both the needs of the patient and the caregiver have to be discussed. Home care might not be able to provide as many hours as you would like. Relatives and friends are often willing, but hesitant, to offer assistance because they don't know what to do. However, if tasks are discussed and delegated on an individual basis, a win/win situation is created—you as the caregiver will receive the help you need and the support team feels useful providing it.

Initially, members of this team might save you the time and effort of tracking down information you need. For example, is there a barber or hairdresser who does house calls? Is there a volunteer-based service to provide respite care? Can you access Meals on Wheels or another food service? If you don't have a car, is volunteer transportation (for medical appointments) available through a community agency? Would the in-home services of an occupational therapist, speech therapist, or physiotherapist be available if required?

When It's Time to Make Tough Decisions

Difficult decisions surround our elders, and at times we need their blessing to move ahead. Expect resistance. Here are some ideas about how to approach the inevitable.

Suggestion: *Practice patience* (perhaps it's time you took up meditation or yoga to reduce your stress level). Be realistic. Don't expect a decision today. This process, especially in times of good health and wellness or when early health management decisions are on the horizon, may be frustratingly slow for us.

Slow down: Even if you're ahead of them, decision-making and laying out options may need to be broken up into baby steps with the goal of a gentler flow. (Plan for a series of discussions if you have the luxury of time.) Deal with health-care wishes. Gradually review assets. Discuss home and long-term care options. Decide which member of the family (i.e., which child) is going to take the lead.

Remember:

- This isn't about what your elders are going to leave you and your siblings, it's all about arranging for their care and the quality of their later life.

- Draw up a road map now to save yourself and them long-term trauma. Even if plans have to change, at least you've got markers going in the right direction that'll guide your way.

- Maintain dignity—yours and theirs—at all cost.

- Seek outside advice whenever possible. There's often support available through provincial health ministries and not-for-profit associations. Alternatively, if you can afford it, legal and medical experts can be hired on assignment or by the hour. Your goal: To have some of the tricky questions asked by someone else and the options outlined in a non-judgmental, choice-focused way.

Know You're Not Alone

By choice, by instinct, or by a process of elimination, we become responsible for our elders. It's often a juggling act, sometimes a pleasure. All told, it's a lot of extra work that requires more "know how" than most people expect. Can we become smart caregivers? Here's some must-have advice, compiled from our gurus, who've been there and have the stories to prove it.

Most of us are not equipped with the necessary knowledge or tools to take on the role of caregiver when the time comes. Each situation is different. Family dynamics and history play a significant role in how your particular experience will evolve.

With a little time and good advice, you can begin by equipping yourself with as much knowledge as possible, gathering information on your parents' abilities and disabilities, their needs (both present and future), and the services that are available to help you both. An often-neglected part of planning is determining exactly where and how you fit in. You need to understand your strengths and weaknesses and identify what you will need to be successful in your role (including the help of family, friends, neighbours, and community agencies).

Equally important to the responsibilities you have to your loved one are your "rights" as the caregiver. At the onset you are filled with hope and have ideals, energy, and the motivation to make things happen. You may be able to survive on less sleep, reduced leisure time, leaves of absences from work, and so forth, but this regimen will not be sustainable.

Avoiding Caregiver Burnout

Balance Your Responsibilities

Thinking that you can do it all can lead to exhaustion, stress, and burnout. Although burnout may not be evident until up to 6 to 18 months later, there are early warning signs. Perhaps you're not sleeping well. You might be experiencing headaches and lingering colds and social withdrawal. Caregiving by its nature is not something that can be added on top of your daily cycle of activity in a neat package. It must be integrated with many other responsibilities. The key to surviving lies in finding the balance between the roles and responsibilities of caregiving and other important activities.

Never underestimate the need for caregiver relief or respite. Investigate what relief services or respite care can do for you, look for support groups, and develop your own coping skills. Be aware that there may be waiting lists for services and facilities.

To make home care really work, it is vital to research and prepare a care plan. Identify one family member as the coordinator of the care plan—it will help things to run more smoothly. By planning ahead, you can avoid worry, guilt, and uncertainty and make the home-care experience a more positive and rewarding one for all involved.

fast facts

Women watch out!

- The wives of elderly men have traditionally been the primary source of support and care.

- Men tend to marry younger women and women have longer life expectancies.

- Wives often outlive their husbands and, in the process, have often cared for their husbands.

- By the time women need assistance, their husbands have died and they must rely on help from their children, primarily daughters or daughters-in-law.

- Changes in family size over time have also meant that there are fewer children to provide help to a frail mother.

- Often, the responsibility for caregiving tends to fall on one child. To help understand the complexities of caregiving, it is useful to be aware of the main phases that many caregivers experience.

Further Reading

The Three Rs of Caregiving

Carol Edwards

For effective and compassionate care, you must follow the "three Rs" of effective caregiving—respect, realistic expectations, and respite. The three Rs, especially respect, address both your needs as the caregiver, and those of the parent or elderly relative. How do these three principles work? The best way to illustrate is to show them in action and, equally importantly, what happens when they are not applied.

Take the case of John, a married high school teacher with two kids living in Winnipeg, who was faced with serving as the unofficial care coordinator for his aging parents. John's parents were in their 70s. Both were physically strong and active, still participating in outdoor activities, and living independently in their own home. John and his mother, however, noticed a decline in his father's mental state—the first signs of Alzheimer's disease. It was not long before his mother could no longer cope with his father's aggressive outbursts and constant wandering. She asked for help with looking after her husband at home.

John made the decision to sell his parents' home and move both parents to live with him and his family. John would be his parents' caregiver. This act of family loyalty and kindness may have seemed the natural thing to do at the time, yet the consequences were almost devastating. Eventually, John's father was placed in a long-term-care facility while his mother moved into a rented apartment. John's marriage did survive, but his relationship with his parents was irrevocably damaged. The mistake that John, his parents, and family made—although well intentioned—was essentially to ignore those vitally important three Rs.

Respect

Aside from keeping your sanity, respect is the most important principle to keep in mind when accepting the role and responsibilities of caregiving. Respect comes in many forms, including:

Respect for aging: The attitude of the caregiver toward aging can have a tremendous impact on the elderly. Despite her advancing years, John's mother was still very active, mentally astute, and capable of independent living. To John, however, his mother was "old" and needed his help, which came on his terms. An effective caregiver respects that aging is not a "disease" but merely a slowing down of life, and assists in creating a sense of purpose through maintained independence. Aging is a family affair. It has a ripple effect on the entire family.

Respect for an individual's roles: Understand that living with or being cared for by family can threaten the status of the older person. The "reversal of roles," going from looking after a son or daughter (even though actual caregiving may have ended decades ago) to being looked after by one, can cause resentment and angry feelings to develop. An aging parent may be slower in step and thought, but has a long life of experience and wisdom to draw upon.

A successful caregiving arrangement often includes the fact that the elder perceives that the decisions being made are hers or his.

Respect for a person's wishes: Whether it be the wishes written in a living will or those wishes expressed daily, they are important and should be honored whenever possible. Acknowledge that an elderly parent may not have the same set of values. John's parents were prepared financially to stay in their home until "the end." However, John was blinded by the problems he saw his parents facing and therefore did not help his mother explore the services that would be available in her own home.

Respect for professional advice: Annual evaluations by a doctor are invaluable. Changes in the early stages of Alzheimer's disease are subtle. Many elderly find it difficult to consult a doctor when there is no obvious physical problem, as they struggle to conceal their mental difficulties. In the same way, many children are reluctant to concede that their parents are aging. John could have benefited from a realistic overview of his father's condition and the challenges involved. It would have also been wise for him to accompany his parents on their visits to the doctor.

Realistic Expectations

John's mother had been struggling for some months before coming to John for help. The role of being primary caregiver to her husband was becoming overwhelming. She did not wish to seek help from her son. She was valiantly trying to respect the wish of her husband to stay in his own home. Finally, her approach to John led to the outcome she had feared. John assumed the role of caregiver without understanding the challenge and what he was capable of doing or not doing.

John failed to be realistic in his evaluation. He underestimated the level of independence his mother was capable of if she had the proper help and support. And he overestimated how well he and his own family could cope with the many challenges of caring for his parents. He also underestimated how such an arrangement would strain his relationship with his wife and children.

Limits need to be set in any caregiving situation, or else conflicts are bound to arise. The first step in setting limits is to examine all possibilities and recognize what is within your capabilities, and what may be beyond you.

This goes back to respect—a respect for your own limitations. The caregiver should work together with the elder, if possible, in developing realistic goals and plans, acknowledging their time and knowledge deficits.

Respite

An increased number of family members are providing more complex care in the home setting than ever before. This is not easy. It requires considerable mental and physical effort. At times it can be exhausting, and many people keep going, without a break. In too many cases, caregivers are overwhelmed by their responsibilities. The result can be burnout. John came close to burning out. The efforts required to care for his parents, combined with the demands of work and family life, were too much, leaving him physically tired, mentally dull, and withdrawn from his wife and children.

Regular short respite for John's father arranged through a local long-term-care facility may have been all John and his mother required to avoid being overwhelmed.

Experts almost universally promote the importance of respite for caregivers. Respite services are available in most communities to ensure the caregiver receives adequate rest, sleep, exercise, nutrition, socialization, social support, and even financial aid and health management.

Help is available from a variety of resources, including community and senior centres, advocacy associations (e.g., the Alzheimer Society and Parkinson Society), Friendly Visitor programs, nursing agencies, and other support services. Professional care managers can help to access these services and generally assist in ensuring all the pieces of effective caring are in place.

The prospect of caring for an aging parent is a reality for many of us today. It is never too early to prepare for your parent's aging. Start by stepping back and taking a look at the big picture, including your needs as well as those of the elder person. And make sure any plans you make take the three Rs of caregiving into consideration.

Source: Solutions Magazine

CHAPTER 3

Housing Options for Dependent Parents

Home sweet home—that's where your parents want to be and surprise, surprise, if they can't live there on their own, research tells us that they're expecting to live with you. Better think fast!

A recent study by the MacArthur Foundation points out that older people are much more likely to age well than to become decrepit and dependent if they live alone in their own home. Of those surveyed between the ages of 65 and 74, 89% reported no disability, and even in advanced old age, a surprising number had little functional disability. (Much of this is a result of the gradual reduction of infectious illnesses, and recent management of high blood pressure, high cholesterol, and smoking-related disease.)

Traditional housing was not designed to accommodate changes that are demanded as people age. As we age, we should consider adapting our homes to make them more supportive, or we may need to choose other housing options. The reality is, many of our elders are at risk.

Knowing when to intervene on behalf of an aging loved one is one of life's most difficult decisions. Let's take a look at some alternatives.

Clues That Your Intervention Might Be Needed

This may well be a fragile period in your parent's life. Changes may occur on a daily basis, and behaviours may be inconsistent or hard to read. Your parents may hide or cover problems to avoid worrying you. Be diligent. Keep your eye out for one or more of these changes that may signal that all is not well:

Activity Levels: Suddenly Mom is a glass-half-empty gal, focusing on the negative. You notice that she is no longer pursuing hobbies or social interests that once provided her with pleasure.

Personal Grooming: Few things raise the spirit like newly coiffed hair, a trimmed beard, or a freshly laundered shirt. However, when people are depressed, personal hygiene and grooming are often the first daily activities to fall by the wayside.

Bill Paying: If your parent is recently widowed and is having difficulty with the bills, your elder may just need a helping hand until he or she can master these new skills. On the other hand, if your parent was a good cook or housekeeper or very conscientious about paying the bills and you see a marked change in these habits, there is reason for concern.

Health Watch: Many symptoms of a decline in health can be attributed to medical conditions that can be treated. Medical intervention may be required if your loved one shows a marked loss of appetite, a change in sleeping patterns, loss of hearing or incontinence, or is becoming accident prone.

Medication Management: Is your parent using medication inappropriately? Perhaps there are so many drugs now that he or she can't remember which does what. While a good medication regimen has positive effects, taking medications improperly can have unfortunate and sometimes deadly results.

Confused: Your parent may have become confused, suspicious, or fearful. If this has not been part of your elder's personality in the past, or the fears seem exaggerated, this is a sign there is a problem.

Forgetfulness: Dad can't remember the names of longstanding friends or family or goes to a familiar place and can't get home.

Suddenly Single

It's an all-too-common situation. One of your parents has died, leaving the other facing the daunting prospect of a life alone. When one parent dies, there's a tendency to expect the survivor to move in with the children. This may not, however, always be the best or most practical solution. Rather, expect a period of adjustment for everyone and try to understand that what is really needed is a little time and help in getting reestablished.

My Story: Mom's Move

When my father died, the first thing my mother wanted to do was sell or give everything away and move out of their recently purchased home into a small, maintenance-free apartment. Before we knew it, the neighbours were happily carting off my father's tools. The garden hose and lawn chairs went off in the back of my brother's friend's truck, and the local antique dealers had an auctioneer's heyday. The next few years consisted of several unrewarding moves and constant complaints about rental properties and landlords. We saw our mother progressively becoming more unhappy and in smaller, less attractive spaces that belonged to other people.

To our surprise, she called one day to say she'd bought another house and was starting again. Financially, this was a huge stretch, and to this day I wonder how she got a mortgage at age 65 on a limited income. Nonetheless, when all was said and done, she was much happier in her cute little house where she planted a charming garden, complete with a fishpond, which my husband was coerced into digging. My mother, Margaret, spent the next eight or nine years cheerfully "making house" and entertaining friends. The gentleman friend whom she met after a few years maintained his own home a few blocks away—on any given day the pair of them would be off to Home Depot or the garden centre to complete one project or another to keep each other's house in good shape.

Elderly Couples: A Unit of Care

In a study of six elderly couples living in their own homes and married an average of 48 years, Frances E. Racher, an associate professor in the School of Health Studies at Brandon University, asked the couples to provide insight into their long-term partnership relationships; their adaptability and decision-making and problem-solving capacities as they managed challenge and change; the issues of daily living that they encountered; and their experiences in accessing health services and other resources.

"Age is mind over matter. As long as you don't mind it, it don't matter."
—*Muhammad Ali*

What was discovered was that a couple's support for each other enhances the capacity of the couple to manage more effectively than either partner could manage on his or her own. Spouses account for an increasing proportion of each other's social interactions as the frequency of social contacts with others decreases.

According to Racher, while couples appreciate the support and assistance of family members and health professionals, they do not appreciate what they view as interference in making decisions or managing their lives. These couples with extensive life experience, committed partnerships, and sound problem-solving abilities believe they deserve the respect of others and report frustration when members of their social networks do not support their rights and abilities to make their own life choices.

Elderly couples value autonomy. They desire choice, the right to make choices, and respect for their choices. When families express faith and trust in their parents' abilities to manage their lives effectively, their tendency to interfere is diminished. Family members and others who recognize the impact of their attitudes and behaviours and behave in truly supportive manners contribute positively to the quality of life of elderly couples.

Access to Health Services

Deteriorating health and increasing need for health services are burdensome for elderly couples. Access to health services is a growing concern. Couples worry about access to physicians, other health professionals, and home-care services. They are apprehensive about the rising costs of medications and assistive devices. Elderly veterans praise the Department of Veterans Affairs (DVA) for the support provided to them as veterans, while recognizing how support to them as couples would be even more beneficial. Some new programs for seniors seem to meet the needs of individual seniors while not addressing the unique needs of elderly couples. Couples worry about the cost of maintaining two households should one spouse require placement in a personal-care home. Further, the need for supportive accommodation that maintains the couple as a unit when one spouse needs increased care requires attention and the development of creative ways to keep them together.

Creating a Sense of Security

When older adults are living on their own, even during a transition period, it will be easier for everyone if you know that they are living in a safe, secure environment. Start by doing a security audit to make sure entrances and windows are secure and encourage them to be "security conscious." For example, any elderly person living alone should remember the following tips:

- Ensure all windows and doors are closed at night, even balcony doors and high windows. A "closing-up" checklist can be helpful.

- Don't let too many people know that he or she is living alone.

- Never use the phrase "We are not home" on the answering machine. Just simply say, "We can't take your call right now."

- Never open the door to strangers.

- Be wary of telephone solicitations.

- Keep emergency and family phone numbers handy by the telephone.

- If appropriate, get to know the neighbours, so they will watch out for them.

- Sign up for any local police or community crime alert programs (call your local police department for details).

    For more information about anti-fraud programs, visit www.e-volunteering.org/aboutfraud.

Look for Alternatives

Be there for your elders in times of transition. What I've learned is that one size doesn't fit all, so be prepared to change your ideas in changing circumstances. What's right for today may not work tomorrow given emerging health or financial concerns. For example, if you're looking for alternatives to your relative being alone, investigate house sharing or moving into a seniors' living community or residence. Sometimes these options work out to have financial advantages as well.

If your relatives enjoy social activity, help them to find a place where they can feel safe, can continue to meet friends, and can participate in activities and volunteerism. According to a 1998 General Social Survey, 48% of people who spent less than two hours alone on an average day were very happy compared to 37% who spent eight or more hours by themselves.

Choosing Housing Options

Independent Living Tops the List

Do elderly Canadians value their independence? The answer is a resounding yes.

A study conducted in Victoria, B.C., by the University of Victoria Centre on Aging found that seniors—even those who have chronic illnesses or disabilities—prefer to remain as self-reliant as possible. This means taking care of daily tasks, such as shopping, cleaning, and meal preparation, themselves. They also prefer to fend for themselves when it comes to minor health issues, such as headaches and colds.

Many of the 1,000 Victoria-area seniors studied noted that they had or would be willing to alter their living environment in some way to make it easier to care for themselves. While many need to lean on family members, volunteers, or health-care professionals to help them cope, they would prefer this to be a support, rather than a substitute, for self-care.

Independent living describes housing in single houses, apartments, cooperatives, townhouses, and condominiums with design adaptations. Here are more ideas about options for independent living for your aging relative:

In-law apartments and suites: An in-law apartment, also known as a granny flat, is typically attached to or built inside another home. It may have its own appliances, along with separate kitchen and bathroom facilities. Many have private entrances as well. For many adult children, in-law apartments can be a suitable solution when parents are unable to live alone but are not yet ready to move into a nursing home.

Moving to a smaller house or condo: Downsizing can offer affordable, safe, and easy-care living. Pride in ownership of property is retained.

Retirement apartment: Apartment complexes with one-bedroom or two-bedroom units designed for the elderly exist across Canada. Some are subsidized for individuals who qualify (usually income-based). Activity and leisure programs are included, and many have other useful services, such as buses to local shopping or health professionals who visit regularly.

Retirement community: These are more comprehensive than retirement apartments and usually contain a variety of housing (from apartments to townhouses). They may offer additional features, such as meal or maid services. Many of these communities are designed to offer expandable levels of care. For example, as a person loses independence or becomes frail, medical or nursing assistance can be made available. These communities tend to be privately operated (although some are subsidized). Some require an upfront financial investment as well as payment of fees on a regular basis. Many of these communities, especially those in urban areas, have a waiting list.

Mobile homes: This type of housing provides a quite inexpensive way to enjoy community living. Mobile homes today are modern and practical, as well as convenient. In addition, residents often share community recreation facilities, gardens, and security services. Units are small and easy to maintain.

Condominiums or cooperative rentals: A good alternative, if your parents like the idea of having their own home but don't want to have to worry about the upkeep. In exchange for dues or fees, a condominium association takes care of worrisome maintenance (for example, snow removal, lawn care) and provides shared recreation facilities and, often, private bus services to shopping malls and recreational areas.

Staying Put!

With support from friends and family, seniors usually prefer to live in their own homes and communities for as long as possible. When

A Home Safety Checklist

It is important to ensure the house or apartment is "senior safe." The following considerations are particularly important when choosing accommodations (more detailed tips are included in the next chapter). Make any repairs or modifications that are necessary. Alterations that can prevent a fall or other accident are a wise investment.

✓ Are all stairs and railings in good condition?

✓ Are all doors, windows, and locks secure?

✓ Are there working smoke and carbon monoxide detectors in the home?

✓ Are all carpets and rugs secure?

✓ Are electrical appliances and cords in good condition?

✓ Is lighting adequate?

✓ Do neighbours or landlords know how to reach family members?

✓ Are there non-slip mats in the tub and bathroom?

✓ Is the kitchen "senior safe"? Think about helpful devices such as self-shutoff kettles, unbreakable plastic jugs and dishes, and easy-to-grip ergonomic utensils.

✓ Are snow and ice cleared in the winter?

✓ Are emergency telephone numbers by the phone?

their health declines, they often require additional support services delivered by community-based agencies. Some of these services include Meals on Wheels, homemaking, transportation, friendly visiting, help with errands, and telephone assurance.

If your relative is staying at home and you're on the hook, here's what you need to do:

• Identify important medical concerns, health-care needs, and safety issues, usually in consultation with the physician, therapist, and other involved professionals.

• Work out the financial costs of having your parents stay at home through sickness and health based on their life expectancy. Consult with legal and financial advisers if necessary.

• Provide a detailed plan of care, identifying problems and the potential need for special services.

• Research, arrange, and plan to monitor in-home care from personal support workers and homemakers.

• Be mentally prepared for a crisis to happen at any time and have a plan for who is going to be in charge.

• Ensure your relative is following a healthy diet, which is critical to his or her well-being, by planning menus, organizing meal preparation, and providing specific recipes for the home help to prepare.

• Be ready to go to doctors' and other appointments to provide interpretations and follow-up if referrals to other professionals are necessary.

• Assess the safety level in the home and implement any needed improvements.

- Organize referrals to other health-care professionals such as physiotherapists, occupational therapists, podiatrists, psychiatrists, and dentists.

- Act as a liaison to other family members who live far away, ensuring that things are going well and alerting families to problems. (A personal note here—e-mail is fabulous! When the last family member finally got e-mail, it just made things so much easier to keep everyone informed...one e-mail went to four, sometimes five, other people.)

- Arrange for around-the-clock palliative care in the familiar comfort of the elder's own home when his or her health fails.

Source: Careable, Inc.

Semi-independent Living

Your parents might be able to remain living comfortably in their home by using services to help them with homemaking, personal care, meal preparation, and shopping. Often, they are not aware of the services that are available and neither are we, their children. It's worth the time to do some careful research into services available in your area that can help maintain your parents' lifestyle. A move to a residence that offers additional care services or hiring home helpers are two popular and practical ways to help parents maintain an independent yet supported lifestyle. Semi-independent living options include the following:

A continuing care retirement community (also known as life-care) provides various types of accommodation and services, including independent rental units. These communities also offer 24-hour skilled nursing care, so residents can change the nature of their care as their needs change. Although residents do pay significant entrance fees, they also enter into a binding legal agreement or life-care contract that will, for the duration of their lives, guarantee nursing and health-related services. Watch for hidden or rising costs of care when budgeting.

Both retirement apartments and communities tend to be advertised in newspapers or magazines aimed at mature adults.

Churches and non-profit social agencies are also good sources of referrals, as some residences are affiliated with these organizations.

Supportive housing or assisted living is a community support program that assists older adults with their activities of daily living. On-site personal support and essential homemaking services are available 24 hours a day.

Home Care

If you feel home care or some support is needed even on a part-time basis for your elder, call your local government home-care program listed in the blue pages of the phone book under the Ministry of Health and Long-Term Care or a private nursing agency or eldercare service provider. An assessment will be done of the individual's medical and nursing condition, the family support, and the home environment. The assessment will be used to ascertain the level of care the individual needs.

If publicly funded services are determined to be required, a formal care plan will be developed. The individual and family will be informed of the services that will be provided and the commitments the family or individual needs to make for home-care services to be implemented (e.g., a family member may need to provide some assistance, or a home environment may need to be modified).

If services are not available or sufficient from the publicly funded health-care system, or if an individual or family feels that additional services are required, they can be purchased privately through home health-care providers. Insurance plans and veterans affairs may also be a source of funding.

Types of Home Care

Professional care is clinical or specific care provided by a registered health-care professional, such as a nurse, physiotherapist, occupational therapist, nutritionist, or social worker.

Homemaker services refer to help with regular day-to-day activities, including dressing, shopping, cleaning, and meal preparation.

Companions are individuals who spend time with an elderly person. Tasks can range from reading to them to preparing simple meals to taking them on outings. Many companions are volunteers from community, service, or religious groups.

Adult day care is a program designed usually for the elderly or individuals with disorders such as Alzheimer's disease that offer away-from-the-home care during working hours. These programs are usually held in local hospitals or community centres, and the services provided vary.

Full-time attendants are people hired to provide daily one-on-one care for a person in his or her home. The qualifications of attendants vary according to the tasks they need to perform. They can range from professional companions to qualified nurses.

Respite care is provided by special programs that are designed to give family caregivers a break from the stresses and rigours of caring, or to fill in if the caregiver is sick. These programs provide experienced people to look after your loved one on a temporary basis, either in your home or at their location.

Full-time Residential Care

Nursing homes and long-term care facilities provide a continuum of care in a secure setting, 24 hours a day, seven days a week. They take care of people who are no longer able to live independently in their own homes, even with a wide range of community support. A Ministry of Health case manager or social worker can assist you with choosing a long-term care facility that best suits the needs of your loved one and preparing applications for acceptance. When contemplating long-term care, caregivers are often consumed with guilt. This is a normal reaction, but discuss your feelings with a health professional to ensure you do not suffer any long-term effects or depression.

"Destiny is not necessarily what we get out of life, but rather what we give."
—Cary Grant

Nursing, Municipal, or Charitable Home?

Long-term care facilities are also called municipal homes for the aged or nursing homes. For quick reference:

- Nursing homes are usually privately run but provincially regulated.

- Municipal homes for the aged are owned and managed by local (municipal) town councils.

- Charitable homes are run by not-for-profit faith, ethnic, and cultural organizations.

Long-term care facilities offer a variety of accommodation options. Residents of the facility pay a fee based on the type or style of accommodation. "Preferred" accommodation is a term used to describe private or semi-private rooms with special features, whereas basic or standard accommodation refers to shared accomodations. All long-term care facilities have dining rooms or common rooms, and they also usually have facilities such as a lounge, beauty salon, chapel, garden, or gift shop. The basic package includes the following services:

- furnishings (e.g., bed, chair), meals (including special diets), bed linens and laundry services, personal hygiene supplies, medical or clinical supplies and devices (e.g., walkers, wheelchairs for occasional use), housekeeping, pastoral services, social and recreational programs, medication administration, and assistance with the essential activities of daily living

- nursing and personal care on a 24-hour basis and access to a physician and other health professionals

Optional services are usually available for a fee. They may include hairdressing, cable TV and telephone services, transportation, etc.

Facilities must prepare a "plan of care" for each resident, outlining the care requirements and levels of service offered. This plan should be reviewed by the care team at least every three months and adapted as health needs change.

Two different terms are used to define the length of time a person stays in a facility:

1. **Long stay** refers to accommodations that are obtained for an indefinite period of time.

2. **Short stay** refers to temporary stays at a facility. The maximum number of days a person can stay on short stays is 90 days per year. There are two types of short stay:

   • The short-stay respite service provides a caregiver with a break from caregiving duties.

   • The supportive care service provides the resident support to regain strength and confidence, usually following a stay in a hospital.

What Is Palliative Care?

Palliative care is for patients who have chronic or life-threatening illnesses and involves the provision of pain management and comfort to a dying person. Palliative care eases the symptoms of a disease, rather than attempting to cure it. It is a team-oriented approach that deals with the physical, psychological, and spiritual needs of patients and their families, allowing them to live life to the fullest each day. Just as births can take place in a hospital, at a birthing centre, or at home, palliative care can be given anywhere. It can take place in hospitals, hospices, nursing homes, or at home, depending on the family and community resources and the patient's wishes. Arrangements and preferences can be discussed with the care team to best meet everyone's concerns.

The pain management and comfort needs of every patient are only partially medical. Nursing care, homemaking services, occupational therapy, speech therapy and physiotherapy, nutrition assistance, and counselling as well as pain medication administration fit into palliative care service.

Palliative care in rural areas faces particular challenges. "In a rural setting, a large part of the comfort component comes from staying in the community, surrounded by familiar faces," says Michael MacLean, director of AgeWise Inc., a consulting firm researching the health and social issues of aging.

Given the long distances, impact of adverse weather, and scarcity of health-care resources in the rural environment, supporting a patient and his or her family within the community can be difficult. In addition, since palliative care is tailored to and dependent on a patient's individual needs and wishes, it usually doesn't fit into a narrowly defined health-care system or program.

Rural palliative care is primarily administered by a family member with support from community and hospital services. Faced with the responsibility of caring for a terminally ill family member in addition to the demanding work of running a farm, what do most families do? It seems they just work harder.

"They can't neglect the farm work, and they can't neglect the patient," says MacLean. This can lead to stress, exhaustion, burnout, and physical illness in these caregivers, so caregivers need to take care of themselves as well as their family member.

Caregiver Hint: Use respite-care programs if they are available. Typically, respite-care programs offer alternative caregivers, short-term nursing home stays, or day programs to give the primary caregiver some rest.

When Moving Can't Be Avoided

When all signs point to a change in residence for your parents, your role as caregiver is pivotal in helping them make the right decisions and plans for the long term. Be sure that the decisions you make allow for their personal preferences and changing needs. Some questions to ask landlords, residence directors, or intake staff include those regarding affordability, availability, cost of maintenance, access to leisure and social activities, and the details of any necessary agreements. For your elder's comfort, also inquire about proximity of shopping, banking, and churches and about special programs and services. There are also some physical considerations, including accessibility, comfort in winter, and quality of nearby medical facilities.

Walking the Line

When to step in and when to leave well enough alone is a sensitive issue that often ruffles feathers. There's a delicate balance between independence and risk and between what's okay and what's not.

Selling the "Family Farm"

One of the most difficult decisions to make is what to do with the family home when elderly parents can no longer continue to live there. Urban or rural, the underlying premise for selling your parents' home is still the same. If it can't stay in the family, try to make the process as painless as possible for all concerned.

When the home is sold, you'll have your hands full with helping them to pack and move. If your parents are anything like mine, you'll find collections of Tupperware, children's toys, craft and hobby paraphernalia, and assorted memorabilia mixed in with antiques and family heirlooms. Your job is to decide what stays and what goes. Hopefully, this is done in concert with your parents' wishes and those of other family members. Chances are, there'll be some disagreements as to what goes where and who gets what.

When you have decided to buy or sell a home, the services of a qualified real estate professional are of utmost importance. The ideal sales agent will have a good working knowledge of local real estate market conditions, be prepared to deliver a high standard of service to customers, and have the support of an established real estate company. Most importantly, a good agent will save you time and money. Selected real estate agents specialize in eldercare services with special attention to accessibility and home care.

Use this helpful checklist as a reminder of the things you need to do before your parents move.

✓ Book the movers: You can choose to have the movers pack everything, or just the breakables, or you can pack everything yourself. It's a good idea to obtain estimates from several different companies. (Remember, this might be an emotional time, so think about limiting your involvement if possible.)

✓ If they own: Arrange to have gas, water, and electric meters read on the day your parents leave and have the bills forwarded to your address or your parents' new one. Have the oil tank filled before the sale closes, and provide a receipt to your legal professional if required. If the water heater or furnace is rented, arrange for a transfer of the rental agreement to the purchaser. Disconnect the telephone, cable TV, and water softener.

✓ If they rent: Give necessary written notice to the landlord and make arrangements for the return of any monies on deposit. Examine the lease as soon as possible. Knowing when it expires will allow you to establish a timetable for your parents' move.

Each province and territory has different rules on getting out of a lease in the event of the death of one of the residents. However, be warned that in most provinces the terms of the lease are binding (as in Ontario), even if the surviving spouse is unable to afford the rent. Ending the lease early is at the discretion of the landlord. Subletting is an option in most areas, although again, the rules vary by province.

✓ Get "Change of Address" cards from the post office and send them out well before moving day.

✓ Cancel any contracted services and pre-authorized cheques.

✓ Inform all home services, including nursing or home help, insurance companies, gardening, dry cleaning, garbage pickup, newspapers, magazines, etc.

✓ Make arrangements for trust or bank accounts and securities. Sometimes a simple address change and electronic banking does the trick. My mother still has her bank account in Coburg though the banking is done through a branch here in Toronto. It was a lot easier to do this than to close her account there, and notify all the organizations that paid pensions and so forth directly into this account. It's worked extremely well.

✓ Inform social, athletic, civic, religious, or business affiliations and memberships of the move and cancel anything or request refunds for any activities no longer required.

✓ Arrange for transfer of medical, dental, prescription, and optical records if changes are required based on a new location or to meet procedures that are required by the new residence.

✓ Change the address on or cancel the driver's licence and car insurance effective the day of the move.

✓ Collect all items that have been sent out for cleaning, repair, or storage—things such as fur coats and dry cleaning items.

✓ Make special arrangements for the moving of perishables, such as plants.

✓ Make special arrangements for the moving and care of pets.

✓ Dispose safely of all flammable liquids as it is illegal for movers to carry them.

Source: Royal LePage

Moving Checklist

Move Date		
Who Is Helping		
Name	Phone	E-mail
Expenses		
Item/Service		Cost

Item/Service	Cost

What Needs to Be Done (Always a good idea to follow up after completion)				
Task	Who Is Doing It?	Date	Arranged	Completed

Examples of Tasks to Divide

• Audit what can go, be moved, sold, or donated to charity

• Review and purge personal papers, bill, photos, slides, etc.

• Do a clothing inventory and donate unwanted items to Salvation Army or Goodwill

• Check garden tools and items in the garage

• Do a basement cleanup

• Get packing boxes, wrap, and markers

• Create new address labels

• Notify the post office

- Send change of address notes to:
  - Insurance companies
  - Pension providers
  - Bank
  - Credit card companies
  - Magazines and newspapers
  - Care providers
  - Family doctors
  - Utility companies (gas, electric, phone)
- Find out any car-related details (insurance, registration, location of all keys, etc.)

Relocation and Your Elder

You're applying for a new job that will involve moving from Calgary to just outside of Toronto. You've moved several times before and have dealt successfully with the challenges of resettling your husband and two boys. This time, the kids aren't the issue, it's your father-in-law.

Today, a large number of relocations discussions centre on "soft issues" such as eldercare. Thoughtful employers recognize that no two families will have the same concerns, but they realize that caring for Mom and Dad is becoming higher on the agenda. Eldercare services or programs are often available from employers with "on-line and live" advice, and many banks, realtors, and financial advisers now offer special services for elders.

What are the options you should consider when a job offer that involves a move from your community is on your mind and there's an older person in your life?

- **Take them along**. Consider moving your parents with the family to the new location. This keeps the family unit whole and minimizes out-of-town worrying. Costs are, of course, increased by the additional moving expenses, which will vary by personal circumstances. (Some enlightened employers cover these as well.) If your job postings are outside the country, check immigration procedures and medical coverage.

Often widowed parents (especially mothers) are happy to make a change, and I know some families who have had a lot of fun finding or renovating homes with in-law apartments for relatives. In other cases, the dynamics of living together are disastrous. Think carefully before you offer this option and, if and when you do, make sure your spouse also agrees that it's a good idea.

- **Upgrade locally**. If your parent is happy in the community but not necessarily well placed for the future, think about looking for a new, more supportive housing environment that is close by. No rush, just a gradual process to make sure that current and longer-term needs are on the table. If existing support and care can be expanded without further moves or changes, it's less disruptive for all of you. Your parents can be left to happily "age in place."

- **Negotiate family-focused trips home**. When you agree to take the new job, try to plan your time around making regular visits back home. Ask for the flexibility to leave quickly in an emergency situation and check your company's policy on "caregiving leave." Long-distance caregiving is unpredictable. Try to keep your options open and be ready for an emergency. Keep money available for sudden, unplanned trips to take care of eldercare situations. Be sure you have thought ahead about somewhere comfortable to stay when you're back in town.

- **Discuss and delegate**. Go over your plans with all concerned. Are other family members willing and able to fill in while you're out of town? Sometimes we get so used to doing things ourselves we forget that others may be willing to help. Try to find a designated person who will take over as the primary caregiver in your absence. If this isn't possible, make other suitable arrangements so that you and your parents are not left scrambling and you have an open and direct line of communication at all times.

- **Stay involved**. Make a concerted effort and commitment to be in touch regularly and predictably. With today's on-line and wireless options you can be in touch any time of the day or night if necessary. Schedule your calls so your elderly family member will always know when to expect to hear from you. Your calls are an event to look forward to and a time for catching up for all.

- **Hire help**. Geriatric care managers and eldercare accountants and lawyers, as well as nursing services, offer part-time or round-the-clock service advice and intervention. From paying the bills and mowing the lawn to preparing meals or taking Dad to the doctor's or the emergency room at the hospital, there's a full range of professional services that will keep things running smoothly in your absence. And, for the record, you can expect very timely, detailed reports from these professionals to keep you up to date.

- **Review costs carefully**. Will you or your parent incur additional costs because you're out of town? Are you currently underwriting certain expenses or providing services that will require cash in the future? Take a look at the budgets, arrange for easy-access banking services, and make sure there's no way your parent will suffer financially or be taken advantage of while you're not there.

> **My Story: Beware the Extras!**
>
> I had a not-so-pleasant surprise when I received my three-month "extras" bill from the nursing home. Besides costs of medicines not covered by OHIP, I found weekly hairdressers' fees, footcare bills, and charges for extra socks, underwear, and personal care items. I'd got a bill for cable TV and the snack shop. All told, I was on the hook for an extra $630— unbudgeted!

My Story:
The Best Alternative

My mother fought for years for her right to live alone and managed to do so, despite a number of incidents that were both frightening and costly to the health system. After she had a stroke, the doctor felt strongly that long-term care was the best option. Mom would still tell you she'd rather head home and try to struggle through on her own. But I think that she's come to realize over time that full-time care is her best alternative. Thankfully, now that she has accepted long-term care, it is far less stressful for the family. She's safer now and well cared for. We can relax knowing there's professional care 24 hours a day, seven days a week that's better than we could provide.

CHAPTER 4

Home Safe Home: Safety Measures and Accessibility

Imagine this scenario. Your mom has been discharged from the hospital with a prescription for a manual wheelchair, a bath seat, and toilet rails. However, she can't get in and out of the front door, let alone the bathroom! How do you make your home more accessible?

Start with the Basics

Depending on your situation, there is a range of no-cost and low-cost solutions—as well as more expensive alternatives. If someone is using a wheelchair, living at home can be challenging. Answer yes to three basic questions and your elderly relative will be home-free.

1. Can he or she get into the house using a wheelchair?

2. Can he or she get through the doorways?

3. Can he or she get into and manoeuvre within the bathroom?

If no is the answer to any of these questions, you'd better read on. Simply put, you've got to consider your elderly relative's options. Is it possible to move to a more accessible home? Is it possible to renovate or remodel? To help you decide whether it's better to remodel, move, or build, think carefully about your loved one's situation today and in the near future.

- Is your parent's medical situation stable?

- Will housing changes be required in the future if your parent's abilities decline?

- What are his or her goals for independent living?

- What housing modifications are needed?

- Will daily assistance be needed from a family member or outside caregiver? Does space need to be planned for helpers to work or live in the home?

- Do you need to postpone housing decisions until a caregiving routine has been established?

- What is the structural condition of the home? Is it safe? Is it worth the investment to make it safe?

- Can modifications be made without destroying the architectural appearance or resale value of the home? Is the home's appearance important to you or your parent?

- Does your parent have enough money or funding to live independently and safely?

- Would home care or moving to an appropriate facility be easier, safer, and less expensive with a better quality of life?

If you decide to relocate your parent, think about finding a realtor or property manager who can help you locate an apartment or house that much better meets your parent's current needs. Whether you decide to look for a new place, remodel, or build your own home, the following section will provide you with some practical guidelines.

Adapting the Home

If you have an aging parent, relative, or friend, you may want to consider making modifications to his or her home to allow more independence and a greater sense of security.

In reviewing home improvement projects to achieve easier mobility, remember that everything should be planned to fit the needs of the occupants, with an eye for accessibility, comfort, and safety.

Low-Cost Solutions

Getting in: Look for at least one accessible entrance with no steps or a suitable way to navigate around existing steps. A barrier-free entrance is one that will accommodate people in wheelchairs and walkers. To do this, a level or gently sloping pathway is needed, or a ramp without steps.

- Use portable ramps as a temporary solution.

- Build a ramp with no more than a 1-inch rise for every 12 inches in length (check with the ramp manufacturer for specific guidelines).

- Re-grade the site to make a ground-level entrance without steps. Make sure this does not compromise the foundation by allowing water to build up against the house. Check with your municipality to see if this kind of change is allowed and if special permits are required.

- Consider building a "bridge" to connect the house and yard on a sloping site so your parent can enjoy the outdoors more easily.

- You may need to make changes to the driveway so that the wheelchair lift in your van opens directly onto a deck, porch, or landing pad.

- If funds permit, you may be able to install a weather-resistant lift or elevator outside to get up to a front or back entrance. (You may also need to provide a protective structure over the elevator.)

Go wide: Doorways need at least a 32-inch clear opening to roll a wheelchair through a doorway under a person's own power. Here are some ways to make an existing doorway wider:

- Take the door off temporarily.

- Install swing-away hinges or change the swing of the door to allow it to open wider.

- Remove woodwork from around the door.

- Remodel the door to create a wider doorway.

Staying put: Before you go all-out, hit the panic button, and call the mover or the contractor for additional remodelling, consider no-cost or low-cost ways to relocate activities, restructure tasks, and rearrange furnishings. If your parent lives in a two-story or split-level house, activities for eating, sleeping, bathing, and living can be confined to one floor. If some of the household tasks your elder used to do are no longer accessible, think about eliminating these tasks or having someone else do them. For example, other members of the household could get the mail or do the laundry, and the elder could assume some of their responsibilities in turn. Finally, less "stuff" means more space. A wheelchair or walker will take up more space to manoeuvre in the home. Large pieces of furniture may block access to rooms or make it difficult to get around. Rearrange furnishings and decrease clutter to create straight, easy-to-follow "traffic lanes."

Falls, Public Enemy #1

Think the world outside is fraught with hazards? When it comes to older adults, the home is a real danger zone—at least when it comes to falls, slips, and other accidents. Despite being the most preventable health risk, falls are the leading cause of injuries among seniors and account for more than half of all serious injuries. In fact, 85% of falls occur within the supposed safety of seniors' homes. Many falls lead to serious injury, such as broken wrists or fractured hips; they can also lead to a loss of independence. We are also told that nervousness concerning additional falls often limits our elders from enjoying life to its fullest as they begin to avoid going out or staying in touch with friends for fear of falling again.

"Middle age is an awkward period when Father Time starts catching up with Mother Nature."
—Harold Coffin

What causes these falls? Two out of five household accidents happen in the bathroom. The culprits are not hard to spot—loose rugs, wet surfaces, slippery tiles, and other, all too common, household scenarios. Fortunately, by taking a few smart steps, you can go a long way to ensure that their home is much safer.

Watch Your Step!

A declining sense of balance and weakening strength abilities in combination with poor vision and high daily dosages of medication dramatically increase the risk of falling among elders.

- More than 30% of Canadians 65 and over experience at least one fall every year.

- While falls often result in a loss of independence, they also account for up to 20% of injury or deaths among seniors. Injury and death rates rise steeply with age.

- Stairs, steps, and floors (in addition to other construction features of homes or buildings) are identified more often as the cause of an injury than any household product.

- Hip fractures are the most common fall injury among seniors.

- The annual direct health-care costs of falls are estimated at $2.4 billion. Forty-one percent of total costs ($1 billion) are spent caring for injured seniors.

Source: Health Canada, Division of Aging and Seniors

Before any falls or incidents occur, a caregiver can launch a pre-emptive strike against falls. A good first step is obtaining an appropriate in-home needs assessment. The same kind of assessment can be applied to retirement or long-term care centres. Carried out by a health professional such as an occupational therapist, physiotherapist, or visiting nurse, these tests measure ability to perform an activity (often called level of function) and identify weaknesses at the same time as recommending changes to the environment, lifestyle, and day-to-day habits that will reduce risk.

The Importance of Listening

A caregiver should listen carefully when elders suggest they're in pain or experiencing discomfort. A fall might be in store if your elder has feelings of light-headedness or dizziness, or a history of falling, losing balance, or tiredness and fatigue. Also, keep an eye on any new prescriptions or side effects from existing medications. Being neglectful about taking medications also contributes to accidents or confusion (ask your parent's doctor if medications can have this effect). Falls may also be caused by poor vision, so have your elder's vision and hearing tested regularly. Balance may also be affected by the use of alcohol, which may not mix well with medications. Make sure your elder wears sturdy, properly fitting footwear with wide rubber soles. By taking these measures, you will help reduce the possibility of any falls and ease both your and your parent's minds.

Read on to find out how you can prevent falls and increase safety generally in all areas of the home.

Getting a Good Night's Sleep

Not surprisingly, falling out of bed or tripping over clothes or other bedroom obstacles in the dark is high on the list of unnecessary mishaps.

Bedroom Safety Tips

- Keep a charged flashlight handy in the bedroom. A mini-flashlight within easy reach of the bed is a useful aid to getting to the bathroom or kitchen during the night.

- Non-slip mats and, if needed, grab bars work well beside the bed.

- For increased comfort and safety, find out about a special home-care lift and tilt bed. It can be one of the best investments you make.

- A small humidifier or air-filtration system can enhance night-time breathing.

- Items such as a magnifier (to make reading easier), long-handled reachers, and specially designed dressing aids can be very convenient.

- Install side rails on both sides of the bed to increase safety and prevent accidents for tossers and turners.

- Use a night-light and make sure bedside lamps are easily reachable and have easy-to-operate switches. Many falls occur when someone gets up in the night for a midnight snack or a trip to the bathroom.

- Use a firm mattress for added support.

Hallways and Lighting

When it comes to lighting, you can't have too much. Add rocker switches, which can be turned on and off using an elbow, in place of wall switches in hallways, near the bed, and outside the bathroom. Line hallways and stairwells with motion-activated night-lights and install motion-sensitive lights to front and rear entryways. Also, light-coloured carpeting is easier to see, as are light-coloured handrails in stairways.

Guess Who's in the Kitchen

In the morning, at mealtimes, and during a midnight snack, the kitchen is often a hub of activity. Combine this busyness with electrical appliances, water, and tiles, and there's a real potential for accidents. If the kitchen is used by an older family member living alone or at risk, do a safety check.

Appliance Guidelines

- Make appliances more accessible by lowering or raising them to a height more suitable for the chef. For instance, by lowering a section of countertop and leaving the space beneath it clear, you can make it easier for a wheelchair-bound person to use the counter as a work surface. Installing a dishwasher about six inches off the floor makes it easier for everyone to load and unload.

- If you can, add roll-out shelving to kitchen cabinets.

- Look for a kettle that switches off automatically after it boils.

Top 20 Kitchen Safety Tips

Stop accidents before they start by following these proactive steps to accident-proof the kitchen:

1. Turn pot handles away from the edge of the stove, counter-top, or table.

2. Keep the oven and stove top clean—residue grease and food can easily catch fire.

3. Never leave cooking unattended (a "watched pot" does boil).

4. Secure electrical cords behind cupboards and appliances. Avoid extension cords because they can overload circuits, causing a fire hazard.

5. Discourage older family members from wearing especially loose clothing while cooking or working near the stove. You can buy special flame-resistant aprons from many cooking supply stores for extra safety.

6. Set the temperature of the hot water heater at 120 degrees Fahrenheit (49 degrees Celsius) to avoid hot water burns.

7. Don't stack plates or dishes in the fridge. Keep frequently used items—like butter and milk—near the front.

8. Respect the microwave. Check for non-metal items that might inadvertently be put in the microwave. Also, people are frequently burned because they don't expect microwave-heated items to present the same risk as food heated or cooked on the stove or in the oven. The steam that can build up in a covered container heated in the microwave can cause burns.

9. Don't put glasses, cans, and mugs near the edge of counters, tables, and shelves. Place "everyday" dishes on lower shelves, especially if your loved one frequently uses the kitchen on his or her own. Remove any items that can break easily.

10. Don't leave sharp objects unattended, and load utensils "points down" into the dishwasher.

11. Store sharp knives somewhere safe or even out of the reach of family members who may be easily confused.

12. Move cleaning supplies from below the kitchen sink to upper shelves or into the garage or workshop.

13. Remove medications from the kitchen and store them in a cool dry place. Your relative may become confused about dosages and their timing if the drugs are always visible. Also, humidity, which can sometimes be a problem in kitchens, can reduce the drugs' effectiveness.

14. Don't use high-gloss (and slippery) floor waxes or finishes on the kitchen floor.

15. Consider putting a non-slip mat in front of the sink. Clean up spills quickly.

16. Try to find useful items like "reachers," which are designed to take light items down from higher shelves, and "grippers" to help open tight jars or bottles. They can be purchased at your local health-care store.

17. Keep a fire extinguisher in the kitchen and learn how to use it. Add overhead sprinklers for extra safety.

18. Install smoke detectors. Replace smoke detectors that are older than nine years, and check the batteries once a month.

19. Buy a sturdy rubber stool with rubber feet, and a long-handled reacher. Discourage unnecessary climbing and reaching for out-of-the-way items.

20. Post a large, easy to read list of emergency telephone numbers on the fridge. In case of an accident, you need to be able to reach help fast!

The Living Room

Just being in the living room, the social centre of the house, can help improve an older person's outlook and well-being. Comfort is key, as well as safety and positioning:

- Attractive easy chairs (often referred to as lift chairs) sometimes come with heat and massage options and have options to help the user to stand up and sit down by automatically tilting. Chairs equipped with back rests and neck rolls make sitting more comfortable.

- Floor-to-ceiling transfer poles, similar to ones in buses and subway cars, set up beside the couch, bed, or toilet can also help make sitting and standing easier. Many come with special easy-to-grip surfaces.

- Remove throw rugs and secure all other rugs with tacks or two-sided tape.

- Secure all telephone and cable cords, wires, etc., so that they are out of the way.

- Mark transitions from one room surface to another (for example, from a carpet to tiles) with coloured tape for increased visibility, especially if they are similar in colour.

- Older people have trouble hearing when there is too much background noise. Keep volume levels low when radios, TVs, and computers are on to avoid discomfort and confusion for the older person.

Remember that noise and activity can be overwhelming. Sometimes the comfort, peace, and quiet of the living room provide a welcome solace and simply a change of scenery for someone who is frail or unwell. At other times, a visit to the "active" part of the house can provide much needed stimulation and an opportunity to share in family activities.

Caregiver Hint: Plan activities but be mindful of sudden tiredness, confusion, or extra noise that may be too much. Also, be mindful that many seniors wear hearing aids that may amplify even normal background noise.

Bathroom Safety

As a caregiver, I find the bathroom is my number one enemy. I've learned to cope by using some of the following tips regarding basic bathroom setup, tub and shower safety, toileting, and accessibility.

Caregiver Hint: Never leave a frail family member alone in the bathroom—not even for a second, even for something as innocuous as fetching toilet paper or other supplies from a nearby closet.

Basic Bathroom Setup

- Grab bars or safety bars are important. Install a grab bar on the side wall and another on the back of the shower or tub, as well as next to the toilet. Both ends should be mounted to wall studs, and not merely screwed into drywall.

- Install lever-type faucets, which require little pressure at the sink and tub or shower. Preset water heater thermostat controls to prevent scalding. Clearly mark hot and cold water handles.

- Remove or adapt the door lock to prevent accidental locking and to permit easy entry in case of emergency.

- Make sure that any cane or walker used in the bathroom has a wide rubber tip, and that it's kept dry.

- Ensure that the area is well lit.

- Remove area rugs. If the bathroom is carpeted, make sure the carpet is glued down.

Bathtub and Shower Safety 101

In the bathroom, a stall shower may make all the difference in the world to someone who has no easy way to climb into a tub. It may cost a few dollars more, but adding a seat makes showering safer for older bathers. Non-skid rubber mats or self-adhesive strips on the bottom of the tub or shower stall reduce chances of slips and falls, as do rails and grab bars. If showering is too difficult, consider sponge baths instead of tub baths or showers and do bathing in the bedroom.

Hand-held showers with flexible hoses make washing easier for both the elder and the caregiver. They easily attach to your existing shower arm or can be attached with a diverter valve and used in conjunction with the existing shower head. Some of the features are extra-long reinforced hoses and convenient wall-mounting brackets, and on/off valves built into the handle to allow control of water flow.

Fall Prevention

- Apply non-slip stickers or a slip-resistant mat to the floor of the tub or shower to increase grip while bathing.

- Place a mat with a non-slip rubber backing outside the shower or tub.

- Install grab bars and shower rails to make entering and exiting the tub or shower safe and easy.

Slip-resistant mats and stickers help, but if your elder has difficulty standing in the tub or would rather sit while bathing, here's what to buy:

- Bath and shower seats are available in blow-molded plastic for sturdier, safer seating or padded vinyl for added comfort; they are available with height adjustments and slip-resistant rubber feet. Protect the rubber feet from oil or talc.

- Transfer tub benches extend beyond the edge of the tub for non-ambulatory patients who have difficulty stepping over the side of the tub safely. Leg extensions are available to fit bath and shower seats and transfer benches are made to accommodate old-style bathtubs.

- Consider purchasing a battery- or water-powered bath lift for additional comfort and safety. Portable, easy-to-use bath lifts offer the reclining backrests and lateral supports for positioning.

Toilet Tales

If being on the throne is no longer a simple matter for your elder, here are some helpful suggestions, depending on his or her requirements:

- Raise the toilet seat. A few extra inches of height may make sitting down safer, especially for someone with a recent hip fracture or anyone who has difficulty getting up from a low seat. Home health-care stores carry these extensions that can be easily used with the existing toilet bowl.

- Consider using adult diapers at nighttime.

- Try using a bedside commode.

What Is a Bedside Commode?

People who have difficulty getting to the bathroom are helped by these bedside toilet facilities. A commode is a movable toilet that is usually placed on wheels. Basically a chair with a toilet seat, it is made out of metal or plastic and equipped with a removable container under the toilet seat that can be cleaned after use. Generally, a commode can be rolled away when not in use and its wheels can be locked to prevent it moving while it's being used.

"Middle age is when you have two temptations and you choose the one that will get you home earlier."
—Anonymous

Anyone who is too weak to get to a bathroom, particularly those who are in bed most of the time, could benefit from a commode. A commode should also be considered for people who cannot use bedpans or in cases where transferring the person to a bathroom would be too difficult for the caregiver.

Depending on the physical limitations of the patient, you can choose from a number of different models.

Basic, with fixed arms: This is for people who can walk, stand, and sit down safely, but may have trouble accessing a bathroom because of stairs or distance.

Drop-arm: This model is for non-walkers who need help sliding into the commode from a wheelchair or bed.

Over toilet: In addition to bedside use, this model can also be placed over a regular bathroom toilet with the container removed.

Caregiver Hint: Always ensure that the container is securely under the seat and be sure to lock the wheels before use.

Toileting Risk Assessment

When does it become risky for an elder to continue to use the toilet independently? Each case and level of care required is different. A yes to any of these four questions means help is needed.

1. When seated, can your elder reach down to pick up objects from the floor without falling? Does the elder have satisfactory sitting balance—that is, with one hand holding on for support?

2. Is your elder able to stand independently without holding onto any furniture or is he or she able to stand only with a walking aid or if there is something to hold on to?

3. Is Mom or Dad able to walk independently or does he or she require a walking aid or helper?

4. Can your elder get up and go—eat, dress, groom, shower, and toilet—independently or does your parent use assistive devices (e.g., long-handle brush) for certain tasks? Would he or she be able to stand and transfer to a bedside commode chair or would standby supervision or help for feeding, grooming, dressing, showering, and toileting be required?

Issues Beyond Safety

Here are some additional issues that you may encounter in the bathroom, particularly when caring for someone with Alzheimer's disease or a related condition:

Shortened attention span: People with cognition limitations can forget they are sitting on the toilet and begin to stand up and leave or they can become distracted by the slightest noise and become startled or upset.

Refusal to bathe: Resistance to bathing is one of the more frustrating behaviours that caregivers face. A bathtub full of water can be terrifying to an Alzheimer's patient. Others may be concerned about getting their hair or bandages wet or soap in their eyes. The water may appear to be too deep. Being forced to bathe against their will may prompt some elders to try to escape or resist. Installing soft, protective edges on counters and corners, and using shower curtains (instead of shower doors) are all bathroom modifications that can minimize injury or avert a fall when an elder is agitated or frustrated.

Caregiver Hint: A coloured bath mat on the bottom of the tub can make the bottom easier to see and make the water appear more shallow. Face a person with Alzheimer's away from the visible exit and involve them in the showering process by installing a grab bar on the wall opposite the door and asking them to help by holding onto it with both hands.

Cues to finding the bathroom: Pathways on the floor (made with coloured electrical tape) or wall railings can guide and direct a person to the bathroom and back to the bedroom. Negative guides, or modifications to discourage going the wrong ways, are also helpful. Consider putting up "Stop" signs on doors other than the one leading to the bathroom. If the only room with a light on or open door is the bathroom, it could attract your loved one's attention and guide him or her there. Make the most important rooms stand out and be the hardest to miss. A bright-coloured doorway is one way to attract attention.

Bathroom comfort: What makes a bathroom pleasant, comfy, and homelike? Add soft and colourful towels, carpeting, curtains, shades, potpourri, pictures on the wall (framed with non-reflective plastic, not glass), colourful wallpaper borders, etc. An accessible warm blanket, stored under the sink or the laundry cupboard, would be welcome on those cold nights when sitting on the john may not be too pleasant.

Caregiver Hint: Water rushing out of the faucet, the flushing toilet, or the exhaust fan may cause too much noise and discomfort. Close the window, wait until later to flush the toilet, and turn off the fan if your family member becomes agitated easily or resistant.

Need to Accommodate a Wheelchair?

A 60-inch (152.4-cm) diameter circle of manoeuvring space in the bathroom area is needed so the individual can reach fixtures. To achieve more usable floor space, try the following:

- Arrange for the door to swing out instead of into the bathroom.

- Replace the existing door with a folding door.

- Use a curtain for privacy instead of the door.

- Remove undersink cabinets to provide knee space.

- Change fixture locations to create more floor space.

- Replace the tub with an easy-to-access shower unit.

- Relocate the toilet or shower to a corner of the bedroom.

Consider how you will transfer your family member from a wheelchair to a toilet, shower, or tub. You'll need room to move the chair close enough to the sink to wash your loved one or brush his or her teeth. Most important, make sure the wheelchair can get through the door.

Don't overlook the threshold at the bathroom door. These small "bumps" are high enough to stop even the most modern wheelchair. Normally 3/4 of an inch (2 cm) high, they can be replaced with special thresholds, which are only 1/4 inch to 1/2 inch high (0.5 to 1.3 cm) and tapered. Add some tile or carpeting, and you barely have a bump at all.

Clear space to the side of and in front of the toilet. Transferring to and from a wheelchair can take place from in front of the toilet or from one side. Helping a family member stand from a sitting position requires plenty of space in front of the toilet. You need room to grasp the person's arms or hands and lean backward, lifting him or her up.

"Accessible" also means "close by." A second-floor bathroom may have several drawbacks. It can require the caregiver to go up and down the stairs several times a day or it may simply be too far for your loved one to get to. Stairs can be a silent cause for incontinence—if you can't get to the bathroom, you can't use it!

Upstairs Downstairs—Stairlifts Work Wonders

While stairs can be a real nuisance or even a hazard, moving into a bungalow or limiting access to one floor of your home may not be options. If you find yourself in this situation, you'll probably want to look into installing some sort of stairlift.

When looking for a stairlift, you may find yourself confused by technical jargon and the wide range of models available. You should be able to get informed advice from an occupational therapist or other home-care pro in your area. To get you started, here is some basic info about what's available and what you should consider when buying a lift.

There are three basic stairlift types:

1. **Conventional stairlift**: This is the most common type of lift and it's generally used by people who can walk, but who have trouble with stairs. Fixed to a straight or curved track, these lifts can usually be mounted on either side of the staircase. While most lifts come with a chair, there are models for people who prefer to stand or perch on the lift. Here are two options to think about:

     • **Folding armrests and foot plates**: Many lifts block off quite a bit of the stair area, so you may need to fold away foot plates, armrests, and the seat while the lift is not being used. If you're going to need to fold the foot plates, make sure that this can be done safely and easily as it may need to be done several times each day and it can be a very tricky task!

- **Swivel seats**: When getting off the lift, the person using it needs to turn around to face away from the stairs. A swivel seat can make this manoeuvre much easier. Check for models that can be operated either manually or electrically depending on your needs.

If you choose a conventional stairlift for someone with a wheelchair, there are some questions about access you'll need to address:

- How will the person get the wheelchair on and off the lift?
- Is there enough room at the top and bottom of the stairs to get the wheelchair on the lift?
- Will you need two wheelchairs—one at the top and one at the bottom?
- Is there enough room on the lift for the person, the wheelchair, and a helper if necessary?

2. **Wheelchair platform lift**: These lifts, specially designed to handle wheelchairs, are often the most practical option for someone who needs to get up and down the stairs without leaving the wheelchair. If you're considering this option, note that you may need to lower the area at the bottom of the stairs to provide level access for the wheelchair over the platform. Also make sure that there's enough space at the top and the bottom of the stairs for the wheelchair to turn around when the person is getting off. Think about how other people may be inconvenienced by the lift.

3. **Vertical or through-floor lift**: Check out this option if there's not enough room around the stairs for a regular lift or a wheelchair platform lift. This lift will carry the person from a place like the living room on the lower floor up to a bedroom or landing. The lift can be either fully or partially enclosed and can be constructed with or without a shaft depending on your needs. Do note that this option can be quite expensive as renovations are often required!

Special Considerations about Lifts

In most cases, families are able to adjust quickly and easily to stair-lift additions, but be sure everyone understands the effect the new equipment can have.

- **Space**: Stairlifts run on tracks and generally take up quite a bit of room on the stairs. Be sure to ask sales representatives how much room the lift will take up on the stairs and whether any parts can be folded away easily to make more room.

- **Safety**: Stairlifts will stop if they encounter any object or person obstructing the stairs. Through-floor lifts and wheelchair platform lifts also have mechanisms to prevent anyone being crushed by them. Lifts also generally have guards to prevent fingers from moving parts.

Caregiver Hint: Be especially careful in your selection of lift if your house is home to small children and/or pets!

Purchasing Tips

- **Seek advice**. Ask an occupational therapist to advise you on the best choice of lift for your home. When purchasing, be sure to ask as many questions as you need to about the lifts as installing a lift can have a significant impact on your home configuration and lifestyle.

- **Try before you buy**. Purchasing and installing a lift can be a significant investment. Be sure to try out any model before buying to make sure it suits your needs.

- **Ask for a home demonstration**. A sales representative may be able to arrange for you to visit someone's home so that you can see firsthand what a stairlift or through-floor lift is like. Take this opportunity if it's offered!

- **Consider funding options**. Lifts and structural adaptations are expensive. Think about funding options before you decide to make a purchase. Some benefits or insurance packages cover home modifications and lifts but often only if labour costs and equipment purchases are pre-approved.

CHAPTER 5

Hiring Help in Your Elder's Home

Finding a reliable and qualified care provider or home-helper for your parent requires research. The best advice I can give is to be relentless and don't compromise on the quality of care, training, and expertise of care providers and their availability to fit your schedule. Your parent's well-being is linked to stability and routine in this area. And your stress can be reduced with qualified home-health-care professionals by your side.

Getting Started

List the job tasks clearly and ask applicants to check off those that they are willing and able to perform. (One family told me that their caregiver refused to toilet their 80-year-old mother.) Address subjects like benefits and wages, frequency of paydays, lateness, absences, vacations, and notice time. Make sure the applicant has reliable transportation to get to and from work on time. If you work and are heavily dependent on the home-care assistant, emphasize the importance of reliability in the interview and be sure to have a back-up plan in case the caregiver does not show up.

> "You can't turn back the clock, but you can wind it up again."
> —Bonnie Pruden

You may wish to consult a family physician, hospital discharge planner, or geriatric case manager to help you locate home-care providers in your area. Think carefully about your elder's needs before you venture into the world of interviewing and hiring. It's just like finding suitable childcare—with the right person or people, things are well under control at home and you can head off to work without additional worries. If the dynamics are wrong, it'll be nothing but trouble, so make a change and put yourself out of your misery as soon as you can.

Finding the "Right" Caregiver

Relative as caregiver: Your elder may prefer care from a relative rather than a stranger. Perhaps someone in your family can offer care without receiving any compensation or will agree to live rent-free in exchange for providing care. It might be a perfect arrangement for someone who is finishing school, is between jobs or marriages, or is ready for a change.

Some families treat this arrangement as an officially paid position with a written agreement and benefits.

Private agencies: Paid caregivers with training are referred and managed by home-health-care or nursing agencies in your region. Some of these agencies are branches of larger national firms, while others are very local. Find out if the caregiver provided by the agency is an employee of the agency or an independent contractor. Avoid up-front deposits and payments in advance. Check references, understand qualifications and job descriptions, and ask for financial arrangements in writing. Some agencies charge a one-time finder's fee and offer a 30- to 60-day guarantee. Others charge by the hour or pay period.

Recruiting locally: To find a caregiver or personal support worker locally, run an ad in the daily newspaper or search the Yellow Pages under home care, hospice, or nurses. Ask other caregivers for referrals. You can also talk to employment agencies that specialize in placing workers who are trained to work with seniors.

Be Clear about Your Elder's Needs

Establish a list of your elder's basic needs and "nice to have" extras. Your first priority is to determine what kind of help is necessary. The easiest way to do this is to create a list of circumstances and tasks. This should allow you to narrow down the key areas where a professional can be of assistance. A personal support worker could provide assistance with bathing, laundry, or meal preparation.

Try to match the personality of the caregiver with that of the person receiving care. Can they get along? Will they work together? Are they patient and friendly with each other? There are other questions to ask. Is the caregiver capable and strong enough for moving and lifting? Can he or she cook the food that your parent likes? Does your loved one need a nurse for medical treatments—dressing changes on wounds or pressure sores, IV therapy, diabetes monitoring? Will driving be required? What about shopping and banking?

It may take a few tries before a good match is made. In general, it's the cheerful, positive helpers that make the most difference in your life and that of your elders.

Caregiver Hint: Language, menus, tradition, and family values are pivotal in making a selection. Pay attention to the cultural or religious issues that will make your loved one most comfortable. Don't expect your Hungarian father to suddenly fall in love with Chinese food.

Check References

Credentials do matter. Screen applicants carefully to ensure that they have the necessary qualifications, training, and/or temperament. Your interview should include a full discussion of the client's needs and limitations as well as yours as it relates to time away and other responsibilities. Have a written copy of the eldercare job description, conduct a careful review of the care worker's home-health-care training and experience, and take time for a discussion of his or her expectations and availability. (For example, is he or she looking for a short-term or long-term placement?)

Have applicants fill out an employment form that includes name, address, phone numbers (home and cell), date of birth, social insurance number, educational background, work history, and references. Have applicants provide a driver's licence, school and training certificates, and citizenship and photo ID. Also be sure that you have detailed information on previous employers and watch for gaps in their work history. With the applicant's permission, conduct a criminal background check.

How to Screen an Agency

For the most part, agencies expect you to trust their expertise in finding the right person for the job. It can be a little off-putting when a stranger shows up at the door for the first day of work when you and your relative have never met him or her before. (Specify if you have a gender preference or you might have a surprise.) However, with careful matching on the agency's part, it usually works out, so my advice is to find a reputable agency and work with them. When you call, ask these basic questions to get the conversation going with the placement consultant or case manager on the other end of the telephone.

- How long has this company been serving the community?

- How are employees selected and trained?

- Are there written policies and procedures for staff?

- Does the company carry malpractice insurance coverage?

- Will the company provide literature explaining its services, eligibility requirements, and fees?

- Is there a "patient bill of rights"?

- Will you be charged hourly or weekly?

- Is there a supervisor to oversee the quality of care that patients are receiving at home?

- What are the provider's emergency procedures?

- Is there coverage 24 hours a day, seven days a week?

- Are nurses and therapists able to evaluate in consultation with doctors and specialists?

- Can they ensure patient confidentiality?

- Do you have references where cases are similar to yours?

Hiring an Agency? Use These Quick Reference Q & A's

Q. Is the agency bonded and insured?

A. Agencies providing homecare should be insured against any losses or liabilities as a result of their employees' actions.

Q. How are nursing and care staff chosen?

A. The agency will verify the education and skills of their staff as well as screen them for physical health. Top agencies will provide ongoing training so that staff can upgrade their skills.

Q. Will an in-home assessment be completed?

A. Some agencies offer a complimentary in-home assessment by a registered nurse. This assessment is a valuable opportunity for you to evaluate the agency's ability to develop a care plan and schedule to meet the needs of the family.

Q. What are the costs?

A. This will vary depending upon the type of care you need. Most personal-care services are paid by the hour, while professional services are paid by the visit. It is important to clearly understand the distinction and any premiums you are paying for.

Q. Will the agency send the same person all the time?

A. Consistency and continuity of staff are key indicators of quality service. Although it's ideal, it is not always possible to have the same agency staff member providing care each time. Good agencies will monitor and minimize the number of different staff involved in providing care.

Q. Are any of these services covered?

A. Provincial government funding is available if you qualify. In addition, some private plans do cover home-care service. Most agencies will coordinate and optimize their service by working with the funders.

Special Extras to Consider

Heavy lifting: If the older person needs to be transferred from a wheelchair to a commode or lifted into bed, make sure the aide knows how to do this safely. A lifting device may be requested as many agencies and individuals follow a zero-lift policy to protect their backs.

Full time plus: Don't try to hire someone on a seven-days-a-week basis. Not only is it against the law but also no one can manage to remain effective without a break. Aides who live in or sleep over cannot be expected to be on call 24 hours a day. If your relative needs frequent help or nighttime supervision, consider hiring a second person or have family members fill in.

Ensuring personal security: However trustworthy you feel your caregiver might be, it is essential to protect your parent's assets and precious items. Put private papers and valuables in a safety deposit box or safe and put a few proactive procedures in place such as the following:

- Check the phone bill regularly for unauthorized long-distance or 1-900 calls.

- Set a limit on cheques and credit cards for household accounts if money must be handled at all.

- Don't leave cash around the house, and insist on receipts for all purchases.

- Have mail sent to your home or a postal box where you can pick it up.

Protecting against abuse: Although abusive situations are not common, you can usually prevent poor treatment by workers if you make sure the workers are not depressed or overburdened and that there is someone regularly checking on the person receiving care. Even within the family it is wise to be alert to unfortunate signs that your loved one is being neglected or not properly cared for. Some warning signals are the following:

- The elder is whimpering, crying, or refusing to talk.

- The elder has bruises, fractures, burns, or pressure sores that can't be explained.

- The elder has poor personal hygiene with an unkempt personal appearance.

- The elder's living quarters are dirty or chaotic.

- The elder has weight loss for no medical reason.

- The elder shows personality changes and is more fearful.

- The elder exhibits confusion, excessive sleeping, or other symptoms of extra sedation.

Even if you aren't sure, it's best to find ways to ask for a supervisor's assistance when an agency is involved, or if you're in a private situation, replace the home-care worker as quickly as possible. If it's a family situation, ask the doctor for advice. Beyond a doubt, your parent should be as comfortable as possible with the home-care situation and deserves appropriate, professional care.

"When it comes to age we're all in the same boat, only some of us have been aboard longer."
—Leo Probst

If possible, involve your parent in initial selection decisions to ensure that he or she is comfortable and feels safe with the candidate. Check in with Mom and Dad on a regular basis to confirm that his or her needs are being met, discuss any potential concerns, and verify that your parent is being treated with dignity and respect.

Long-Distance Caregiving

All's been well for the last few years, and then suddenly, in the middle of the night, the dreaded phone call comes to say that Mom, who lives in another province, seems confused and unable to care for herself. Her helpful neighbours who watch over her well-being have taken her to the hospital. You're on the next flight. Welcome to the world of long-distance caregiving.

I n today's fast-paced world, many families find themselves separated by distance. It's not unusual for family members to live in different cities or provinces, sometimes even different countries, and that trend is not about to change. Research predicts that the number of long-distance caregivers will double over the next 15 years.

There's good news, though. A wealth of knowledge is now available to help those who are trying to manage from far away. If you live more than an hour away from your parents, you'll find this chapter helpful. If you're in another town, read carefully. If you and your parent live at different ends of the country, this is your new bible.

> "You know you're getting old when history books include events you remember reading about in the newspaper."
> —*Anonymous*

On the Road...Again

The average age of a long-distance caregiver is 46, and the average age of the care recipient is 78. Adult children find themselves helping from a distance and travelling back and forth with a certain amount of regularity. If this sounds like you, you're not alone. On average, caregivers spend four hours travelling to their parent and invest 35 hours of care each month. Delve into these valuable ideas that'll help you to come to grips with "the rules of the road."

Step 1: Don't panic. Navigation is generally more important than speed. Think before you act.

Step 2: Realize that conditions change and that, given your distance, you'll probably find the changes in your elder more dramatic than do those who are involved on a daily basis.

Step 3: Gather information. Be ready to share what you know with other family members and health professionals and keep track of all your conversations and decision points.

Step 4: Take care of yourself. Travelling and charging back and forth can be stressful. Be sure to slow down, eat well, and make your health a priority.

A Beginner's Checklist

When you arrive on your parent's doorstep, whip through this handy list as you jump-start your caregiving efforts. It'll tune you in to priorities and give you a quick assessment of where help is needed this time.

✓ Understand the current medical situation and the risk factors.

✓ Review medical appointments and/or consultations with doctors and other health professionals.

✓ Connect with other family members or significant others to determine their roles and willingness to help.

✓ Check medications and make sure your elder is taking them on time (is your medication list up to date?). Know the location of the local pharmacy and who holds prescription renewals. Know about any other alternative, vitamin, or herbal treatments that are part of your parent's daily regimen.

✓ Ascertain the schedules of other caregivers and family members.

✓ Find out about how personal care such as dressing and bathing routines is being handled.

✓ Review meal planning (Meals on Wheels, grocery shopping, etc.).

✓ Assess chores to be done: laundry, yard work, and household maintenance and arrange for someone to look after them.

✓ Arrange regular transportation to appointments, church, social events, etc.

✓ Do a quick check of finances. Are there bills that need to be paid?

✓ Locate and put all essential documents (powers of attorney for personal care, wills, and banking information) in a safe place.

✓ Recognize the importance of and arrange for social visits from friends, family, and volunteers.

✓ Check for financial assistance or insurance funding that might be available.

✓ Know where to find and who has access to house keys and any home security codes.

✓ Review driving safety issues (status of licence, insurance, and location of car keys).

Being miles away from older parents can also mean feeling frustrated and helpless when trying to access services from afar. There are no simple answers, but there are a number of practical things you can do to make your task more manageable.

Be Prepared

When you visit your parents while they are well, anticipate future health or safety problems. Privately paid case managers and occupational therapists are available through nursing agencies or, if you qualify, through provincial health authorities to help older people and their family members decide when assistance might be needed. These services are called in-home assessments and can be arranged through your elder's family doctor. Involve your parents in the assessment of their needs and help them understand the value of being proactive. Simple changes made now can prevent accidents or crises in the future.

Gather Information

Look for community services that are available in their region. There's usually home care and Meals on Wheels. You can get this kind of information over the phone or on the Internet. Prepare to be patient and persistent and have as much information as possible on hand about your relative's situation. It's a good idea to write down the name of the person you spoke to, on what day, and what follow-up is needed. Get referrals, if you can, for any new services or care providers that are needed. One-stop shopping with a single retail supplier for equipment or care manager for services is often the best way to go if you are coordinating from afar. See the section on health-care professionals and services.

Ask Questions

When you investigate local resources, be ready to take notes on topics such as these:

- how to apply for a particular service (is there any paperwork, verifications, or certificates that you will need to supply)

- services that the government or provincial health system offers

- any private services that are available

- any assessments that are needed and who is readily available to help with decision-making

- fees and how they are calculated

- whether there is a waiting list

- how to link up with care providers (home care, long-term care, respite and palliative care)

- what not-for-profit associations exist that are applicable to your parent's condition (e.g., Alzheimer's Society, Heart and Stroke Foundation, Parkinson's Society)

- how to bridge gaps between service providers

- who is in charge and how will they report to you

- banking and bill-paying options (find out about banking and bill-paying using on-line or direct deposit)

Keep a Record

You need to know the who, what, when, where, and why of medical, financial, personal, and other issues. Get a blank journal or exercise book or make a separate place on your computer or electronic organizer and start collecting this information so that it is both readily available and portable. Make a list of all family members and their key contact information, as well as the names and numbers of all caregivers and family doctors.

Get to Know Neighbours and Friends

It is virtually impossible to go it alone when arranging care. Instead, work to build a reliable team of caregivers for your loved one. This could include hired help or staff through a nursing agency, an accountant, and a geriatric care manager. Neighbours, caring cousins or other relatives, and friends should be part of the team, too. If you can't reach your parent, knowing you can call these people will be a godsend.

Caregiver Hint: Plan ahead and start meeting neighbours, friends, and care agencies next time you are in town so you are better prepared should an incident or emergency occur. Talk to others who are in the same situation as you, for they may already have quick solutions to some of your problems.

Be Sensitive to Your Parents' Views

Even though dealing with parent-care issues and logistics can be time-consuming and frustrating, it's important to try to maintain a positive focus and reach consensus. One of the best ways to influence your parents' decision-making is to explain any services or support that is available. Sometimes it is helpful to have someone your parents respect like a pastor, lawyer, or accountant recommend or help explain the services that are needed. If your parents are able to understand, it is important to share schedules, details, costs, and quality-control measures to help them feel more secure. In many families, it is a challenge to get parents to initially accept help, so don't be surprised if you encounter resistance.

When You're Not There

Long-distance caregiving has its own special challenges for both the caregiver and the care receiver, so here are a few things to consider when you are faced with eldercare responsibilities:

- Are publicly funded services available in the community where your elder lives?

- Are these services easily accessible?

- Is there a professional within the local community available if the person requires help accessing these services? (e.g., geriatric care manager, family accountant, lawyer)

- Does the person have a relative or friend in the community who can help?

- As a caregiver, is your energy level up to the stress and fatigue of travelling back and forth?

- How will your eldercare commitment and time away affect your family?

- Are you in a career or work situation that allows you to take time off?

- Are you financially able to handle the costs of long-distance caregiving?

- Are you strong emotionally and able to take charge on the spur of the moment?

- Are you patient and assertive enough to be able get things done from afar?

Considering a Move?

Sometimes family discussions are centred on a quick-fix solution: moving a loved one closer to you or other family members. This may be a good idea, but keep in mind a number of important issues. Will Mom or Dad be happy in a strange community? Will your parent have enough social connection during the day if he or she is living at your house? Will your brothers and sisters be able to continue visiting your parent? How do your spouse and kids feel about your increased involvement? Is your home suitable for your relative? Would your parent be better off in a local nursing home, surrounded by friends and activities, or will it be better to start again in a home closer to yours? What happens if you or your husband gets a job offer that involves a transfer?

Caregiver Hint: Not so fast! Too often, we uproot older people and disrupt their lives, only to find that the families they moved to be with are divorcing or moving again. Obviously a second move or breakup of households will create a whole new set of problems.

Making Arrangements

Sometimes caregivers prefer to have a trusted observer look in regularly on their parent. This is especially helpful when formal care is not really needed on a regular basis. Often, you can pay building superintendents, neighbours, or local students to run errands, shop, and provide regular visits.

Wonders of Modern Technology

Despite the hurdles that being miles away creates, staying in touch is much easier these days. If you use the phone wisely, the cost of even frequent calling shouldn't be too expensive. If your elder is computer-savvy and comfortable using e-mail, send regular, easy-to-read e-mails that are more like the letters that they are used to. Avoid short, snappy business lingo. For most of our parents, the written word is still treasured and reread. Send a card, include photos of the kids, pets, and day-to-day events. You may also find it easier to get your kids to send their grandparents letters when they are sent via e-mail rather than picking up pen or pencil.

Caregiver Hint: The more involved you can be in your parents' lives, the easier it will be to spot and resolve challenges and issues as they arise.

Things Change, Keep in Touch

Regular contact or visits are vital. If you are unable to manage them, arrange for others to provide this service. Things can go downhill very quickly, and it is important that parents are not left alone for extended periods of time. Commit to calling on a routine basis and be disciplined about sticking to this schedule. Remember, a personal call with a few discreet questions is the best way to find out how things are going.

Scheduling Visits

Notwithstanding the reality of your over-hectic life, the importance of paying visits to an aged or ailing parent cannot be stressed enough. The less frequently such visits take place, the more extended they ought to be. These visits are crucial to re-assessing a situation, providing respite for other caregivers, and reconnecting with your parent.

These are times to establish whether their driving is still safe, they are managing with meals, and medicines and household chores are on track.

Medical emergencies or accidents usually require an immediate visit and perhaps a longer stay. It's a good idea to have a contingency fund and a few days of holiday banked for such eventualities.

Divide Responsibilities between Family Members

Often, due to logistics, relationships, and so forth, one family member (usually an older daughter) will assume a leadership role, especially when it comes to talking to health professionals. It's important, though, that all family members are involved and informed, so meet and chat with others as often—and as early in the process—as possible. Ensure that everybody who wants to be involved is included in the decision-making process and that you all have a common understanding of goals, tasks, and responsibilities. Getting together provides an opportunity to ask each other for support and air feelings or concerns. Focus the discussion on care issues and avoid accusations and blaming. If the meeting is likely to be difficult, consider inviting a trusted person to facilitate.

Circulate a tentative list of tasks that will need to be done, such as accompanying relatives to doctor appointments, handling care, and handling finances, so that everyone will understand the responsibilities involved and be able to ask questions.

Further Reading

When Parents Won't Accept Help

After 55 years of marriage, Doreen Davis missed her late husband dreadfully, but she kept up with her friends and hobbies, continued driving, and stayed busy. That changed dramatically when a fall sent her to hospital with a broken hip.

A week before her discharge date, the family held a conference. Her children came up with excellent ideas about Doreen's care, so her adult daughter was feeling quite pleased with herself as she arrived from her home an hour away to outline their plans. These included a support worker for baths; a homemaker for meals, cleaning, and laundry; friendly visits; telephone monitoring; and an alarm necklace for emergencies—"You'll never be alone at all, Mom."

Doreen's angry response shocked her daughter. A broken hip obviously didn't mean a broken tongue—and where did our gentle Doreen learn that kind of language?

One of the most difficult and sensitive topics to broach with a parent is the notion of getting help for him or her in the home. You may have tried home help in the past and experienced problems with inconsistency or reliability that made it difficult to integrate care into your parent's daily routine. You've heard all the objections:

- I don't want strangers in my house!

- Our last try at getting even a cleaning lady didn't work out.

- What will I get her to do and what will it cost?

- Your father would never accept help—it'll hurt his pride.

- I can do all this myself, it just takes me a little longer.

- Never mind, I'll soldier on...

Did You Know...

Caregivers Are on the Move

- Nearly half a million Canadians moved to care for someone with a long-term illness.

- In nearly one in five cases, people moved closer to provide care for a friend.

Source: Statistics Canada's General Social Survey (1996)

Let Your Fingers Do the Walking...

Here are a few tips on tracking down the telephone numbers of health and service providers in other cities:

- Pick up an extra copy of the local phone book or Yellow Pages next time you are in town. Extra copies are available from the Bell Store or from larger reference libraries. Look under headings such as Nursing Homes, Senior Citizens' Lodges and Homes, and Senior Citizens' Services and Centres.

- Check out the Web for services, refining your search to include the city and/or province you are looking in.

- The Yellow Pages Web site, www.yellow-pages.ca, lets you search for businesses and services across Canada on-line.

What's Really Going On?

Think about how you feel when things get out of control at work, or you're forced to accept something new that's outside your comfort level. Imagine, then, feeling that way all the time, and you'll have an idea of how many elders experience the world. The elder years bring great satisfaction and rewards, but they are also years of loss—the death of friends and spouses, and cumulative losses such as no longer being able to drive, a decline in basic mobility, changes in surroundings, and loss of general confidence and optimism.

Life Changes

The five stages of grief described so many years ago by Dr. Elisabeth Kubler-Ross—anger, denial, bargaining, depression, acceptance—apply not only to death, but also to any dramatic change in life. Anger and denial, for example, are immediately evident to any adult child who has tried to suggest that a parent give up driving! But what's really going on is a well-justified fear of change and resentment over lost control of daily activities. Bargaining is a familiar response—agreeing to a cleaning lady when what's really needed is a nurse. Depression is a serious problem among the elderly and is often attributed to "just grief," so that medical help is not sought. It's important to anticipate, recognize, and deal with these stages to help your parent move forward.

Education is also on the agenda. Home care has changed over the past 10 years, as have all aspects of eldercare. There are options between the extremes of "alone at home" and "going to an institution." You owe it yourself, and your parent, to find out the most current information available.

A Different Approach

So what went wrong in the case of Doreen? Her children had the right answers—but like all things in life, presentation is everything! What is the best way to present your suggestions so they're considered thoughtfully?

You are probably aware that a legally competent person cannot be forced to accept help. It is your task, then, to objectively assess your parent's needs, identify where help could make his or her life easier, then research the services that are available to meet the need.

Anyone coping with eldercare is no stranger to family dynamics. Ask yourself—are you really the best person to be doing this? Get professional help if you need it, rather than risking a false start with a poor result. Plan your approach beforehand and think all options through before acting. The six-point plan outlined below can help you get started and minimize problems.

Give It Time

And what about Doreen? She returned home from hospital to minimal care. Her daughter called several times a day and visited daily, but within a few weeks, Doreen's world had shrunk to a bedroom, night table, and TV. She didn't change out of her nightgown, the shades were down all day, and she took all her meals on a tray.

Finally, there was an evening of sharp words, then tears and hugs, and some apologies.

The next day the daughter called in an eldercare consultant to work with both mother and daughter on a realistic plan of action. The three of them determined that personal care and meals were a top priority, and that Doreen jealously guarded her privacy. A few options were described in detail to Doreen, focusing on how her daily life would be affected and allowing her to ask questions, voice objections, and understand the costs. A short checklist of what both mother and daughter hoped to accomplish was drawn up. It was decided to introduce daily help for a trial period, based on the checklist, with the plan to be reviewed after two weeks of support.

This was only part of the equation, though—who exactly was to carry out these duties? The eldercare consultant suggested two experienced caregivers. The daughter preferred the first candidate; however, after three days, her mother felt "fussed over" and told the woman not to return. This naturally prompted another lively mother-daughter discussion! The second candidate, equally qualified, somehow made the care seem less invasive and was pronounced a success.

A Happy Ending

Six months later, Doreen's caregiver comes in from 8 a.m. to 1 p.m. daily. She gets Doreen up and dressed, takes her to activities in her wheelchair, prepares and serves two meals, and organizes an evening meal. Doreen is managing in her apartment with a walker, uses the microwave, and enjoys a good dinner every night in privacy. She has a sense of control over her routine and it's given her, and her adult daughter, their lives back.

As her daughter says, there is no sweeter irony than hearing your mother say, "Dear, why didn't we do this years ago?"

With thanks to Pat M. Irwin, a former financial services consultant who is the founder and president of WorkingWomen+, a consulting service assisting adult children in dealing with aging parents.

> "Purpose is the most powerful motivator in the world."
> —Ghandi

Helping Out: A Six-Point Plan for Smoother Sailing

1. **Know your options**. Assess the real need by observing your parent through the day. Where do they think the challenges lie? Compare notes.

2. **Choose your team**. Inform yourself about the many resources available, including private, volunteer, public-sector, and community services; their features, advantages, and availability.

3. **Do the math**. Depression-era parents often have deeply rooted money anxiety. Get a range of prices for each type of service, compare it to your requirements, and do the arithmetic up-front.

4. **Write it down**. It is essential to document your requirements: the type of service you need, at what level, for what frequency. It's a good idea to develop an outline to clarify for all three parties—caregiver, parent, and adult child—what's expected, and what's not included.

5. **Get it done**. The key to successful implementation is to manage expectations—yours and your parent's. Do this by reviewing your requirements and establishing clear goals that you

want to accomplish; for example, getting help once a week for grocery shopping.

6. **Keep in touch**. No system is foolproof and backsliding is to be expected—"I'm coping fine now, dear." Even in the most ideal circumstances, needs will change over time. Carefully monitor what's happening, listen to your mom and to the caregiver, and expect to do some fine-tuning.

Source: Working Women+

CHAPTER 7

When the Chips Are Down: Crisis Management

Who does what, when? This chapter will examine ways for you and your family to make eldercare arrangements during difficult times after a diagnosis, an incident such as a fall, or hospitalization. Prompt decision-making is often important. Juggling and coping are the mantras of this stage of care.

Best advice: Look before you leap. Get second opinions, take notes, and make sure your decisions, however quickly you make them, are well thought out. Don't close any doors.

Where to Go for Immediate Help

Oftentimes, the need to care for our elders is caused by an "accident" or "incident." Suddenly, we find ourselves face to face with a doctor in the emergency room or rushing home from work to deal with a crisis. At times like this, it is important to do the following:

- Call your family physician for advice.

- Contact your local nursing or community support agency.

- Call family and friends for assistance.

- Be sure to understand medical coverage and benefits programs to avoid unexpected bills.

Take the time to understand all the options available to your loved one. Frequently, we are stressed and rushed at times like these and have trouble remembering what was said by experts. Take notes. Don't hesitate to ask nurses and clinicians to write down a diagnosis and rehabilitation instructions. If in doubt, call back later. Don't be pushed into making decisions too quickly. Barring a major health crisis or safety issue, waiting a few hours or overnight won't make a huge difference. In fact, taking extra time and thought will help you develop the best long-term plan.

"I just got lost in thought. It was unfamiliar territory."
—Anonymous

Dealing with Hospitalization or Rehab

It's a whole new world for you and your elder when he or she suddenly needs the care and support of others. Hospitals and rehabilitation centres encourage and mobilize patients to return home and resume the normal activities of daily living as soon as possible. In addition to the medical and nursing regimen, treatments and programs will include a range of occupational and physiotherapy activities as well as a social and recreational focus. How do you make sure your parent is getting the best care and advice? Here are some wise words to help you make it through this challenging time.

1. **Connect with health professionals.** Get to know the experts and talk with them a lot. Ask questions and give them as much information as you can about your parent's situation and condition. Be patient and pleasant, recognizing that your loved one is one of many in an often overcrowded system. While the squeaky wheel often gets the grease, it's important to remember that you will catch more flies with honey than vinegar.

2. **Make visits meaningful.** Visit your elder as often as you can, even if the visits are brief, so your parent is assured of your support. Leave little reminders of your visit so when your parent wakes up, he or she will remember you were there. Simple items like cards, small flower arrangements, a colourful box of tissues, or family pictures will provide comfort.

3. **Get friends to visit.** If your loved one is up to it, reduce the pressure on yourself by asking your parent's friends to visit as often as they can. On those days, give yourself a break. Make it easy by providing directions and helpful hints about what to take and how long to stay. Reduce shock and surprises by

briefly explaining physical changes in your elder and current levels of cognition. Remember, visitors may be elderly as well.

4. **Find volunteer help.** Ask the hospital for a volunteer to spend time with your parent or, if needed, hire someone to spend a few hours with him or her two or three times a week. If your parent is religious, most facilities have a chaplain or pastoral care available on request. Students or women's auxiliary members may also be on hand to visit.

5. **Maintain good grooming and appearance.** Arrange for your parent's hair to be done regularly, nails trimmed and polished, and other grooming practices so your parent feels better about how she or he looks. Take some favourite items of clothing and surprise him or her with something new to wear as often as possible.

6. **Encourage and praise.** Recovery is often difficult and rehabilitation is hard work, especially in an unfamiliar environment with what may seem to be a demanding team of physiotherapists and occupational therapists. There will be goals and expectations to meet in regaining optimum physical, mental, and functional levels. As your parent makes progress, acknowledge it often. Expect your parent to be tired and often disillusioned, especially at the end of the day when the hospital or rehab centre is quiet. Let your parent know how much you're rooting for her or him, and how happy you are with the progress. Telephone with words of encouragement when you can't be there in person.

Taking Mom or Dad Home

After an "incident," especially one that has involved hospital care, most elders are eager to go home. It is the shared responsibility of health-care providers and families to inquire about next steps. Usually, the hospital or rehab facility's staff, discharge planners, or social workers are assigned to this role, and when the system is working at its best, there is a very close working relationship between these advisers and your community service providers. A word of caution: Be tenacious and don't expect too much from the public system. It's often not quite enough to meet people's all-round needs, especially if you hope to leave Mom or Dad home on his or her own and go back to work. Expect to have to hire private care or make highly organized care arrangements.

Time for Home Care

Once home-care service providers start coming into your elder's home, it is very important that you keep a written record of needs and a schedule so you will know when help is arriving and what responsibilities they must carry out.

Although you may have the best of intentions, there are many things you may not have considered or may have missed along the way. Sit down for a moment and discuss these overarching issues with family and health team members.

How can you best use the available help?

If you feel overwhelmed or frustrated making arrangements, a geriatric care manager or case manager, who can be referred by a doctor or social worker/discharge planner, is well equipped to work out an overall written plan. You may choose to be a little less formal and make some basic decisions and arrangements, keeping the following issues in mind.

Will the medical condition or disease progress?

- How is it affected by aging?

- If it's a progressive illness, will plans include both short-term and long-term needs?

- What education will you need?

- What are the medical needs that may require special nursing skills or special medical equipment or supplies (e.g., catheter, IV, medications)?

- Are there primarily physical and/or mental issues to consider (e.g., Alzheimer's, stroke, depression, mobility)?

What are the legal and financial implications of the change in condition?

- Is there an existing legal care plan or power of attorney?

- Do you need the services of a lawyer or accountant?

- Are funds available to rent or purchase equipment, make home renovations, and cover the costs of transportation?

- What will happen to your parent's house or apartment?

- Is insurance coverage in place when the house is empty?

If appropriate, approach funding agencies such as March of Dimes, your elder's Extended Health Insurance or benefits plan (e.g., Clarica, Blue Cross), Department of Veterans' Affairs, the local social services, the provincial department of health's assistive devices program or equipment rebate plan, or diagnosis-specific agencies (e.g., the MS Society).

Is your parent's doctor able to make home visits and answer calls promptly?

More than half of Canada's family doctors do make home visits. Family physicians in rural areas are most likely to make house calls—73% of them report that they do! Don't be afraid to ask.

While a whopping 87% of family doctors feel that home care should be made a more significant part of Canada's health-care system, more than half of the surveyed respondents noted time pressure as their most significant barrier to more active involvement in home-care activities. So recognize that your elder's doctor is extremely busy, too. House calls should be a last resort.

Find out if the doctor is e-mail friendly. See if the doctor responds when you leave a detailed phone message with a request for a callback.

Caregiver Hint: Leave your cell phone number for callback purposes to avoid annoying phone-tag.

Source: The Role of the Family Physician in Home Care (2000) and News Release (October 15, 1998), The College of Family Physicians of Canada

Brown-Bag Checkup

Sometimes your parent will have so many pills at home that it's downright confusing! After an incident, your parent will likely have to take even more prescription medication. Perhaps the specialist will suggest an altogether different therapy than the current one. Should your parent continue to take the old medications too?

Ask your doctor to schedule a Brown-Bag Checkup. In your Brown Bag, take the following:

- any prescription medications your parent is taking, in their bottles from the pharmacy
- over-the-counter medications (like aspirin or Maalox)
- vitamins, herbals, or natural products your parent is taking

During the checkup the doctor will review all the medications and products, including the non-prescription products.

The doctor will check

- to see if medications are the same as those listed on your parent's medical record;
- for the correct dosage strength and the frequency of use;
- to make sure no medication is outdated or to be discontinued;
- whether more than one drug is being used to treat the same condition;
- to make sure drugs are not cancelling each other out or resulting in serious side effects.

A Brown-Bag Checkup is helpful for both your parent and the doctor. The doctor will ensure you know what the medications are, under what conditions they are to be taken, and if there are special circumstances. This is also a good time to ask questions or talk about any special laboratory testing or ongoing diagnostic tests, such as use of diabetes test strips or blood-pressure monitoring.

Caregiver Hint: Have a single doctor in charge or aware of all the pills and products your elder is taking. If this is not possible, given a variety of specialists treating various conditions, keep your list of medications and over-the-counter products up-to-date. Share this information in written form with every doctor or health professional you visit. If you can, fill all your prescriptions at the same pharmacy and let each pharmacist know all the medications your elder is taking, and include over-the-counter, herbal, and mail-order prescriptions.

Managing Difficult Behaviour

Art Linkletter once said, "Old age ain't no place for sissies!" The world becomes a very frightening place for a person who is disoriented. Friends and family members may have unrealistic expectations, and simple tasks that you and I take for granted (getting dressed, having a shower, using the washroom) become stressful undertakings.

A person's response at such moments may be perceived as a difficult behavior, yet in reality it is more often than not fear and frustration. The following are some simple strategies that pros have found effective in neutralizing difficult behaviours:

- **Make the time to listen**. Slow down and listen. You may be able to find the cause of your elder's anxiety.

- **Empathize**. Acknowledge and respect all emotions expressed.

- **Try not to say "No" or "You can't do that."** These are fighting words and can result in a confrontation.

- **Try distractions**. After listening and empathizing, try a change of subject. Focusing on a new topic or interest can relieve tensions.

- **Avoid the stigma of failure**. No one likes to be reminded that an ability to do something is no longer there. Try to give assistance without showing it as a major effort.

- **Break down tasks**. When assisting with dressing, for example, show one item at a time to your elder. Giving two shoes to a person with Alzheimer's disease can result in confusion and frustration. Try one shoe at a time, gently showing which foot it is for.

- **Avoid confrontation**. Whenever necessary, postpone activities, even those in a normal routine, until your parent is receptive to moving forward with the task and ready to accept assistance.

Twenty Take-Charge Tips to Manage an Eldercare Crisis

Here are 20 hints that'll help you keep your head above water during an eldercare crisis!

1. **Knowledge is everything**. The devil you know is better than one you don't. The more information you have, the less likely you are to be guessing and making mistakes. Find out what services are available and what they might cost. Look for sources of general eldercare information as well as for specific conditions. We're info-rich these days. The trick for you is to figure out how to transfer knowledge into coping power. What skills can you acquire to make you eldercare friendly and stress-free?

   Caregiver Hint: Don't reinvent the wheel. Canadian expertise and information are readily available. Be selective. Be objective. The good news is that the basics are pretty well covered by provincial health care. However, as with all insurance programs, how is basic defined? Each family's needs are different. In my family's case, basic wasn't enough and we decided to hire extra help.

My Story: A Good Bridge

When Mom opted to stay in Cobourg, she knew that my brother and I would be too far away to be involved in her hands-on daily care. To facilitate her transition to the nursing home and stabilization, I chose to pay for extra daily visits from a local nursing-care provider, had fresh lunches brought in from the "outside world," and arranged for more than the one bath a week to which she was entitled by the home's guidelines. This left me more worry-free and much more connected.

What did I learn? Once the routine set in, extra help wasn't really necessary. The union staff weren't exactly welcoming of our non-union helper, and potential liability issues surfaced between the home administration and our provider. Our helper wasn't privy to all nursing-home pro tocols. Mom became less anxious and more comfortable as time passed. It was, however, a good bridge to get us started.

2. **Don't be afraid to ask for help**. Initially, a caregiver might get the support he or she needs by confiding in one or two close friends. It is very important to be able to share your thoughts and feelings. Don't isolate yourself. In the first few weeks of caregiving, you may be too busy to even think about joining a support group. However, established support groups offer an alternative outlet for sharing and venting feelings. By acknowledging your feelings, you can begin to understand them. You might find it easier to talk to a group of people who are in the same position as you, who truly understand your situation and can offer emotional support as you carry out your day-to-day responsibilities.

   If the traditional self-help group is not for you, you might prefer a telephone buddy system where one-on-one support is offered, or the anonymity of an on-line support group. For information about the appropriate support network for you, call your local community health centre, speak to your local home-care agency or case manager, or contact relevant groups, such as the Alzheimer's Society or the Arthritis Society.

   Caregiver Hint: Understand that you're not alone. For 70% of Canadians age 30 to 60, caregiving for aging parents is now a reality. More than 70% of informal caregivers are women, most often wives or adult daughters. Half of the informal caregivers in Canada are over 60 years old and 36% are older than 70.

3. **Consider all eventualities**. Though it's often a difficult task to face, it may be necessary to get your parent's financial and legal affairs in order. If you procrastinate too long, your loved one's mental or physical health might deteriorate to the point where he is not able to sign authority over to you. Has power of attorney been assigned to you for your loved one's personal care and financial matters? Do your parents have wills? It would be prudent to get legal advice so that everything is looked after before a crisis occurs.

   Caregiver Hint: Find copies of important documents and check to make sure that you have what you need readily available.

4. **Take notes**. Written records avoid confusion, waffling, and potential discrepancies. Refer to notes for confirmation, instructions, and care plans. It's hard to remember everything and always best to double-check and confirm.

Caregiver Hint: The best way to share the care is with clear instructions and good notes. It will also help health professionals during assessments and appointments if your records are in order.

5. **Time discussions with your parents carefully**. Thanksgiving dinner is not the time or place to drill down about divvying up the family china, medical care, or funeral arrangements. Pick a suitable relaxed time—a free Saturday or Sunday morning in the garden or during a casual afternoon walk or over coffee in the kitchen—to talk to your elder about future choices should his or her health and independence decline. Start with open-ended questions and be ready to listen and gently bring the discussion back to where you'd like it to go. You may not like what you hear and you may need to finesse the details over time, but you have to begin somewhere.

Caregiver Hint: This is not a business meeting; it may not have a tight beginning and end, and it may not be on your terms and at your time. These are your parents—be gentle, but be firm about wanting to make some headway soon.

6. **Privacy matters**. Ask for your parent's agreement to have a more formal discussion at a planned time but perhaps try to get ideas from both of them independently as to what their goals and wishes might be. This is an adult-to-adult discussion and at first should probably involve only the individual who will take primary responsibility.

Caregiver Hint: Expect resistance even in the "talking phase." Many parents want to retain control and independence for as long as possible.

7. **Show respect**. An aging parent may be slower in step and thought but he or she has a lot of life experience and has made a number of lifestyle choices. Change, after all these years, may

be difficult. Don't discount their expertise or wishes. Rely on your knowledge of their past, their preferences, and their right to maintain their dignity and sources of pleasure.

Caregiver Hint: Be ready to make decisions on the run. Expect trepidation and delay tactics. Always try to imagine what they would do and want for themselves and each other if you're unable to involve them in the next steps.

8. **Financial facilitator or decision-maker?** How involved can and will your parents be in financial decision-making? If you know their wishes and they can actively participate, your role is quite different. Who will pay the bills? Decide now that you'll use their assets to pay for their care and think about whether it will be necessary for you to top up funds and if so, by how much. At the end of the day, be careful but let their assets, if any, determine the levels of care. And remember, your parents' lives might have been simpler and more frugal than yours.

> "Life can only be understood backward, but it must be lived forward."
> —Soren Kierkegaard

Caregiver Hint: Make safety, nutrition, necessary equipment, and hygiene top of the list to support comfort and quality of life.

9. **Don't get in between.** When spouses have different needs and express them, it might be tough on you. Don't be surprised when they argue. Don't be awestruck that Dad still drinks and Mom moans about it. Unfortunately, illness and aging don't always bring out the best in us.

Caregiver Hint: Even if they're miserable together, they'd be worse off apart.

10. **Think before you blurt.** Too often, we make up our minds about things and set the train on one track. Yes, loss, sadness, or illness are highly uncomfortable and are certainly personal. Keep your cool. Don't make too many assumptions and don't be rude or threatening if care isn't always available at the drop of a hat. There are always options and often more choices than we think.

Caregiver Hint: Stay focused and calm. It often helps to write a few notes for discussion or take an article with you that makes for a good starting point to discuss your parent's care with others. Remember, communication is the key to getting things done. Be open but tactful.

11. **Opt for safety**. Yours and theirs! Don't take on or support unsafe situations. Early safeguards will deliver solid returns and hopefully prevent unnecessary risks.

   Caregiver Hint: Consider doing regular home safety checks and providing your parent with visual checklists, memory prompts, safe lifting tips, and access to the right home health-care equipment.

12. **Recognize beliefs and ethics**. Where a strong religious or cultural framework may compromise nursing care or recovery, you might want to wait for a vacancy in a culturally centred home (e.g., Ukrainian, Jewish, Finnish, Chinese). There's a delicate balance between maintaining an environment that is familiar and comfortable and providing those services that are available and necessary. If your parents are like many immigrants, they may slip back into speaking only their mother tongue. Being given traditional foods and respect for their customs will help them feel secure as they hold onto the past.

   Caregiver Hint: For as long as possible, encourage parents to continue communicating in English or French or whatever they've chosen as their "official" language. The ability to personally explain to a doctor or medical team member or stay linked to the outside world is worth maintaining if possible.

13. **Manage guilt and obligation**. A sense of duty is often synonymous with parent care. Some parents remind their kids that it's "pay-back time." Act from your heart—do what you believe is fair, manageable, and reasonable. Take on only what you can handle and find innovative ways to have the slack picked up.

   Caregiver Hint: Don't wallow in self-pity and don't be pushed into feeling obliged. Get on with doing what you can.

My Story: A Breakfast Solution

At 7:15 one morning a few weeks ago, my brother called to say he was on his way home to take Mom out of the nursing home for breakfast. The bad news: He'd woken up feeling guilty that he hadn't visited for a few weeks. The good news: He was able to get up and go to see her. The result: A happy Mom and a guilt-free son who can enjoy the rest of his weekend.

14. **Be needs-focused**. Identify and prioritize what is really required in the situation. Chances are you have only some of the skills and knowledge to adequately provide what's needed. Outside help may be just what will make the situation more palatable and calmer for all. How much are those you care about at risk? Think about the potential issues or changes in the short, medium, and long term.

    Caregiver Hint: Work to a plan and be honest about your feelings and ability to cope along the way, especially when one sibling does more care-work than others or caregivers are involved. Communication and defined roles are essential.

15. **Consider geography**. Often times a parent needs to be cared for from a distance. Is someone willing to move to obtain the benefits of having family close by? Consider the consequences of staying put vs. packing and moving.

Charlotte's Story

Charlotte had lived in Welland for most of her married life, and she'd raised her children there. Recently widowed and living on her own, she saw an opportunity to be a part of her son's family when they moved back to Ottawa from Toronto.

Planning and decorating was a family affair, with Charlotte's daughter-in-law working to help her fit a house full of treasures into 600 square feet.

The result: a custom-built, ultra-comfortable granny flat. Charlotte now enjoys the company of three generations and is happy and secure.

Caregiver Hint: Don't feel guilty if you can't be there. Remaining in a town far from where you live is often your parent's choice because of familiar surroundings, memories, and friendships. Embrace long-distance caregiving and set aside some special time each week to make the most of the situation by phone, e-mail, or planned visits.

16. **Ask insiders: When in need...** A significant number of people are employed in the health-care field in your community, so seek out advice and opinions on local programs, facilities, and home health-care equipment suppliers on an informal basis—especially if your need is urgent or your options seem limited or too expensive. Connect with some of your parent's friends, neighbours, and their families who may have already or are currently walking this road. Ask about their ideas, solutions, and plans. Solicit feedback. It's amazing what you can learn in a few hours by chatting with someone who has "been there, done that."

    Caregiver Hint: Fast-track yourself to local resources and innovative ideas and support services.

17. **Share research.** Knowledge is a powerful tool that will help you to explore and narrow the choices you may face as the result of the crisis. If you share information with an aging relative or friend and other family members, or encourage them to do some of their own research, this can assist everyone in moving decision-making to the next step.

    Caregiver Hint: Share what you learned. Base your decisions on reliable information and pass it on. Sometimes the help of a geriatric care manager or a family physician may be needed to present options in an unbiased way—especially when time is of the essence.

18. **Set some ground rules.** Be clear about your role, time availability, and the expectations that will be either placed upon you or self-inflicted. Know your limits and don't be afraid to adjust them as time goes on. Will you change adult diapers, help with bathing, clean house, garden, pay bills? If not, it's

better to be realistic, let others know your position, and put an alternate plan in place.

Caregiver Hint: Eldercare can be rewarding but it also loads on the stress. Statistically, caregiving interferes with your time at work and ability to be productive—not to mention time with your own family.

19. **Measure impact**. How much impact will you allow your elder-care responsibilities to have on you? Remember, your health and well-being are priorities. If you burn out or run dry, you're no good to your parents or yourself.

    Will eldercare affect your...

		Yes	No
a.	marriage	Yes ❑	No ❑
b.	work	Yes ❑	No ❑
c.	children	Yes ❑	No ❑
d.	volunteer activities	Yes ❑	No ❑
e.	financial situation	Yes ❑	No ❑
f.	day-to-day life	Yes ❑	No ❑
g.	health	Yes ❑	No ❑
h.	recreation	Yes ❑	No ❑
i.	transportation	Yes ❑	No ❑

    Caregiver Hint: Look at the areas where you're being affected and weigh the costs. If you have checked "yes" more than twice, you're well on your way to trying to do too much. If you've got any areas in the "too much" category, get help quickly. Plan now before the mountain is too hard to climb.

20. **Work to a plan**. If you hire service providers to come into your home or your parents' home, it is very important that you plan ahead and keep a detailed written schedule so you and your parents will know when help is arriving and what they are to do. You will also need a system to keep track of medical information over time.

    Caregiver Hint: Check out a few of the forms that are available in the back of this book.

Further Reading

Mom's in Rehab...What Now?

Pat M. Irwin

When a person suffers a stroke and embarks on a recovery program, the family must prepare for the many changes that may lie ahead.

Muriel Norfolk suffered a stroke in her home, pressed her personal alarm, and was taken to hospital. After three weeks in an acute stroke unit, her two adult children were called to the hospital to sign forms for her transfer to a rehabilitation hospital.

That weekend, her son, Ken, unlocked the door to his mother's empty condo, set down a bouquet of flowers and some milk and bread on the counter, and looked in amazement into the living room. There was his sister, Liz, surrounded by books and bed linen, stuffing his mother's clothing into garbage bags.

"What are you doing? Mom's in rehab now; she'll be home soon!"

"Sure, Mom's in rehab now. But she's off to a nursing home. Let's list this place while the market's hot!"

"Are you out of your mind? You never cared about her, anyway."

"Don't be so naive; we'll need this money. You'd better get used to how things are now."

Harsh words, slammed doors and, the next morning, Ken's worried wife called me for help.

What Is Rehab, Anyway?

I met with Ken and Liz at the scene of the argument—a chaotic sight, especially with the wilted flowers scattered over the green bags! The first task was to review their understanding of what rehab is all about. Rehabilitation is the transition phase following an acute illness that prepares the patient to return to the community. Whether it's a rock star drying out after too much high living, your mother recovering from a broken hip or your dad from a stroke, it has four aspects:

1. physical recovery that occurs in therapy sessions;

2. social, emotional, and spiritual recovery activities such as socializing with other patients, recreation, visiting with friends and family, and being involved in personal care;

3. practical recovery—using new equipment and learning new ways of doing things in order to become as independent as possible;

4. planning and facilitating access to appropriate community services, care, and housing options.

Rehab is offered in many hospitals and in specialized centres. Admission is made by the acute-care hospital, based on availability and location. Interdisciplinary teams staff rehab units and typically include an attending physician, physiotherapists, occupational therapists, speech and language pathologists, psychologists, social workers, dietitians, and recreation directors, along with one or more nurses.

When a patient is admitted, each team member makes an assessment of needs. Then a care plan is developed and its progress is tracked in regular team meetings. The number of therapy hours is carefully designed to maximize progress: adding more therapy will not result in faster recovery. The average stay is 65 days but may vary from one to three months.

Admission

The hospital's social worker had explained Mrs. Norfolk's options for rehab to her, but her children's reactions were causing her confusion and anxiety. I visited her, with Ken and Liz in tow, and described the rehab hospital she was going to, showed pictures from its Web site, and explained exactly how she'd spend her days. Mrs. Norfolk's speech had been affected by the stroke but her cognition was fine and she struggled to ask a lot of questions. We decided that Liz would accompany her mother in the wheelchair taxi to the new location and get her settled in.

I contacted the rehab hospital's social worker, who arranged for a meeting with the family and care team a few days after admission. She had some excellent suggestions. The family was to be given information about the illness so they would know what to expect. Then they worked with the rehab team, benefiting from the team's expertise. The family members were also told to participate in the program by accompanying Mrs. Norfolk to her therapy sessions and observing what was going on and learning to recognize the progress.

So Far, So Good

Mrs. Norfolk settled in to the unit fairly well, but her children continued to squabble over her care. Liz arranged for a private caregiver in the mornings so her elegant mother would feel clean and well-groomed ("Liz, I thought we were supposed to save her money") while Ken leased a large-screen TV and VCR to keep her company in the long evenings ("Ken, you know Mother hates anything mechanical"). Ken's business kept him busy all day so he liked to drop in at about 8 p.m. and stay until midnight and expected Liz to take the day shift so their mother would never be alone.

Very soon the social worker intervened to limit family involvement. While participating in therapy and helping at mealtimes is productive for both patients and families, 24-hour attendance is actually counterproductive because it prevents the patient from regaining independence with the support of the rehab team.

A Turning Point

Both Liz and Ken were interested in the goals set by the rehab team and each was eager to review the progress at the next family-team meeting, a month after admission. All the team members updated the goals they were working on with Mrs. Norfolk, such as eating without assistance, assisting with personal grooming and dressing, and moving smoothly from bed to wheelchair and back with the assistance of only one trained person. The team's consensus was that progress was good and Mrs. Norfolk was congratulated on her hard work and willing participation.

Ken spoke up. "There's one goal I don't see here—walking."

The social worker explained that this was not a goal in this situation; the goals had been based on detailed assessments and reviewed carefully with Mrs. Norfolk, who understood them and their implications. But Ken and Liz had not understood that their mother would never walk again, even though she herself knew it.

So the family learned the importance of a sound assessment and participating in the setting of realistic goals. They also learned it's important to focus on strengths rather than deficits: It's natural to be overwhelmed by abilities that have been lost, even temporarily, but progress should be celebrated.

Preparing for Discharge

That meeting marked a change in the Norfolk family dynamic. Ken and Liz were in awe of their mother's ability to accept her new disability; they tried harder to decipher her speech and listen to her wishes. She had specific ideas about what her new life should be and sent them off to some of the retirement homes that had assisted daily living facilities where some of her friends had already moved. She dictated which possessions should go with her, signed the sales agreement on her condo with a shaky but confident signature, and set her sights firmly on her new home.

Her family learned that they needed to be realistic about outcomes and that home visits are excellent preparation for discharge, as they quickly demonstrate if adjustments are possible and what will be needed. It is also important that care plans should begin well in advance of the discharge date.

The rehab team will work with the family to understand the options but it will not discharge a patient until it is confident that suitable accommodation is in place.

A Happy Ending

Mrs. Norfolk now lives on a retirement home's complex-care floor and engages fully in all activities and makes regular shopping trips with a private caregiver using Wheel-trans. Her condo sold for an excellent profit, which helps to finance these extras.

Many of her extra possessions went into storage, where her children continue to enjoy arguing over their dispersal. Some things never change!

The author is grateful to Peggy Arden, MSW, RSW, Senior Social Worker, Baycrest Centre for Geriatric Care, for her assistance and information.

Source: Solutions Magazine

Dad's in Rehab, Too

His goal is to walk out the door when discharged from Toronto Rehab's Spinal Cord Rehabilitation Program this summer. And, at the rate he's going, he may do just that. Six months ago, Justin Wadden's family learned that emergency surgery was required to save his life. At midnight on Christmas Day, 2001, neurosurgeons at Toronto Western Hospital began what turned out to be a six-and-a-half-hour operation to remove two cysts from his spinal cord. The infected cysts had encircled and compressed his spine, leaving him paralyzed from the neck down.

Today, the 67-year-old retired research chemist credits his remarkable progress to the nurses and to therapists, Mona and Sylvia in particular, whom he's worked diligently with since being admitted to Lyndhurst Centre last January.

When he arrived, he couldn't sit up by himself or lift his legs, but within a month, he was sitting up on his own. About a month later, he stood up. By April, Justin was walking short distances with the support of a walker, and looking forward to attending his granddaughter Christine's fifth birthday party. Her greatest gift that day was seeing her grandfather walk through the door.

Quick Tip

Physically inactive people older than 30 years lose approximately 3% to 5% of muscle mass per decade and experience a parallel decline in muscle strength.

—C.A. Vella, IDEA Personal Trainer

The Seven Stages of Caregiving
Judy Cutler and Bill Gleberzon

Over 2 million Canadians provide informal care at home to elders, according to a recent Statistics Canada study. I was one of them. I cared for my mother at home on a full-time basis during the last two years of her life.

My role as an informal caregiver was painful, of course, but more than that, it was personal, profound, even sacred. My mother and I really got to know each other—unconditionally. There were no barriers between us as individuals, and we went beyond defining each other by our relationship. We were just two people trying to make it through a rough time together, but in fact being totally isolated with individual suffering. The actual details are a blur in many ways as I have tried to put them behind me and get on with life. Still, to dig deep into it all feels important on many levels: to really bring closure to the trauma of the experience, to hopefully benefit other informal caregivers, and in some way to pay tribute to what my mother and I shared.

I have often been asked what those intense years as an informal caregiver for my mother were like. This has led to a mission to share my experience with others who might find themselves suddenly and unexpectedly conscripted as an informal caregiver for a loved one. With an aging population and increasing focus on home care, this will become a more likely scenario for many people.

I spent a long time wondering how to put what happened during my years of caregiving into words. My challenge was to do this in a meaningful way. Then, suddenly, for some inexplicable reason, Shakespeare's description of the seven ages of man flashed through my mind. Where this inspiration came from was a mystery. My long background in theatre? Or some spiritual insight? Whatever it was, it gave me the idea to explore the stages that I had gone through as I cared for my mother. Without trying, I came up with the seven stages of caregiving. Thank you, Shakespeare!

The first stage was, of course, *shock and numbness*. My mind froze as I heard the doctor tell my mother that she had colon cancer and that immediate surgery was essential. However, my body went into action. I took care of the required planning with the hospital and called my sister and my son; the rest of the family had to wait for a less numb moment. And, of course, I could hear myself saying all the right things to my mother. It felt like a dream—someone else's life. The truth was that my mother's illness propelled me into unfamiliar territory and an unforeseen occupation—and preoccupation.

The second stage hit me quite quickly and I went into a *practical mode*. With the surgery, we won the battle, but not the war. Her cancer had already metastasized. I entered a process with my mother that would last just over two years—every day and every night, through the bad and the better times. It was stark reality with no escape for either of us. I put my career on hold and threw myself totally and completely into the task at hand. I became a caregiver, taking one step at a time and one challenge at a time.

Today I look back and think that I probably qualified for some kind of degree, if only honorary, because I became so proficient in contributing to medical assessments and at times solutions—after all, I was well placed to see subtle signs. My advocacy skills became honed as I fought for quick and effective responses to my mother's needs. I was an integral part of the medical team right from the beginning at home and in the regular hospital stays. My duties included coordinating social visits—not too many guests at a time, not too many gloom and doom faces around the bed, and always enough food to create a festive atmosphere. I also tried to maintain some semblance of normal living in the house—and humour. My mother kept asking me what she would do without me. I dread to think what those last years would have been like for her had I not been there.

By the time I slid into the third stage, *automatic pilot*, I did not even think about what came next. I just did it. Shopping. Cleaning. Planning meals, but actually eating little—I eat only when I'm happy. I acquired the facility to do therapeutic procedures and learn the medical jargon. The days and nights blended, and I slept when I could, and most of the time didn't. Eventually I slept beside my mother because it was easier to roll over and check her out rather than move from one room to another. Even when I did have a few hours away from the "scene" once in a while, when my sister came over from Scotland or my son took over, there were no breaks from my emotional or practical preoccupation—and responsibility. I remember going to a concert with my son. Sitting there, I remarked to myself how amazing that everyone there was upright.

As my mother's health deteriorated and we had to endure regular and long waits in the emergency rooms until a bed was found for her, I slipped into the double-edged stage of *resignation* to the situation and *burnout*. It was harder and harder to relate to friends and family, who were trying to distract me when all I wanted to do, and could do, was to focus on the situation at hand. I was constantly in a fog of exhaustion and emotional depletion, and besides, I had nothing to talk about except medical shoptalk. In fact, my strength came from the health-care workers who had become pals with me—and my mother. We turned to their world to provide a structure and some objectivity in the situation—as well as hugs, laughs, and even tears from three or four doctors and nurses who really became close to us. But underneath was the constant adrenaline rush, softened temporarily by little treats such as chocolate cake, a bubble bath, a walk in the sunshine. My little comfort cushions.

Near the end, the emaciated body I was caring for (at home and finally in the hospital) wasn't the person I knew. Only my mother's voice remained poignantly familiar. My all-consuming exhaustion and ultimate sense of helplessness, not to mention the long anticipation of the inevitable, took their toll. My resilience was beginning to wane. I have to admit that my mother's death brought a momentary *sense of relief* for me. This brief stage ended our tough—but very special—passage together.

Of course, the next stage kicked in immediately as *grief* took over with a deep sense of loss—and another change in my life. Time heals all, it is said. It took me a year just to begin to recover physically and mentally. I had lost a lot of weight and any real sense of who I was. Although I had used up all my savings, it was impossible to rush back to anything. I just didn't have the stamina. I mortgaged my house and eventually sold it, living off the proceeds for as long as I could.

In many ways, the hardest part of the healing process, however, was the final stage of caregiving: *re-entry*. After so many years secluded in a very private space, it was no small feat to face society, the world—the job market. I certainly wasn't the same person I had been. And I became aware that everything around me had changed too. Three years is a long time. I remember the first job interview I had. It felt like I had come from another planet. It became clear to me that I had to reinvent myself, to redefine myself in order to renew my inner strength.

I eventually got a job in a field different from the one in which I had worked for over 30 years, before my mother's final illness. It wasn't easy but I managed to successfully transfer the skills that I had honed in my previous occupation to a new world. My executive position with a national seniors' organization gave me the opportunity to speak and intervene in practical ways on behalf of informal caregivers—described as "the silent victims in a silent system" in a national study on home care I helped to coordinate.

Knowing what I know now, would I do it again? Could I do it again?

At the time there was never a question of whether or not to care for my mother. When the need arose, I just did what seemed the natural thing to do.

The key lesson I learned from this experience is not especially profound. Since I am here to tell the tale, I'm convinced that what I learned works and I continue to be guided by it—take one day at a time and one challenge at a time. It's as simple and difficult as that.

How can I sum up those last years with my mother? Moving from Shakespeare to Charles Dickens, "It was the best of times, it was the worst of times...."

Source: Solutions Magazine

Daily Living Redefined

Sharpen your mind and theirs while catching up with the girls. Gabbing is good for your brain. Schmoozing actually leads to better memory power and decision-making ability, according to recent studies.

Experts usually suggest things like reading or doing crossword puzzles to enhance memory function, says University of Michigan's lead researcher and psychologist Oscar Ybarra. "I found just chatting and sharing concerns to also be effective."

In one study of 3,600 people, Ybarra found that the more people visited with others, the better their memory performance was. In another study of nearly 2,000 older residents in four Middle Eastern countries, he discovered that the more social they were, the more they participated in everyday decision-making.

Source: Working Mother *June/July 2002*

Staying active and in touch with family and friends is a large part of maintaining both physical and mental health. For many of our elders, maintaining an independent lifestyle and getting out and about with ease becomes a bigger challenge with age. Often, safety, fear of falling, and fatigue are worries that lead to isolation. Sociability and peer contact, as well as the arrangement of suitable support services, are often part of a family caregiver's new responsibilities.

In this chapter, you'll find information about how everyday living will change for your elder—things like driving, meal preparation, and fitness. Come along for the ride as we share ways to reduce risk while keeping bodies and minds sharp and active.

Hanging Up the Keys

Safety and the older driver is a much talked-about topic as insurers and families begin to get concerned about the number of elderly drivers in Canada. Driving can play a big role in the lives of older adults. It's about freedom and independence—all the things that were the motivators for driving when they (and we) were 16. As many of us have noticed, some older adults on the road pose serious risks both to themselves and others. Now it's not someone else's mother slowing down traffic and making illegal left-hand turns—it's yours.

A recent study of 165 elderly individuals suffering from some form of dementia revealed that over 80% of those involved in an accident continued to drive and close to 40% of these were involved in another crash.

What causes an older person to lose his or her driving skills? For many, the reason is strictly medical. Conditions such as Parkinson's, Alzheimer's, and related dementias associated with advanced age can result in cognitive impairments. Stroke, a heart condition, or similar problems can also affect roadworthiness. More common factors associated with age, such as declining distance vision, reduced physical strength, slowed reflexes, and even certain medications that are commonly taken (e.g., antipsychotics, antihistamines, and some analgesics) are also culprits.

More often than not, the individual in question doesn't realize that he or she has become a potential hazard. Over time, they may gradually recognize the change from safe to poor driving behaviours but unless a specific serious accident occurs, they will ignore these slow changes.

"For older individuals, being able to drive is central to maintaining their independence so it's difficult to encourage them to quit without a fuss," explains Dr. Allan Dobbs, a researcher from the Northern Alberta Regional Geriatric Program in Edmonton and an expert in the field. His colleague, Lynda Dunal, an occupational therapist at the Baycrest Centre for Geriatric Care, concurs. "For anyone who has been driving for 60 or 70 years, a car has much more meaning than a set of wheels. Driving is strongly tied up with a person's sense of self. It means freedom, independence, and mobility."

Erika's Story

For nearly a decade, Erika realized her grandfather was a road hazard and tried to encourage him to give up driving. For years, with the support of her grandmother, he stubbornly refused. Eventually, her worst fear came true and her grandfather made a fatal left-hand turn into oncoming traffic. "Grandpa was fine, but my grandmother, 84 years young, was killed," Erica recalls. "Granddad has since passed away but from the time of the accident until his death, he was a broken man. He could never forgive himself." Erika's message is when you find yourself in a similar situation, don't ignore the problem. It's not a matter of if, it's when will there be an accident. Recognize the danger, talk about it, and take charge—before it's too late.

Breaking the News

If you have a concern about your elder's driving habits, Dobbs recommends taking a ride with the elderly relative you believe is at risk and watch for the signs. "Early warnings may be failure to yield right of way, making a left turn without looking, difficulty in back up or turning, and slow response times. Any situations where other people responded by honking, or the traffic had to adjust, are early indicators of potential trouble.

"The loss of driving privileges is one of the most emotional and difficult issues for cognitively or age-impaired individuals," says Dobbs. Some will recognize their own failing ability and stop driving on their own because they don't feel safe on the road. Others may feel their skills slipping but are less willing to give up. And there are those who will sincerely believe that, regardless of the circumstances and warning signs, there is no problem and insist on continuing to drive.

The challenge is to help the driver realize how dangerous his or her driving has become and how much of a risk the driver is taking.

Talking may not work; showing will. Experts suggest driving behind the person and using a video camera to demonstrate how his or her driving safety has declined. If the problem continues, more drastic options can be used, such as disabling or selling the vehicle to prevent its use.

When It's Time to Take Away the Keys

Fortunately, experts have some proactive suggestions for family members with elders who shouldn't be on the road.

- Involve others who are in a position of authority, such as a family doctor or occupational therapist, to help deliver the message.

- Encourage a re-test from the local government driving authority if there is any doubt.

- If possible, make the withdrawal from driving a gradual process by reducing night and highway driving.

- Be honest and fair, recognizing that this is a difficult process.

- Try to ensure that other options for transportation are readily available and affordable.

- Sell or disable the vehicle.

- Know you're emotional, know they're scared.

What to Do?

A number of centres across Canada offer driver re-testing services for a fee. (See the list below.) For example, Dobbs has developed a computer-based test specifically designed for the cognitively impaired. Called the DriveAble test, it involves a touch screen computer test and a road test and is available across Canada. Many driver-training centres provide written reports and optional remedial lessons and education when needed.

DriveAble Test Locations

Vancouver	(604) 921-3355
Edmonton	(780) 433-1494
Calgary	(403) 252-2243
Lethbridge	(403) 317-1463
Toronto	(416) 498-6429
Montreal	(514) 733-1414
Laval	(450) 688-9550 ext. 4435

My Story: Out for a Drive

Mom was active in the community and quite a good cook. Consequently, people began asking her to cook and deliver for them, and this turned into quite a nice little part-time job. Despite a few kitchen accidents, she managed quite well. The delivery part was another story. As the route expanded and clients became seemingly more demanding, she became more accident-prone. Late again one lunchtime, she got caught speeding—75 miles (120 kilometers) in a school zone. Why? She told the rather surprised young officer that her hurry was because she had to keep Mr. Jones's sausage rolls warm. Then, just a few days later, she backed out of the garage and scraped the entire side of the car along the house wall, nearly knocking off the porch. She tried to hide the scrapes and fix them up herself. Parking lot bumps and dents were ongoing. Of course, it was always the other guy who was at fault.

Just as I was beginning discussions with our family doctor and setting up an account with a local taxi company, Mom had a stroke. Ten days later, even before she left the hospital, her driver's licence was temporarily suspended. It was the only comforting news that week!

When Seniors Drink

Since his wife died a year ago, Arthur, age 80, has started to drink more and more. Recently, he hasn't been meeting friends and isn't bothering to shower or change his clothes. He's eating less and less and is angry and tired during visits.

Sadly, the number of elders who use alcohol to deal with grief and loneliness is on the rise with many families caught off guard when they find out. Identifying the problem is difficult, and many of us are pushed away or lied to when we ask questions. Often, family members hesitate to interfere—even when mishaps or falls at home are too frequent or car accidents become a cause for concern.

Arthur might have what is called late-onset alcoholism, a new drinking problem that is not easy to spot. Until now, his family has been unaware of his growing alcohol consumption. Like other children, they attributed his confused, forgetful behaviour to normal signs of grief and aging and his aches and pains to old age. Although this is a serious concern for many, the good news is that late-onset drinkers are more stable and respond better to treatment than lifetime excessive drinkers.

To make matters worse for elderly drinkers, though, some people tend to ignore or shun older people who have drinking problems, leaving them to their own devices with a "let them enjoy the time they have left" approach to the problem. Others try to keep them happy or make them feel included by serving them drinks at get-togethers.

Does Alcohol Affect Older People Differently?

The effects of alcohol vary with age. Slower reflexes and response times, vision and hearing impairment, and low tolerance to alcohol's effects put elders at higher risk for car crashes, falls, and other kinds of injuries that may result from drinking.

Mixing alcohol with medicine can be fatal. Older people usually take more prescription and over-the-counter medicines than younger people, which puts them at a high risk if they do consume alcohol.

Needless to say, many therapists and nurses are reluctant to work with older alcoholics or heavy drinkers as they already have their hands full with the daily care and treatment plans for other patients, without taking on the "extras" that come with a drinker (e.g., medication reactions from drinking on top of taking a number of prescription meds, increased soiling, verbal or physical abuse, lack of motivation, increased physical challenges, mental deterioration, etc.).

"If you must choose between two evils, pick the one you've never tried before." —Senior Friendly Toolkit

Be passionate and patient—but be willing to act. Persons with drinking problems have the same needs as others—food, shelter, clothing, health care, social contact, and the need for self-confidence, self-worth, and dignity. Experience proves that preaching doesn't work. A nudge or a push shows that you care—especially when the person must choose between losing his or her family and going to treatment. You may not be able to cure the illness, but when the crucial moment comes you can guide the person to competent help.

How to Know If Someone Has a Drinking Problem

Not all problem drinkers drink every day and not everyone who drinks regularly has a drinking problem. If an elder you care for has the following symptoms, you may want to look into getting some outside counselling and support:

- A significant life event that triggers excessive alcohol use

- Little interest in food

- Trying to hide or lie about drinking habits (secret drinking)

- At risk of or actually hurting themselves or others

- Gulping down drinks to calm nerves, forget worries, or reduce depression

- Feeling irritable, resentful, or unreasonable when not drinking

- Has medical, social, or financial worries caused by drinking

- Prior history of drinking and/or treatment

Caregiver Hint: Don't contribute to or facilitate drinking. Be aware of and watch for early warning signs of excessive drinking. The truth is that with alcohol and other drug problems, as with other kinds of acute and chronic illness, early recognition and treatment intervention are essential—and rewarding. Ask for help—treatment programs and support programs are available in most communities. Of note: Be sensitive to the conditions that outside caregivers are facing when caring for your elder who uses alcohol or other drugs.

Did You Know...

The National Institute of Health recommends that people over the age of 65 who choose to drink have no more than one drink a day.

If you know an older person who is considering getting help with his or her drinking habits, you may wish to contact Alcoholics Anonymous (AA) to find a group in your area.

Alcoholics Anonymous

Visit http://www.aa.org

Beating the Stress of Meal Preparation

How do you ensure that those in your care are eating well? As a busy caregiver, you may not have the time to prepare meals in advance or be home at mealtime. When pizza delivery and other take-out options just don't cut it, you can arrange for "senior friendly," inexpensive, nutritious, and regularly available meals to be delivered to an elder's home. Depending on the service, the meals will be home-style hot meals or frozen entrées for convenient re-heating.

Partially subsidized by provincial Ministries of Health, local service clubs, and donations from clients, volunteers, and corporate sponsors, Meals on Wheels is a service that is considered affordable for most seniors. This community service provides home delivery of meals to anyone in need. Generally, referrals are accepted directly from individuals themselves or from relatives, neighbours, social workers, and health-care professionals.

Friendly, reliable volunteers are the backbone of such non-profit programs. Across Canada, thousands of people from all walks of life generously give their time to deliver nutritious meals and cheery smiles to independent seniors at lunchtime.

It Does a Body Good!

Amply covering the four food groups, Meals on Wheels lunches and dinners offer 25% to 40% of the recommended daily nutritional intake. Hot meals are usually made up of soup, an "entrée of the day," bread, beverage, and dessert, but the menu may vary from community to community. For instance, Meals on Wheels in London, Ontario, has an extensive 22-day meal rotation, as well as a daily meal alternative for those "extra-picky" eaters. Their motto: as long as they eat! Clients who are vegetarians or diabetics with strict restrictions can order from a specialty diet.

There may not be a pickle on the side, but the low cost, convenience of these meals could be your ticket to not worrying about your loved one's lunch while you're at work. There's also security in knowing that a friendly volunteer will check on your parent's well-being on a delivery day and will respond quickly if an emergency arises.

Diners Club Luncheons: Double the Service, Double the Fun!

Whoever said only millionaires have chauffeurs? Meals on Wheels Diners Club is a special-event program that picks up participants at their front door and takes them to a local restaurant to enjoy a satisfying full-course meal, lively entertainment, and friendly chitchat with other seniors and volunteers. Participants pay for their own meals or order from a pre-arranged set-fee menu. Programs and frequency of events vary from community to community.

For many seniors and their families, the thought of leaving the security of home initiates safety and health concerns, as well as fears of embarrassment. Many worry about things such as the following:

- What if my asthma kicks in and I'm nowhere near my medication?

- What if I experience chest pain on the bus and I can't get to a hospital?

These concerns often restrict an elder's activity and lead to social withdrawal. The thought of a friendly Diners Club volunteer who picks you up right at your door and whisks you away for a few hours of leisurely conversation and a good lunch is reassuring. Diners Club is not available everywhere, however. Contact your area Meals on Wheels organization via the provincial Ministry of Health or seniors' centre to find out if Diners Club is available in your community.

Meals on Wheels

Here's what Meals on Wheels has to offer your family:

- Home delivery: no need to worry about going out to shop

- Flexibility and choice: you decide what program and meal delivery schedule best suits your lifestyle

- Convenience: home delivered, ready to eat

- Safety: avoid the risk of accidents in the kitchen

- Social contact: meals are delivered "one smile at a time"

- Nutritious food: a variety of menu choices and special meals

- Short-term service: for seniors recovering from surgery or other temporary problems

- Deliveries: Monday to Friday between 11:00 a.m. and 1:00 p.m.

Who Qualifies?

Take this test to determine if the person you're caring for is a candidate for Meals on Wheels. Residents who, due to illness, disability or advanced age, or lack of adequate cooking facilities, are unable to prepare hot meals for themselves may qualify. Also, the recipient must be willing to accept the service and be able to pay a nominal fee for the meals.

Eldercare Situation	Points
Is there an illness or condition that changes the kind and/or amount of food eaten?	2
Are fewer than two meals eaten per day? (A meal consists of food from at least three of the four food groups)	3
Are fewer than two servings of milk and/or milk products consumed per day? (Examples of one serving: 1 cup (250 mL) milk, 3/4 cup (175 mL) yogurt, 1.5 ounces (50 grams) cheese)	1
Are fewer than five servings of fruits or vegetables consumed per day? (Examples of one serving: 1 potato, 1 medium banana, 1/2 cup (125 mL) juice, 1/2 cup (125 mL) vegetables)	1
Does the person you care for have three or more drinks of beer, liquor, or wine almost every day?	2
Are there tooth or mouth problems that make it hard to eat?	2
Eating alone most of the time?	1
Are three or more different prescribed or over-the-counter drugs taken per day?	1
Without wanting to, has the person lost or gained 10 pounds (4.5 kilograms) in the last six months?	2
Is the person sometimes unable to obtain groceries or prepare food?	2
Total points for your elder's nutritional score	

If your elder's nutritional score is:

0 to 2 points: There's a low nutritional risk. Meals on Wheels is not really needed at this time.

3 to 5 points: Consider the nutritional risk moderate. Meals on Wheels might be provided at this time, and other available community services or supports should be reviewed. Recheck nutritional score in three to six months.

6+ points: This person is at high nutritional risk. Meals on Wheels should be requested daily. Suggest referral to doctor, dietitian, or other qualified health professional as well. Other community services or supports should be immediately reviewed and the nutritional score rechecked in three to six months.

Exercise to Keep Fit

According to Health Canada, it's best to aim for 30 to 60 minutes of physical activity a day—and this applies to you as well as your elder. As a caregiver, it might be hard to fit this level of exercise into your busy work-life juggle, so try combining some manageable exercises with a visit to Mom and Dad. There are three types of exercise we all need: endurance, flexibility, and strength and balance.

Endurance activities should be practiced four to seven days a week. These include activities like walking, cycling, skiing, dancing, skating, or hiking, which are great for heart, lungs, circulation, muscles, increasing energy, and in some cases even improving chronic diseases and their symptoms. Wear comfortable, supportive footwear, and as capability improves, increase the activity.

Flexibility activities of some sort, like stretching, gardening, cleaning, golf, yard work, yoga, or bowling, should be practiced every day. This will help increase independence and the ability to tie shoes, clip nails, and get in and out of the tub.

Strength and balance activities should be done two to four times a week and can be part of a routine, like carrying groceries, doing laundry, piling wood, lifting weights or soup cans, doing wall push-ups, or even taking weight-training classes. These daily activities will increase strength, enabling you to do more, decrease risk of bone breaks, improve balance, and prevent falls and injuries, even in your 90s. Remember not to hold your breath while lifting and start with small objects you can comfortably lift in repetitions of 10.

Top 10 Exercises to Share with a Parent

1. Aqua fitness	6. Golf
2. Walking	7. Chair aerobics
3. Dancing	8. Bowling
4. Yoga	9. Gardening
5. Swimming	10. Shopping

Fitness Matters

The value of exercise has no age limit, and lack of activity at any age is not good. Changes that occur with aging can include weight gain or loss, weakening of muscles, and loss of flexibility. Experts agree that physical activity helps maintain a youthful lifestyle, prevents and delays certain diseases, and even improves current symptoms. The bottom line: Being fit reduces the risk for falls and injuries and helps with better sleep, more energy, and regular elimination. At the same time, getting moving enhances mood and relieves stress and depression.

Whatever Works for Them

Suggest that your elder start with reasonable expectations and build from there. Think about how to describe your parent's situation—is inactive, mildly active, moderately active, or very active the best descriptor? Get some advice by talking to a fitness expert or physiotherapist in conjunction with the family doctor before any exercise routine is undertaken. Discuss whether the social aspect of being with others would provide more motivation and fun; if so, look for classes in your local community centre. Group fitness doesn't have to be carried out in a class, either. Many malls have walking programs for young and old. Your elder can do a video exercise break at the bridge game or start a walking club with their friends. It's whatever works for them. Experts suggest that every moment of movement is beneficial, so even gentle movement will improve range of motion and level of ability as well. If your elder is in no condition to jump up and join a formal class or head to the gym, consider light chores or chair aerobics as a beginning point. The best exercise plans are built slowly and are most helpful if they are consistent over time.

Caregiver Hint: As your elder's confidence builds, there may be an opportunity to add some variety to the routine. If your parent misses a day, tell him or her not to give up; just start again tomorrow. Unless the doctor recommends otherwise, there are few reasons why you and your parent can't exercise.

Exercise Safety Tips

- Check with a physician before you or your parent starts exercising.
- Wait two to three hours after a large meal before exercising.
- Avoid exercising in extreme temperatures, hot or cold.
- Always warm muscles with slow walking, and then stretching without strain.
- Drink plenty of water.
- Use safety equipment, like kneepads or a helmet.

Source: The Encyclopedia of Health and Aging (*Firefly Books, 2001*)

Exercises for the Elderly

Your parent may be reluctant to participate at first but don't let up. Just as with kids, once seniors get started, they tend to adjust and start to love it. Exercise classes for the elderly offer light aerobics, yoga, aquafit, Ex-and-Flex, Pilates, and simple stretches. From what I've seen, these classes provide a simple, pressure-free environment without too much emphasis on speed or flexibility. Certainly there's not the youthful panic about what to wear. Daytime classes are usually available. There's often music, which is uplifting, other elders attending from outside the facility, and positive young people and students around to lead and participate in classes.

In a wheelchair? No problem. Wheeling is as beneficial as walking, and a number of classes and moves are adapted for seniors that can be done while sitting in their chairs.

Arthritis aches and pains? Keep moving to avoid stiffness by walking, dancing, or doing Tai Chi.

Osteoporosis? Adapt strength programs to a manageable level without straining. Challenging bones and muscle is important for gaining strength and preventing falls and breaks.

What about heart or stroke problems? Check with a physician. Most doctors recommend activities like walking or dancing because they stimulate circulation, improve heart health, energize muscles, and strengthen lungs.

Not so steady on his or her feet? Start with exercising on a bed, in a chair, or against a wall until your elder has enough balance for other things. Exercise will improve balance over time.

Afraid of ice and snow? Get boots with cleats, join a mall walking club, or work out indoors during the winter at a local community centre or YMCA. Seniors in the community are often invited to attend exercise programs at local long-term care facilities or homes.

Did You Know...

The Canadian Society for Exercise Physiology in partnership with Health Canada put together a rich resource, an interactive Web site with everything you need to know to get your elder started on an exercise program, with advice from doctors specifically for older adults, a list of fitness resources, helpful pointers, and has an interactive quiz and downloadable versions of the Physical Activity Guide for Older Adults. Or you can order the guide and handbook free at 1-888-334-9769. Visit: **http://www.hc-sc.gc.ca/hpppaguide/**

Memory—And Those Senior Moments

Is losing one's memory a normal part of aging? Whether it's forgetting where you put your keys or whether you locked the front door, it's natural to be concerned or frightened. Yes, there are changes in the way memory works that are a normal part of aging.

Memory begins to slip in middle age and continues to decline, especially after age 75. In older adults, long-term memory tends to go unchanged, while short-term or working memory tends to slow down.

One of the changes identified throughout the literature on the subject is that memory actually becomes more accurate with age.

Information may be processed at a slower speed, but there may be some silver lining found with slower processing. After all, isn't wisdom more a function of accuracy than speed? As we age, we have more information to sift through before we can recall the greater awareness of nuances, shades of grey, or alternative perspectives. The wisdom we acquire through aging allows us to see things from a wider perspective. We have more internal data to bring into our working memory for comparisons before final decisions are made. Did you know that older adults have been shown to have a greater sense of understanding of these subtle qualities of life than younger adults? Research has shown that if elders are in an environment in which they must keep their mental skills sharp, they are probably more likely to retain memory skills as well.

Minding Your Elder's Memory

Your elder can't find her car keys, remember her best friend's phone number, or what she went to the store for in the first place. Ever wonder if it's the onset of Alzheimer's? Not to worry. As we age, this type of forgetfulness is very common. If your elder finds a friend about as familiar as a stranger from the bus, or forgets what even goes on in a store, then it might be time to see the doctor. Otherwise, your elder should stick to these great preventatives:

- **Treat high blood pressure.** See the doctor for advice.

- **Eat a balanced diet.** Include flaxseed, wild salmon, trout, and walnuts.

- **Burn those calories.** That exercise bike is great for some aerobic action.

- **Check the medicine cabinet.** Drugs for ulcers, pain, depression, anxiety, or hypertension should be discussed with the doctor.

- **Hit the hay.** Sleep hygiene is important for recalling information and concentration.

- **Stay smart.** Encourage your elder to learn a new language, play chess, or read. Watching TV is not effective.

- **Get a head start on safety.** Your elder should eliminate household hazards and wear activity-appropriate headgear.

Source: The John Hopkins Medical Letter *August 2003*

Use It or Lose It

In their recent work, *The Memory Workbook*, Douglas J. Mason and Michael Lee Kohn aptly emphasize the need for us to recognize and accept that memory is imperfect at any age. They compare the aging memory to an out-of-shape muscle, debilitated by years of flabby thinking habits, that needs to be exercised and revitalized with a new regimen of skill building and positive attitude development. After all, there is truth to the aphorism "use it or lose it." The brain is like any other part of the body in its need for exercise, and we need to find new ways to flex its capacity to remember.

Later life changes in memory may be bothersome, but they are not debilitating. We must change the false presumption that we lose the capacity to remember as we age. To compensate for the natural changes in your memory, you must take your attention off autopilot and place it on manual. You must help to manually move the information from working memory into long-term memory.

Improving Memory

Often an elder's memory can be improved by relearning how to focus their attention, eliminating distractions, and practicing good recall skills. Don't embarrass or blame them. Simply offer memory-improving strategies to do together. When you're motivated, you tend to pay more attention. Mental exercise is as important as physical exercise. There are fun ways to stay on the ball. Board games such as backgammon, chess, or checkers provide mental stimulation and require the player to focus and think ahead to anticipate the next moves. Crossword puzzles and card games also require recall and transfer of information from long-term to short-term memory.

Lifestyle changes such as retirement, moving, grief, and financial challenges, as well as changing medical conditions, add to the list of things to watch for that will affect your elder's ability to remember. Keep an eye on these causes:

Nutritional efficacy: Adequate food and fluid intake are important to good health. Shortages of essential nutrients such as B vitamins, especially riboflavin, carotene, zinc, and iron may impair memory. Foods known to enhance memory include "brain foods" such as red meat, eggs, and liver, rich both in iron and zinc.

Because these foods are high in cholesterol and fat, however, many older persons avoid them. Also, older persons often have esophageal weaknesses that make swallowing meats difficult or impossible. Try puréeing foods for easier ingestion. Poor-fitting dentures or missing or diseased teeth or diseased gums also interfere with eating.

Drug interactions: Many medications commonly prescribed for older adults cause memory deficits, especially in individuals with low body weight, a history of allergies, or a need for multiple medications.

Divided attention: Concentrating on more than one thing at a time is often a challenge for elders. Multiple conversations or competing activities and background noise may interfere with memory, as well as hearing. For example, during a visit to the family doctor, the elder may just want to ask several questions and will have difficulty refocusing thoughts to answer other questions.

Information retrieval: It may take quite a while for an elder to retrieve information. Slower recall may be attributed to poorer organization of information in the long-term memory. Memory-training techniques that encourage use of more efficient mental organizational skills appear to be beneficial.

Low blood sugar: Overexercising or skipping meals can cause blood sugar to dip. Glucose is needed for memory storage. According to researchers, memory may appear clouded if blood sugar is low.

Stress, anxiety, or depression: Too much stress or pressure, especially when setting priorities or dealing with multiple issues, can cause individuals of all ages to experience memory loss. Grief and loss, as well as changes in marital status, home life, and work, may lead to depression. When elders are isolated, decision-making and change often become inwardly focused with less input from external and environmental influences. This can add unnecessary and lengthy worry and fussing.

Illness: When the body is not functioning well, physical inactivity or illnesses can lead to memory loss. Diseases that are common contributors to memory loss include infections, anemia, thyroid conditions, kidney problems, strokes, emphysema, heart disease, Parkinson's, and strokes. Liver and kidney ailments as well as dehydration can also affect memory function. Both over-the-counter and prescription drugs can cause drowsiness and confusion and interfere with a person's ability to remember. Be especially careful with anti-hypertensives, barbiturates, and anti-diarrhea medications and pain medications that induce sleep. Elders experiencing pain can have more problems paying attention due to the distraction of the pain.

"Age doesn't protect you from love, but love, to some extent, protects you from age."
—Jeanne Moreau

Dementia: Degenerative brain disease can result in irreversible decline in thinking, memory, and behaviours. The onset is often slow, but patients may have difficulty remembering recent events or performing familiar tasks.

Helping Someone Remember

While the process of remembering takes more time, memory is still easily jogged. Many persons who experience a mild memory loss can significantly regain memory function through memory training. Here are some suggestions your elder can follow:

1. Listen carefully and take time to remember.

2. Think about what it is that is to be remembered.

3. Repeat it out loud.

4. Link new things to past memories.

5. Practice using the new information.

6. Write it down and keep it close by.

These techniques are simple and easy to do. Want to learn more? Look into memory training techniques that include association, visualization, and observation.

CHAPTER 9

Mobility
Matters

The physical and cognitive changes that occur with aging are often exacerbated by inactivity. This can lead to muscle weakness, joint problems, and neurological difficulties that add up to walking discomfort. The result: unsteadiness when walking, falls that cause bruises and broken bones, and, in many elders, fear of straying far from home. Sometimes, a number of minor functional limitations build up to create more serious mobility issues.

As a caregiver, concerned relative, or friend, you can help in several ways. First, a caregiver can aid in fall prevention by reducing hazards in the home (see the section on home safety). Offer your support by encouraging your elder to increase activity to improve strength, balance, and stamina. Gentle exercise will also help to improve bones and muscles and help prevent fractures. Next, get out and have fun with your elder! You can also help by finding information and facilitating the purchase or rental of appropriate assistive devices for your elder. Finally, it is important to report to the family physician any recurring incidents or risks pertaining to mobility. Remember, there is no reason for your parent to sacrifice mobility to aging.

Fit, Form, and Function

All of us require tools to enhance and facilitate our passage through the twists and turns of our daily lives. Nowhere is this more evident than for those with mobility restrictions resulting from aging, illness, injury, or disability. Suddenly, you'll be introduced to walkers, scooters, wheelchairs, seating systems, and a range of assistive devices that will become part of your elder's life. Purchasing such mobility equipment can be a difficult, even over-whelming process, but there are a few small steps you can take to make this necessity easier. It is important, first, to determine all of your elder's medical needs, as well as how any new equipment will improve his or her mobility and lifestyle. When choosing any mobility aids, make safety and ease of use your top priorities. It is always wise, also, to obtain advice from health professionals, as well as knowledgeable dealers. When you have access to these valuable individuals, don't be afraid to ask questions! A retailer/home health-care dealer will happily show you a variety of different products, have information about warranties and service, provide an overall assessment with the help of a trained professional, and give your elder the opportunity to try out the equipment.

This chapter will offer tips on how to select equipment, while keeping safety, comfort, and lifestyle in mind. At each stage of the decision-making process, this chapter will guide you through the equipment jargon and help you ask the right questions.

How to Find What They Need

Listen to the experts. Take the advice of the doctor, therapist, or other professional who has prescribed or recommended a piece of home-care or mobility equipment. They have the expertise and experience you can rely on.

Do some homework. You can't be expected to know every-thing about canes, walkers, or wheelchairs, but it helps if you know what questions to ask. Chances are you're already getting medical advice but it's beneficial to ask neighbours and friends about their experience, read industry magazines, visit Web sites of manufacturers and reputable retailers, and ask for profession-al help reviewing product information brochures. Occupational therapists or physiotherapists usually have special training and skills in this area and will perform a needs assessment (see below).

Prevent Trouble—Keep Your Eyes Open!

If you think that someone you care for could improve his or her quality of life by using a simple mobility aid, talk to the physician or other qualified professional to get advice. Also keep your eye on certain conditions in the home to spot any potential problems. These include household hazards, mess and clutter that's in the way, slippery or wet floors, loose rugs or scatter mats, poor lighting, thresholds that are an obstacle, and unsafe bathrooms (see Chapter 4 for more information on safety).

Selecting the Right Equipment

In addition to physically related requirements, equipment selection criteria include current and future needs and goals, budgets, availability, type of use (indoor or outdoor), and the length of time the equipment is required. It's also a good idea to find out about warranties and service. And remember, safety should be at the top of the list!

> *As a rule of thumb, a needs assessment should include the following:*
>
> - the user's physical and cognitive ability
> - lifestyle requirements
> - whether the equipment is for permanent or temporary use
> - whether it is for self or assisted mobility
> - environmental issues or regulations and limitations due to living space
> - seating and positioning options
> - seat to floor height or adjustments for height and weight
> - how needs could change over time
> - pressure reduction needs (for wheelchairs)
> - funding eligibility

Questions for Clients, Families, or Caregivers to Ask

- Will it be appropriate for use at home and work and in the community?
- Does it fit the user's lifestyle and does he or she find it aesthetically pleasing?
- Is the equipment adjustable to meet future needs?
- Will it be easy to maintain and is it durable?
- What about warranties and guarantees?

Include the user in decision-making. Ask questions and discuss how, when, and where he or she will want to use the equipment.

For some, passive indoor use without a lot of transferring and dis-mantling is acceptable. In my mother's case, her equipment is "ready when she is" for a more active lifestyle when we take her out of the nursing home. I can take the wheelchair in a walkathon, a parade, or to a family picnic. It's the standard equipment, along with a commode, that comes along when she stays for a few days at my brother and his wife's cottage.

Take note of colour and style. Today's equipment manufacturers offer finishes and accessories that give us choice. Purple walkers and red wheelchairs are for a certain taste. More neutral colours suit others. If you can, ask your elder which is preferred.

Tips for Making the Right Choice

Ask an expert for assistance. In the highly specialized area of mobility equipment, consumers are faced with an array of options and often find themselves having to choose—often without suffi-cient knowledge. Selecting the appropriate tool for the job often requires help from a variety of sources and a team approach. The client's needs and wants should be combined with the experience of a health-care professional and home health-care retailer who know the equipment's features and benefits. Getting the equipment fitted by an expert so that it satisfies individual needs is essential to obtain maximum function and safety.

Know what the product is expected to do. Make sure you understand the medical purpose of the equipment needed, and discuss with your parent's therapist or dealer how it will be used (i.e., indoors or outdoors, full-time or part-time). It's important that the product be easy for you or your parent to maintain.

One size doesn't fit all. Make sure the product meets the specific needs of the person who will be using it. Just because something is on sale or available used doesn't mean it's right for your parent. Also, make sure correct adjustments are made to ensure the best fit is obtained. (Most equipment allows for some personal adjustments, especially on bigger ticket items, such as walkers and wheelchairs.)

Beware of false economy. Price shouldn't always be the deciding factor. Quality, durability, safety, and function are what matter in the long run. Style may also be a consideration for some elders. Remember your teenager—they'll only wear it or use if they like it.

Buy a reputable brand. Look for products with a good history and a sure future. Ask for testimonials and reviews. Recognized brand names to look for: Invacare Canada (www.invacare.com), Sunrise Medical (www.sunrisemedical.com), Dolomite Home Care Products (www.dolomitehcp.com), to name a few.

Buy or rent from a qualified dealer. Finding a reliable equipment supplier is part of your job as a caregiver. In the case of wheelchairs and similar products, it is vital to purchase the device from a qualified, expert dealer who specializes in home and healthcare products. Learning about equipment and buying from a dealer who is properly trained and has up-to-date product knowledge is vital. Most can speak the language of the physician and therapist (but can still communicate clearly with you). Look for fast, efficient service and a support network that will make the process much easier and safer for everyone involved.

Caregiver Hint: Two home health-care retailers who offer superior service and a variety of products and expertise are the Motion Specialties Group at www.motionspecialties.com and Shoppers Home Health Care at 1-800-SHOPPERS.

Beware of franchises with investor owners or organizations that are unable to afford to pay qualified staff. Loaner, or trial, equipment or rental equipment is sometimes a good way to get started. Try to arrange a visit from the retailer to your parent's home or facility. In smaller centres, look for experts who are willing to travel to you; get in touch with your local occupational therapist or physiotherapist for a referral.

Check out warranties and service plans. Find out up-front what the manufacturer and/or retailer offers and whether service and parts are available locally. Many pharmacies or independently owned small stores are unable to customize or

Five Key Questions to Ask a Home Health-Care Retailer
1. What are your qualifications?
2. Is this really right for my elder's situation?
3. What's the product's or manufacturer's track record?
4. Do you provide free equipment trials?
5. What kind of warranty or service support will I get?

modify equipment for clients and are unable to offer on-site service. My advice: Stick with recognized brands when purchasing must-have items.

The Purchase Decision

Ask about delivery timelines. Depending on your location and brand selected, you may find yourself waiting for delivery. Funding approvals and paperwork rather than a shortage of equipment often cause delays. Check with the home health-care dealer and therapist for their best advice about how to speed up the process.

My Story: Patience Is a Virtue!

It took about 16 weeks to get the correct fit and seat cushion and seat back sorted out for my mother's wheelchair, for a variety of reasons, one of which was my mother's difficulty communicating her needs and preferences. After numerous trials and long-awaited visits from the rural part-time occupational therapist, the appropriate paperwork for the provincial government assistive devices funding was completed. Thankfully, I hadn't waited and had requested a loaner from the home health-care dealer. (The nursing home's standard-issue chairs were less than adequate.) I paid in full for the chair in the early stages of the process and agreed to let the retailer send me a refund when the funding came through. My thinking: better service for a paid-up client. It worked!

Should you customize? It's not as onerous as it sounds. Sometimes a few modifications or special combinations can make all the difference. Today's equipment is pretty versatile and quite adjustable but experienced home health-care pros can often reduce the risk of pressure sores, accidents, or discomfort with a few well-thought-through adjustments. This is especially important for high-risk situations in which clients have skin integrity issues such as pressure sores and deteriorating conditions that make seating and mobility issues especially important.

They won't rush to use it. At times we all need tools or aids to facilitate our journey through life, and using a mobility aid, such as a walker or wheelchair, in later years is no exception. Like any health-care product, its purpose is to improve the well-being, comfort, and quality of life of the user. However, given human pride, social situations, and a fear of losing independence, many elders are reluctant to admit their mobility is decreasing. It's often a struggle to obtain what the industry calls "compliance." Many a well-intentioned adult child has told me that the brand-new walker he just bought his mother is sitting in the corner of the dining room—untouched.

> "Age is something that doesn't matter, unless you're a cheese."
> —*Billie Burke*

My advice is to give it time and ask a professional to help Mom understand the benefits of the walker and how to use it. All the nagging in the world won't get her going before she's good and ready.

A Novice's Guide to Mobility Aids

Walkers

There are a number of lightweight frame walkers designed for the person who is mobile but who may need that little bit of extra walking support to provide balance and conserve energy. Wheeled walkers—also called rollators—are a step up from frame walkers; these are easier to use and manoeuvre indoors and out. They can be a great walking support while shopping, visiting, or even just getting some exercise.

A Walker for Many Reasons

Walkers or rollators can be used by people with many different types of disabilities and lifestyles. Many of them are designed to have a non-institutional look, and by encouraging their use at home, you can help your elder to remain living independently or with minimal assistance. Many people need support when walking or carrying and need to rest along the way. However, the disabilities that are helped by the use of a walker are not only physical but also neurological. For people with the following conditions, walkers offer increased safety, comfort, and autonomy in a variety of ways.

Parkinson's disease: The Parkinsonian patient has a tendency to walk faster and faster until they fall. The rollator will provide the patient with support and a barrier that will push back and slow the patient down, stopping him or her from falling. Adding the optional slow-down brake will assist further when cognition is an issue.

Alzheimer's disease: In the case of Alzheimer's, the patient needs a focal point, a frame of reference. The walker will keep the patient's attention more focused on the environment.

Respiratory conditions: An accessory for holding an oxygen tank clips easily onto the basket of a walker. The seat of the walker provides a place to rest when the user is tired or short of breath.

Broken hip: At times, after breaking a hip or having a hip replacement, the client cannot walk as far as before. Support is needed when walking. In these situations, an uninterrupted walking pattern that's well balanced is important.

Stroke: Some patients who have had a mild stroke can still walk with a rollator, using the one-hand brake and one-forearm support on the affected side.

Arthritis: The arthritic patient requires support when walking and usually cannot walk any great distance without resting. Accessories such as anatomical handles can be added to maximize use and independence while minimizing fatigue.

Osteoporosis: A client with this condition will often stoop and will invariably need help to stand up and walk unsupported. A walker with the handles slightly extended will help the client walk independently and encourage improved breathing and better posture. The walker also helps prevent falls.

Scooters

When the great outdoors beckons—or a day at the local mall sounds tempting—a scooter can be the key to mobility for some people. Scooters provide that extra degree of mobility that many active people need to allow them to live life to the fullest. Scooters fulfil a variety of roles, combining functionality with style. In fact, there is a scooter designed to suit almost every need. Today's scooters are practical, providing a convenient aid for shopping and doing a variety of chores. They are easy to use and feature state-of-the art steering, power packages, and safety features. Today's models offer a variety of accessories, from carriers and raisable seating, to special lighting and medical equipment holders.

Scooters are available in three-wheeled or four-wheeled versions for a variety of uses, whether in the city or country. They are also easy to maintain, store, and transport. Their advanced technology ensures optimum performance and reliability. They are available in contemporary colours and modern styles to suit all tastes and come in a range of prices. Most importantly, however, today's scooters are built with independence in mind. They are designed to help older and other individuals go about their daily tasks with minimal assistance and help them maintain the greatest possible quality of life. Before purchasing, think about the logistics of getting a scooter into the house or storing it in a shed or garage. Remember also, it'll need to be parked near an electrical outlet to recharge its batteries.

Wheelchairs

Lightweight and convenient to transport, manual wheelchairs offer a mobility solution for an elderly person capable of propelling himself or herself, or with a caregiver pushing the chair.

For people who want independence but have difficulty propelling themselves or have limited physical endurance, power wheelchairs are an option; they are motorized, run on battery power and are operated by the user via buttons and controls as opposed to manual manipulation of the wheels. Power chairs are generally recommended by occupational therapists for individuals with more complex conditions. Advances in technology have dramatically improved the function, durability, and practicality of these wheelchairs. These chairs can be modified with environmental controls to turn on lights, open doors, and operate other household appliances.

Seating: The Other Half of the Equation

For health professionals working with the elderly or disabled, the terms "seating" and "mobility" are almost inseparable. Seating consists of cushions, padding, back supports, and other specially designed products for wheelchairs. It determines how comfortable the wheelchair is, how easy it is for the person to operate, and how safe it is. The right seating system can prevent problems, such as skin irritation, pressure sores, and muscular aches, and can enhance posture and improve overall quality of life.

Ask an expert's advice, whether you're considering the purchase of a standard wheelchair, a wheelchair seating cushion, an off-the-shelf positioning product, or a more involved, customized system.

A Few Words about Wheelchairs

Remember this: Don't act without a prescription from a qualified health professional, such as a physician, occupational therapist, or physical therapist.

A health professional will offer expert advice on important issues such as functionality, manoeuvrability, and clinical concerns. However, with today's selection of wheelchairs, the final choice is up to the consumer. Keep in mind the age, personality, and life goals of the person who will be using the product. The wheelchair chosen should reflect these. Experts note that in later middle age (55 to 60), people want the mobility to explore life and challenge themselves. In the advanced years (60 plus), emphasis is more on life enrichment. It's important to maintain an appropriate lifestyle and quality of life, and to interact with others and the environment, both inside and outside the home.

Any mobility product such as a wheelchair must protect the dignity and self-esteem of the user, and above all, assist the user to manage on a day-to-day basis.

Buying and Maintaining a Wheelchair

Just as fit is important in a pair of pants, so it is with wheelchairs, but a bad fit with a wheelchair can have more serious repercussions. So get yourself up to speed by following these few basic hints and consider the following need-to-knows when selecting a wheelchair:

- A wheelchair that is too narrow can cause chafing of the skin from rubbing against the frame.

- A chair that is too wide can cause bad posture. At the most, the seated person should have 1-inch (2.5-centimetre) clearance on each side.

- The chair size should be changed if any significant weight loss or gain is expected.

- Two or 3 inches (5 or 7 centimetres) between the front of the seat and the knee joints helps the weight to be properly distributed and does not interfere with the circulation of blood to the legs.

- When the person is sitting in the chair, the weight should be equally distributed and the trunk and limbs should be balanced.

- Leg rests should clear the floor by about 2 inches (5 centimetres).

- Good-quality seating cushions and back rests are a must.

- A lightweight chair is often easier to take in and out of the car and is better for a person who travels often.

- Make sure seat belts are worn when the wheelchair is in motion or if the person is at risk of sliding.

- Maintain the chair in good working order. Brakes, the air in the tires, and the upholstery should be checked periodically. (Ask your retailers for specific instructions.)

Mobility-Equipped Vehicles: Is a Minivan Right for Your Elder?

Whether a senior is a driver or a passenger, owning an accessible vehicle can be the key to his or her ability to get on the road again to a better quality of life. Many seniors and people with disabilities can benefit from some form of adaptive equipment and will be pleasantly surprised with the options available from specialized mobility manufacturing companies to accommodate wheelchairs, scooters, and other personal mobility equipment required by drivers or passengers of standard minivans.

Depending on the make, model, year, and condition of the vehicle, conversions can be done on both new and used vans. Modifications can range from simply adding a seat that turns and lowers to help a person get in and out, to a complete conversion that includes installing a ramp or lift system for a wheelchair user. A lowered floor design with installed ramp enables passengers to remain in their mobility equipment while the vehicle is in motion.

Passengers usually enter wheelchair-accessible vehicles from the side, but many newer accessible vehicles are now designed so that the passenger enters from the rear of the vehicle. These vehicles, known as rear entry, have become popular with people who use wheelchairs because they provide a more comfortable ride and are considerably less expensive to purchase and maintain than traditional side-entry vehicles. Since the wheelchair user enters and exits from the rear, designated handicap parking isn't necessary. Another plus is that the wheelchair user is always positioned facing

"Not everything that is faced can be changed, but nothing can be changed until it is faced."
—James A. Baldwin

forward, which is far more comfortable and safer. The configuration of rear-entry vehicles permits easier access for larger electric mobility devices. Unlike a side entry, in the rear-entry vehicle, just part of the floor is lowered, allowing wheelchair access to the middle of the vehicle by a ramp that deploys from the rear hatch opening. You can choose ramp systems that deploy automatically or manually; the manual system costs less and requires no maintenance.

Conventional side-loading require modifications such as installing hydraulic lifts to get the wheelchair passenger in and out of the vehicle. The primary advantage of the side entry is that it allows the wheelchair user to also be the driver.

When beginning a search for a qualified mobility expert or van converter, look in the Yellow Pages, in resource guides (or magazines like *Canada's Family Guide to Home Health Care and Wellness, SOLUTIONS*), and on the Internet, using key words such as "wheelchair vans" or "handicap vans." A mobility expert should ask you a variety of questions that can help you determine your equipment needs. For example, is the person with the disability going to be the driver or passenger?

The lowered-floor, rear-entry design of a converted mini-van can accommodate large wheelchairs and scooters, and as many as two wheelchairs. The vehicle may have an aluminum ramp that folds down manually from inside the rear door, virtually eliminating the possibility of being blocked in while parked. The structural integrity of an adapted vehicle is also maintained because there is no need to cut the main unibody frame. An added benefit is that any mechanic or car dealer can address service problems, rather than a specially trained technician.

These vans can range in price from $50,000 to $65,000. Entry-level reconditioned pre-owned models start at $25,000. Pre-owned vehicles are a cost-saving alternative, and manufacturers offer an inventory of such vans that can be shipped immediately and directly to the customer.

My Story:
A Sporty Number

I drive a sporty little car, and my mother is well positioned and comfortable in her funky new manual wheelchair. Thanks to modern design, it folds in half and I can just manage to take off the seat and specially shaped back and stuff it into my trunk. It hangs out the back as I drive. Mom is somewhat low-slung in my car seat, but we make it work. My brother and I believe that we should take her out as much as we can. Thankfully, she's not bothered by the awkward transfers to get her in and out of the car. Instead, she enjoys the outing to its fullest.

Van Search Tips

- Make a list of features that are important to you and questions you want answers to. Identify several manufacturers you are interested in, ask for marketing materials such as brochures, and visit Internet Web sites or call toll-free phone numbers.

- Ask for a written estimate that includes any special features you have discussed and may desire.

- Ensure the modified van meets all government safety standards.

- Calculate the weight of the passenger and equipment to ensure the ramp or lift can support them. Also, calculate the weight of all usual passengers and equipment to confirm the gross vehicle weight capacity will not be exceeded.

- Check the ground around the home, and ensure the vehicle selected will clear any obstructions such as unusually high curbs.

- Check the dimensions of the converted vehicle to ensure the wheelchair passenger and equipment can be manoeuvred along the ramp, will easily fit through the entrance, and once in position will be left with comfortable headroom.

As you know by now, needs and preferences go hand-in-hand when it comes to selecting the right mobility equipment. But it is extremely important to ask questions, fully explore options, and make your desires known before finalizing your van selection. For instance, first-time buyers often aren't aware that many dealers have mobility-equipped vehicles available for you to try. Don't be afraid to ask for a test ride.

You'll also want to ask about the following:

- **References**: Ask for names and telephone numbers of customers who have purchased equipment similar to what you are considering.

- **Warranties**: Inquire about product warranty programs. What's covered, and for how long?

**My Story:
Say Aah!**

My advice: Scout ahead of time. I learned my lesson the hard way when I took my mother to the dentist. Not only was the office not easily accessible (we had to use the freight elevator) but there was barely room to get the wheelchair from the waiting room to the treatment area. Then the fun began as we tried, within a very confined space, to transfer my mom safely into the dentist's chair and keep her upright on the slippery surface. Needless to say, we've since found a more senior-friendly dentist who has taken the time to learn what she and other patients like her need and to modify his office and procedures accordingly.

• **Service programs**: Where are the nearest service centres located? Are service reps and technicians thoroughly trained to perform repairs locally? And what if you're travelling with the equipment? Can work be performed across the country in an emergency without jeopardizing your warranty or resulting in added expense to you?

Automobile and mobility trade shows can also give you a chance to compare the offerings of several manufacturers under one roof. Find out if there are shows coming up in your area.

Source: Liberty Motors

CHAPTER 10

The Role of the Family Doctor

In a recent survey, Canadians told it like it is: the family doctor is number one in their "big picture" view of health care. Home care is a priority, and they'd prefer that their family physician be involved in their hospital care as well. If that's you or your parents, follow this quick guide to getting to first base.

Developing a relationship between a patient and the family doctor is pivotal. The family physician is in charge of a person's medical care and is the first pair of eyes and the first line of defence when looking at a patient's individual health-care issues. The family physician can be critical in identifying issues early and prescribing timely treatment options. This chapter will examine the ins and outs of finding and visiting your family physician, and maintaining the all-important relationship with him or her.

How to Find a Doctor

Fourteen percent of Canadians (imagine, that's 4.2 million people) have reported not having a family doctor, and the reality is that most doctors have lineups at their door. Don't feel sick with dread! It's still not impossible to find a doctor who is taking patients these days. Here's how:

- The Royal College of Physicians and Surgeons, the national organization for physicians and surgeons, runs a "Find a Doctor" service in some provinces.

In Ontario, call 1-800-268-7096 ext. 626 (in Toronto call 416-967-2626) or access the on-line directory at www.ocfp.on.ca to get a list of physicians practicing in your area. For B.C., a directory of accepting physicians is available at www.cpsbc.bc.ca/patient/accepting/AcceptIndex.htm, and in Alberta, access www.cpsa.ab.ca for a listing. A similar service may be offered in other provinces.

- Look in your local Yellow Pages under Physicians and Surgeons.

- Ask the nearest hospital if it has a family practice unit that can refer you.

- Ask friends and family if they like and would recommend their family doctor. We've had success with this plain, old-fashioned word of mouth approach.

Making the Call

Once you have a name or office location in hand, the next step is making the initial call or appointment. First, establish some criteria:

- Would your elder prefer a female or male doctor?

- Is there an issue regarding language?

- How far away is the doctor's office?

Now:

- Is the doctor accepting new patients?

- Have you explained your parents' needs?

- Can you make appointments at a convenient time?

- Is there a medical lab where basic tests can be done?

- Which hospital does the doctor send patients to?

- Does the doctor work closely with the local home-care program?

- Does the doctor make home visits when a person is too sick to leave home?

- Is the doctor in every day?

Making the Appointment

Now that you have that elusive doctor's office on the line, here are a few hot tips for getting the most from a visit.

Schedule enough time. It often takes longer than you think to get your parent to and fro. If you have a complicated problem, or several small problems, tell the receptionist so enough time can be reserved and the doctor isn't overbooked.

Don't be shy. Talk to the receptionist about your parent's needs, asking about the cost of extra services and the doctor's credentials and availability. Ask him or her how to get necessary medical records.

If you hate waiting… Ask for the first appointment in the morning or the first appointment after lunch. Doctors are usually on time for these slots. Also, on the day of your appointment, call ahead to see if the doctor is running behind.

Be Organized

Once the initial contact and appointment have been made, there is a bit of "homework" you can do to get the most out of your parent's upcoming first visit. If you aren't able to go with your parent, make sure he or she has done everything in the following list.

- Make a list (and take it with you) of symptoms and/or concerns. Rank these things in order of importance.

- When you meet with your parent's doctor, hand him or her the list or refer to the list and say, "We need to talk with you about these five things today," then name the five things in order of importance. If something on the list can't be covered during the visit, ask about scheduling a phone call or a second visit.

- Prepare as much medical history as possible (immunization dates, major illnesses, surgery dates, menstrual and menopause history, causes of family death and ages at death, etc.).

- Make a list of the medications and vitamins—prescription and non-prescription. Or you can put all medicine and vitamin containers in a bag and take them to the doctor.

- Make a note of which specialists your parent is seeing and why.

- Have records, lab test results, and x-rays from specialists sent to the family doctor before your parent's first visit, so the complete records are available when you and your parent arrive for the appointment. Before you go to the appointment, phone to make sure the records have been received. If they have not, consider rescheduling the appointment.

What's Up, Doc—The Visit

"You don't stop laughing because you grow old. You grow old because you stop laughing."
—Michael Pritchard

When you and your parent visit the doctor, you will have about 15 minutes to convey all the information that's been amassed, so here's some sage advice to maximize that time. If you are accompanying your parent, be sure you've got all the records and notes listed previously. If your parent is going alone, be sure he or she has the material. Remind your parent of the following:

Think like a doctor. It's time to hand in that medical history that you and your parent had for homework. Doctors follow a specific three-part formula when assessing a patient. First, the doctor listens carefully to a patient's history and a description of the symptoms, then proceeds to an appropriate physical examination, focused on the problem area. Finally, further diagnostic tests and consultations may be required.

Write it down. Covering all your parent's concerns in a short office visit can seem overwhelming, so just as you wrote down the symptoms, write down notes during or immediately after the visit. This will help you and your parent remember and clarify the doctor's instructions and recommendations. If you are unclear about anything at all, just ask.

Encourage your parent to include you. Having a close family member or friend in the exam room helps your parent in several ways. You are a second pair of ears to help your parent remember what was said after the visit is over. Finally, if you are shy, ask a slightly more assertive family member to help in this key role.

And remember...

- The doctor has seen it all before.

- A doctor is not a mind reader.

- Ask questions about the "whats" of your symptoms and the "whys" and "hows" of the recommended treatment.

Working with Your Doctor to Prevent Errors and Misunderstandings

The single most important way you can assist your doctor is by being an active member of your own or your family member's health-care team. That means being prepared to take part in every decision that needs to be made. Research shows that patients who are more involved with their care tend to get better results!

Make sure that all your doctors know about all prescription and over-the-counter medications, dietary supplements, and vitamins and herbs that are being taken. This should help your parent's doctor and pharmacist reduce the chance of contra-indications and unexpected side effects.

On the subject of medication and tests.... Don't wait until you or your parent gets to the pharmacy to understand what the doctor is prescribing. Explaining medications is an important part of his or her role in your loved one's care. Ask questions such as the following about the medicine while you are still in his or her office.

- What is the medicine for?

- Will it be in liquid or easy-to-swallow pill form?

- How is it to be taken and for how long?

- Will there be side effects and how do we handle them?

- Is it okay for my parent to drive or be out while taking this medication?

- What food or drink should be avoided or will cause discomfort?

- What is the medication called and how often is it taken?

- Is there a generic equivalent that will cost less?

- Will it interact with anything else being taken?

- What tests are required and where will they be done?

- How can you avoid waiting lines for tests with your frail elder?
- When can you call the doctor's office for results?
- If appropriate, ask the doctor to explain things to your parent.

Caregiver Hint: When you pick up the medication at the pharmacy, check to make sure it's the right medicine. A study by the Massachusetts College of Pharmacy found that 88 percent of medicine errors involved the wrong drug or the wrong dose.

If Surgery Is in the Cards

Make sure that your elder's family doctor and the surgeon agree on what is to be done and what the longer term prognosis will be. Often there is a disconnect between the family doctor and the hospital specialist, making after-care at home more of a challenge than it needs to be. Personally, I have a great deal of sympathy for family doctors who suddenly get rather ill or recovering patients back in their care with little information or background.

You, as a family caregiver, can prevent this by keeping them in the loop as things happen and conditions change…even simple e-mails with updates are more effective and faster than system paperwork in most cases. Warn the doctor yourself before you bring your parent home again.

Caregiver Hint: Discharge planners or case workers from the hospital are the best people to help you get take-home instructions and paperwork to carry with you if it doesn't come easily from the nursing team on the floor. Expect a family meeting to be called to make arrangements and provide you with details about home care. Make sure you get the phone numbers of who to call when you get home. Never take a wait-and-see approach. (In my case, it took three days for someone to show up from home care. By then Mom was well on her way to being stabilized.)

The Family Doctor and Palliative Care

As the team leader, the family doctor is in charge of a person's medical care. He or she works closely with the person, the family, and the palliative home-care team to optimize patient comfort and care.

Expect the family doctor you choose to have someone on call 24 hours a day and to make home visits when the person you are caring for is too sick to leave the house or residence. This doctor has direct access to hospice care if necessary, the ability to admit a patient to a palliative care unit of a hospital, and the ability to arrange for social work or counselling support for both the patient and caregiving family members.

"The early bird may get the worm, but the second mouse gets the cheese."
—*Anonymous*

Further Reading

Men and Doctor Avoidance: Fear of Doctors or Denial of Medical Need?

Andrea Pennington, M.D.

Two recent reports show that males, especially unmarried males, tend to access medical services less often than females. As a result, they tend to have poor health outcomes, including death from heart attacks.

Are men afraid of docs? Or are they too macho to admit they could use a little help?

The authors of one study found that unmarried men tended to seek routine physical exams less often than their female counterparts. One could speculate that wives tend to badger their husbands into seeking medical care. Or one could argue that married men have more at stake and take their health more seriously.

Another study of men admitted to the hospital for heart attacks showed that less than half of them called for an ambulance right away. Some felt that their symptoms weren't that serious. The study authors speculate that others wanted to avoid the potentially embarrassing ride in an ambulance.

So which is it: fear and avoidance or denial?

Clearly it varies with individuals. If you or a male in your life has not been to see a physician for a yearly physical exam, I highly recommend that you make an appointment—today. Not only can a physical pick up on potentially serious illness, your health-care provider can also help you deal with minor aches and pains, reflux, constipation, chest pain, headaches, or whatever you've been putting up with for what may seem like forever.

Gone are the days of paternalistic medicine. Doctors are part-ners in your good health. Take the first step and pick up the phone, or go on-line and make the appointment. Your life and the enjoy-ment of it depend on it.

Wishing you and your family good health,
Andrea Pennington, MD

Source: Gerontological Society of America annual meeting, November 2002

CHAPTER 11

The Financial Side of Caregiving

When family members or good friends become frail or ill, the care we provide often includes assisting with finances. This chapter offers advice that'll help you avoid awkward, embarrassing, and costly financial problems.

When it comes to finances, a typical caregiver arranges bill paying and bank deposits, overseeing insurance and benefit plans, making savings and investment decisions, and arranging for tax preparation, housing, and day care. Because caregiving can be physically and emotionally exhausting, try to reduce the financial stress by taking these steps before an older relative becomes ill or disabled.

"You can alter the difficulties you face or alter the way you meet them." —Phyllis Bottome

- Get an accurate assessment of your loved one's financial situation by creating a net worth statement, which is a simple listing of all assets and debts. Necessary information is often difficult to extract from elders given the sensitive nature of financial matters (be prepared for surprises, positive or negative).

- Ask for personal and financial documents: Your main concern is to know what documents to look for and where to find them. With this knowledge, you can help protect your elder's assets, including dividends, interest, insurance, pensions, rental income, and the contents of safety deposit boxes.

- Obtain access to banking and brokerage accounts by becoming a co-signer on joint accounts. This will enable you to write cheques or withdraw funds to cover the cost of care in case of a short-term emergency or longer-term disability.

- Consider hassle-free automatic payments for recurring bills. Arrange for water, electric, and other utility bills, along with mortgage, cable TV, and telephone, to be paid electronically out of your loved one's chequing account.

- Arrange direct deposit of pension and benefit cheques. Not only is this a safe and convenient alternative, but there are no delays in getting funds deposited, no cheques lost in the mail, and nothing misplaced or forgotten at home.

- Review insurance coverage. Often our elders buy too much insurance or the wrong kind. Try to make sure that your parents have adequate home and auto insurance as well as health, disability, and long-term care plans. Know how to make a claim.

- Encourage saving and prudent spending. Recognizing today's longer life span for both men and women, and the rising cost of living (especially health-care costs), it's wise to make a detailed monthly budget and a longer-term financial plan.

Be Financially Savvy

Whose money is it anyway? As a caregiver who is also a potential beneficiary of your parent's wealth (great or small), it is difficult not to think of the personal stake that you have in maintaining his or her financial health. Follow these rules:

- Don't feel guilty!

- Spend carefully on his or her behalf.

- Avoid jeopardizing your own financial well-being.

- Keep clear records for other family members.

As long as your loved one's money is being used first and foremost for your parent's personal care and well-being, you can play an important role in helping navigate the maze of cash management, budgeting, and financial planning. This is a journey that must be taken with sensitivity and respect for everyone involved.

Seven Ways to Care for Your Parent's Money

1. Make sure you have general power of attorney.

2. Visit your parent's bank together. Sign the papers allowing you to do the banking and access his or her safety deposit box. Get a debit and/or charge card you can use at your convenience.

3. Save time by arranging for as many monthly/regular bills to be paid through direct withdrawals or on-line.

4. Learn about your parent's various sources of income and when and how payments arrive.

5. Create an estimated monthly budget and monitor it.

6. If your parent has a financial adviser, meet him/her and share plans.

7. Check to see what other benefits and tax breaks are available.

Source: Bart Mindszenthy, Solutions Magazine

Consider Using a Financial Adviser

If an expert isn't already on the job, it may be wise to ask a financial planner or accountant to function in the role of mediator. Creating a healthy environment for dialogue and ensuring that the situation is being looked at objectively should be your main goal. Often, a trusted outsider can bluntly lay all the possible options on the table with no hidden agendas and can play an important role in facilitating timely decision-making in times of emotional upheaval.

It is easier to cope with a crisis when proper planning has already been done. Smart caregivers will make sure that financial matters are in order so their energy can be focused on sensitive medical, emotional, and caregiving issues.

Know Where to Find...

If you're lucky enough to have all these documents organized for you, keep them in a safe place. Hint: It's wise to give advisers copies as well. Here's what you need for a no-surprise future:

- banking information (often there's more than one bank)

- loan records (to whom and how much)

- copies of leases or rental agreements (car, condo, apartment, appliances, furnace, hot water tank)

- government health information (provincial health card)

- insurance policies (health, life)

- investments (RRSPs, stocks, etc.): statements and original certificates

- pension information—government and private

- mortgage on home and cottage, investment properties

- wills and power of attorney for property and personal care

- commitments for charitable donations (regular and upon death)

- birth certificate

- social insurance number

- passport

- veterans Affairs documents

- club memberships or subscriptions

- relatives' addresses and phone numbers

Track Down Low-Cost Assistance Programs

Many lawyers, financial advisers, and other professionals offer free initial consultations. Government agencies also provide counselling, and tax planning for seniors.

Review Executors and Beneficiaries

Do you know the executors of your parent's will and who are designated as beneficiaries? Check it out before it's too late. Find contact information and ask your parent to find current insurance policies and appropriate paperwork to make sure things are up to date.

The Costs of Care
It's Never Too Early to Plan

Many boomers are being introduced to the financial issues of growing old as they help their elderly parents navigate their way through their housing and health-care options. Today, an average 65-year-old Canadian is expected to live for 18 more years, with more than seven of these years expected to be endured with some form of disability. It's fair to assume, then, that a typical Canadian senior will need some form of long-term health care during his or her lifetime.

According to the experts, the cost of private, long-term, facility-based care currently ranges from $2,000 to $7,000 a month. Incontinence products or meal-replacement supplements can cost an additional $2,000 to $3,000 a year, and home health-care equipment varies from a few hundred dollars for a basic walker to $3,500 to $4,000 for a decent manual wheelchair.

With the baby boomers, the largest generation in Canadian history, entering their elder years, costs could skyrocket as demand increases. Today, with the multitude of improvements in modern medicine, seniors are facing a mixed blessing. Better health and increased longevity may also mean a difficult financial reality. Many of our parents are living approximately one-third of a lifetime longer than they expected. The result is that their savings may not match the amount of money they will require to maintain their current standard of living after retirement. It is believed by the investment commnity that income and investments after retirement should equal about 70% to 80% of the amount of income being generated before retirement. However, I've heard people who are retired call to radio phone-in shows to say they live quite comfortably on far less than the guest was advising, and the guest is usually a representative of the financial industry. Also, with the CPP—set aside the idea that it might not be around in a few years—and a possible company pension, an individual may not really need as much as the large amounts investment advisers are predicting. Needless to say, with care and forethought, finances should be in place at the time of retirement to make this possible.

It is important to be aware that if your elder is living alone, further stress will be placed on his or her finances, including increased home health-care or housing costs.

Finding a way to live comfortably well into one's golden years is possible, but requires creating a well-thought-out plan and taking some initial steps, including completing a net worth statement, listing all of one's assets, income, and investments. Next, set a detailed budget of all monthly income minus expenses (see our model budget in "Further Reading"). This will bring the big picture into clearer focus.

Predicting Nursing and Care Costs

It's hard to predict costs for services and equipment over time without professional advice, but here are 10 common items that are bound to make a dent in your pocketbook. Check pricing with local suppliers to compare costs and give you an idea of what to budget.

Eldercare Must-Haves	Price Tag (approximate, Cdn.$)	Your Local Pricing
Nursing care (hourly)	$17 to $65, depending on requirements	
Basic transport wheelchair	$400 to $1,500	
Wheeled walker	$400 and up	
Diabetes test strips (100 strips)	$100	
Extra-large adult diapers (package of 12)	$23.99 to $26.99	
Blood pressure monitor	$99 to $169	
Meal replacement shakes (package of 6)	$6.99 to $8.99	
Personal monitoring device (monthly)	$35 to $40	
Bath lift (entry model)	$1,600 to $1,800	
Portable ramp (6 feet, 2 metres)	$400 to $600	

Who Pays?

It is said that there are only four kinds of people in the world: those who have been caregivers; those who are currently caregivers; those who will be caregivers; and those who will need caregivers.

In whatever caregiver capacity we find ourselves, a wise financial plan should include consideration for the many changing and unknown situations that come with the responsibilities of caregiving. But it's never too early to organize. As the caregiver of a family member, part of your role may be to determine when protection is needed. When and how do you need to take control? What legal issues do you need to be aware of? What are the financial risks and potential issues?

Caregivers who take a leave of absence from work often find themselves out of pocket, as their earnings are depleted and their benefits reduced. Employers lose productivity and skilled workers in visible and invisible ways. As the debate on who should pay (the employer, the government, or the family) continues, it seems clear that while companies and governments may provide some support, relief, and flexibility, the brunt of the pre-chronic expenses will land on the individual family.

Determine your level of preparedness by answering these important questions.

1. With your loved one, have you completed a current realistic budget to include income and expenses that can be projected ahead in case of an emergency?

2. Have you in place a financial risk management plan for you and the person you are or might be caring for?

   • Does your parent have life insurance, critical illness insurance (a relatively new product in Canada), accident and sickness insurance, medical insurance, or long-term care insurance (another new product in Canada)?

   • Review your parent's budget and assets to see if it's flexible enough to include possible caregiving demands and medical expenses. Don't forget the positives, though—he or she could be eligible for benefits such as disability tax credits and attendant care expense deductions at income tax time.

Those on low incomes receive other tax benefits, such as a GST refund paid quarterly.

3. Has your elder's will been updated to take into consideration any new responsibilities or significant changes in relationships, such as the death of a spouse?

- Things to consider include advanced health directives, power of attorney, and guardianship.

What Can You Afford?

Undertake a careful review of your loved one's income and expenses. Draw up a budget and a savings program. Look at investment portfolios. Plan for your parent's future and your own, too. Even with the many health benefits available in most provinces, it is likely that you will have to pay for some caregiving expenses yourself, especially if you are particular about the type of care your elder will require, or if your parent wants to stay at home for an extended period of time with at-home care.

Once you have assessed your loved one's current financial situation to determine whether savings or assets are sufficient to cover an illness or disability, you can evaluate your plans and options carefully. A lot of people can't afford long-term care and/or disability policies that are on the market today but be aware of them and think ahead about whatever coverage you can afford and might need—it's certainly worth the peace of mind.

Take Nothing for Granted

Finally, don't take your own regular income for granted as a factor in the care of your parents or yourself. How many of us could survive for a long period of time without a paycheque?

It's likely too late for your parents to sign up but if you don't have disability insurance, it is well worth considering getting some. When shopping for disability insurance, review the plans carefully for details such as eligibility, coverage (accident and/or illness), waiting period, definitions of disability (total, permanent, temporary, or partial), and any occupational restrictions.

Source: Wayne Taylor, Family Finance and Estate Planning Group

The Financial Realities of Care

Home Care: When the Bill Comes, Who Pays?

Some health-care services are not covered by the province, depending on where you live. Home-care coverage, home health-care products and services, and medications will incur expense. Expect things such as co-payment fees, what's considered basic coverage, which medicines are covered, and coverage for help at home to be a bit of a crapshoot. Finding out what is covered and who qualifies may take some digging.

"Who is going to pay for this?" It is a question asked all too frequently by Canadian families contemplating adding the title of family caregiver to their personal resumés. It is a fair question, given Canada's tradition of subsidized health care. Unfortunately, however, it is not an easy question to answer.

Part of the problem lies in exactly what home care is—or, more accurately, what it isn't. Unlike other aspects of health, home care is not guaranteed under the Canada Health Act. What this means is that if your elderly mother falls and breaks her leg, the basic costs of treatment in a hospital or by the family doctor are guaranteed, so payment is not an issue. You might, however, be expected to pay for the ambulance or transportation when mother comes home, and much of the medical care and equipment she needs might just be on your tab.

Much Talk, Little Funding

To be fair to the federal government, it is not that home care is not considered legitimate; it is just that it simply was not much of an issue when the act was written. As a result, it is left up to each province to decide how to fund home care.

Many critics suggest that the provinces are not funding home care enough. In fact, a 1999 home-care study by researchers at Queen's University in Kingston, Ontario, identified inadequate funding as one of the top two issues facing home care in Canada. "There is definitely a feeling that not enough is being spent across the country," states Dr. Malcolm Anderson, who, along with Karen Parent, conducted the study. "While there is a lot of talk about the need for funding, very little infrastructure is in place, and in many instances, home care still needs to be properly defined."

Still, more than $2 billion annually is made available to Canadians legitimately looking after a loved one at home, and the amount will likely increase as home care has been almost universally identified as a priority across the country. On the surface, this may seem like a lot, but in reality it is less than 4% of total public-health expenditures. The highest percentages were in New Brunswick and Ontario (5.8% and 5.3% respectively) and the lowest in P.E.I. and Quebec, with less than 2.4% each.

Who Qualifies and How Do You Get Financial Support?

Again, the answers are not simple and they vary from province to province across the country. "The bottom line is that the rules for home-care funding are set town by town, region by region, and province by province," notes Dr. Anderson. Finding your way through the maze can be a challenge.

Where home-care funding does exist, it is generally funded by the provinces and territories, either directly or through local organizations. Programs are run by health ministries, regional social service organizations, or municipal health boards. The home-care services themselves may be provided by health care professionals or through contracts with private agencies, both for-profit (such as We Care Home Health Care Services, Bayshore Health Care) and not-for-profit (such as the Victorian Order of Nurses [VON], St. Elizabeth Health Care).

To qualify for financial help, you will have to undergo an assessment conducted by the appropriate agency in your region to determine the type of help that your loved one is qualified to receive. Ask your family doctor for advice as to who to call. In some cases funded programs recognize the caregiver's need for respite and will provide backup to give you a break.

Generally speaking, professional services, such as nurses, physiotherapists, occupational therapists, and personal-care services, qualify for coverage but with a firm ceiling. Other non-professional services, such as companions and house cleaners, are usually paid for by the family.

Many regions expect the family to pick up the tab for a portion of some or all home-care services. These charges tend to be more common on so-called "softer" services, such as house cleaning and Meals on Wheels. Again, many different rules and qualifications apply according to region, family status, income, etc. For low-income families, subsidies can be quite high. In some areas of Canada, Meals on Wheels services cost about a dollar a meal.

The Rules Aren't So Clear

Basically, each province has its own rules, its own definition of home care, and its own levels of care and funding structure. The following chart offers some guidelines, but when you get right down to it, the answer to the question "Who is going to pay for this?" is different in each part of Canada, and the entrance to the home-care funding maze is in a different place in each region. Ask lots of questions and don't give up easily!

Province	Responsibility/ Service Delivery	Funding	Phone Number/ E-mail
BC	6 Regional Health Authorities	Funding plus user fees	www.hlth.gov.bc.ca/seniors (250) 952-3456
AB	17 Regional Health Authorities	Funding available	1-800-860-2742
SASK	33 District Health Boards/Authorities	Funding plus user fees	Ministry of Health (306) 787-3479 www.health.gov.sk.ca/ps_ home_care.html

Province	Responsibility/ Service Delivery	Funding	Phone Number/ E-mail
MAN	12 Regional Health Authorities	Funding available	(Gov't of Manitoba) www.gov.mb.ca/sd (For Homecare) 204-945-6737 www.gov.mb.ca/health/ homecare/index
ON	43 Community Care Access Centres	Funding available with ceilings	1-800-268-1153 www.health.gov.on.ca/ english/public/contact/ccac _mn.html
QUE	151 Centres locaux de service communitaires	Subsidies available	Ministry of Health and Social Services 1-800-361-0635
NB	8 Regional Hospital Corporations	Funding available for medical, subsidies for non-medical	Department of Health and Community Services 506-453-2950
NS	Department of Health 9 District Health Authorities	Funding available, varies with usage and income	Home Care Nova Scotia 1-800-225-7225
PEI	5 Regional Health Boards	Funding plus user fees	Community and Family Services 902-892-2441 www.gov.pe.ca/inforpei/ Seniors

Province	Responsibility/ Service Delivery	Funding	Phone Number/ E-mail
NFLD	6 Regional Community Health Boards	Funding available with ceilings	Department of Health and Community Services 709-729-737-2333
NU	Department of Health and Social Services		Department of Health and Social Services www.gov.nu.ca/hss.htm
NWT	Regional Health and Community Service Boards 8 Boards and Authorities	Funding available with user fees	Department of Health and Social Services West 867-920-6173 East 867-979-7666 or 867-873-7925
YUKON	Social Services Branch, Health and Social Services	Funding available	www.hss.gov.yk.ca/prog/cc/ index.html
VETER-ANS (special)	Veterans Affairs Canada VIP Program	Funding available for veterans with some restrictions	Veterans Affairs Canada 1-800-387-0919 www.vac-acc.gc.ca

The Option to Pay Privately

You always have the option to pay private agencies for whatever extra services you need. These out-of-pocket expenses are entirely up to the individual. You can pay to top up services, such as cleaning, or upgrade professional care (e.g., a 24-hour attendant, when the assessment identifies simple day care as adequate). Some private or group insurance plans may cover these services. Check with the insurer for details. Tax deductions are available for some services that are deemed medical expenses.

Financing Long-Term Care

Check into Home Equity

When deciding the "where" in your elder's caregiving situation, a number of options are available to those who own their own homes. If you can see a nursing home or care facility on the horizon, selling the house is an option, especially if cash is a concern. If the home is in good condition and a good location, your loved one may be pleasantly surprised at the value it has gained over the years. To get a true picture of the home's value, consult several qualified real estate agents.

Caregiver Hint: Take into account any repair costs, realtor's fees, closing costs, and tax implications that are involved.

Cash flow is often a significant issue for elders who are sometimes without cash as they no longer have employment income. They own their own homes but have difficulty meeting their monthly bills, never mind the costs of care.

- **Reverse mortgages**: A 2003 study found that two-thirds of Canadian seniors were homeowners and 90% were mortgage-free. Few seniors had debt, and only 10% were dipping into their capital to finance their lifestyles. A relatively new option available to free up cash is the reverse mortgage. It allows the owner of the house to benefit from the value of the home without having to sell or move out.

  Simply put, equity is the market value of a home minus whatever money may be owing on a mortgage. A reverse mortgage is a loan based on a homeowner's equity. The loan does not have to be repaid as long as the homeowner continues to live in the home. This income can be used by the homeowner to supplement monthly income, pay off debts, attend to home maintenance, or pay for health-related needs. Income from a reverse mortgage can be paid in the form of monthly payments, a single payment of cash, or a line of credit. Through it all, the homeowner's responsibilities do not change, which include maintaining the property, paying taxes, and carrying insurance.

The rules for reverse mortgages vary but they usually require the homeowner to maintain the property as his or her principal residence. If the home is sold or the homeowner moves away permanently, the mortgage will come due automatically. For this reason, it is important to know exactly how long the homeowner is allowed to be away from the home on a temporary basis (for an extended trip or a stay in a nursing home, for example).

• **Renting as a source of income**: If cash is less of an issue and the mortgage is small or paid off, your elder also has the option of renting out the home. The good news is that renting provides income to cover the myriad of long-term-care costs. Renting has two other advantages: it keeps open the option of moving back in should the situation change, and the house can be kept in the family through the will. The bad news is that you also inherit the stress and headaches that go along with being a landlord. If you are unable to assume this responsibility or are caregiving from a distance, investigate hiring local help or a property manager to act in your absence. While this will decrease the rental income, it will save a great deal of trouble. In addition, the rental income will be taxable, although expenses can reduce the taxable amount.

Another rental option is renting out a room or portion of a house. This also has its pros and cons. Apart from the financial boost, sharing a home can be a source of companionship, activity, and security. The success of this option, however, hinges on finding the right personality match and level of responsibility in the prospective renter, whether he or she is a stranger, new friend, or close family member.

Long-Term-Care Insurance

Unlike life insurance, long-term-care insurance plans pay the policy holder benefits while still alive. The plan will pay the policy holder a stated amount (say up to $300) per day in the event that the person requires long-term care in a facility such as a nursing home. This could be due to injury, sickness, cognitive impairment, or the inability to perform two or more activities of daily living. Benefits are usually payable for health care in the home by an approved caregiver.

Two main groups of people find LTC insurance useful. The first are those who are not fully confident that their retirement savings will be sufficient to last their entire lives. These people are worried about outliving their money. They also realize that without money of their own to support them through a period of long-term care, they may end up being a burden on their family. Alternatively, they may have to settle for the base level standard of care provided by the government, a program that may be stretched thin in the future as aging boomers place a heavy demand on facilities and resources.

The other group of people who could benefit from LTC are those who have built up a considerable amount of wealth. They are not concerned about outliving their money, but instead want to preserve that wealth for the beneficiaries of their estate. They realize that a multi-year stay in a long-term-care facility, especially if both spouses require such care, could significantly erode the value of their estate.

So pay attention to the care issues your parents and their friends may be facing. There may be lessons to learn. One of them can be the knowledge of how to better prepare yourself and your immediate family for similar circumstances. Knowing about the benefits of long-term-care insurance now can play a big part in that preparation.

Five Tips for Long-Term-Care Insurance Buyers

1. Purchase a long-term-care insurance policy in your early years. Premiums on such policies can be much cheaper before age 65.

2. Make sure your policy has an increasing benefit, so that the coverage is on par with the cost of service when the time comes.

3. Think about who will take care of you. You may need a full-coverage policy, which includes home care and institutional care.

4. Be aware that long-term care policies are complex—most individuals need professional assistance in determining what coverage, if any, they would need.

5. Don't forget the most important detail of them all: choose a long-term-care policy or any health-care policy, while you are well, not sick.

Source: DJ Korn & Assoc.

Critical Illness Insurance

This insurance provides coverage for a number of critical illnesses, including heart attack, cancer, and loss of independence. If you need to use it, you will be provided a lump-sum amount to spend as you wish.

Extended-Care Health Insurance

In accordance with the particular policy, coverage will be for things such as prescription drugs, dental care, eyewear, specialized care, home care and nursing, medical equipment and supplies, emergency medical health insurance for travellers, hearing aids, personal emergency response, hospital stay, accidental death and dismemberment, and catastrophic coverage. The level of coverage is determined by the package you choose.

Other Coverage to Check For

Traditional accident and sickness insurance is also available as personal coverage or through employer/employee packages. This insurance covers you in the event of a disability, accident, or illness for a designated period of time.

Long-term and short-term indemnity coverage pays you a predetermined lump-sum amount, spread over a designated period of time, in the event of disability, injury, or illness.

How Do I Make a Claim?

The insurance carrier determines how the claims are processed and will explain it in a written agreement (it's wise to request a copy of this to understand your parents' coverage).

In many situations, there is immediate electronic processing of basic prescription and dental coverage.

Tax Tips

The taxman has a few credits available that you may want to delve into. Trying to reduce the federal and provincial income taxes payable can ease the financial burdens of providing care. Take a closer look at these 10 tax credits to see if there's some relief in sight for your elder. (All amounts applicable to the 2003 tax year.)

1. Caregiver Credit

If you maintained a dwelling where you and a dependant lived at any time during the year, you may be eligible for a caregiver credit amount of $3,663.

Your dependant must have been over 18 at the time and

- have a net income of less than $16,172

- been dependent on you due to mental or physical infirmity

- be your child, grandchild, aunt, uncle, brother, sister, niece, nephew, parent, or grandparent and a resident of Canada

- if a parent or grandparent (including in-laws), born in 1938 or earlier

This credit is reduced by your dependant's income in excess of $12,509. You might want to split the claim if you and another person share the support and expenses.

2. Medical Expenses

Eligible expenses include professional medical services, apparatus and materials, medicines, medical treatments, lab exams and tests, hospital services, ambulance, attendant care, private health services, guide or hearing animals, group home and travel expenses for medical treatment.

Total medical expenses within the year must be more than 3% of your net income or $1,755, whichever is less. You must be prepared to supply receipts for these expenses.

You can claim medical expenses that you or your spouse paid for yourself, your spouse, children, grandchildren, parents, grandparents, brothers, sisters, uncles, aunts, or nieces or nephews who depended on you for support for any 12-month period, ending in 2001 and not previously claimed. You can carry forward any unused medical expenses to future years.

3. The Infirm Dependant Deduction

Claim up to $3,663 for each dependent relative. Your dependant must be completely reliant on you at some time during the year by reason of mental or physical infirmity and

- be 18 years of age or older at the end of the year

- be a resident of Canada at some time during the year

- be your or your spouse's father, stepfather, mother, stepmother, grandfather, grandmother, brother, sister, uncle, aunt, niece or nephew

4. Basic Personal Credit

For the year 2003, you are eligible to claim $7,756 as a personal credit.

5. Age Credit

You may claim an age amount of $3,797 if you were 65 years or older by December 31 of the year for which you want to claim the credit. This amount is reduced by 15% of your net income in excess of $28,193. You are not be eligible for any age credit if your net income exceeds $53,440.

6. Spousal Credit

You may claim a spousal amount of $6,586 if you were married or had a common-law spouse, at any time in the year, and if you supported that spouse at any time while you were married. You must have paid a reasonable proportion of the expenses for your spouse.

The spousal amount is reduced by the amount of your spouse's income, if over $659.

7. Equivalent to Spouse Credit

You may claim the equivalent-to-spouse credit of $6,586 if you have a dependant and you were single, divorced, separated, or widowed at any time during the year. The dependant must be

- under 18, your parent or grandparent, or mentally or physically infirm
- related to you by blood, adoption, or marriage
- lived with you in a home that you maintained
- wholly dependent on you for support

8. Personal Disability

A disability credit of $6,297 can be claimed if a qualified person certifies that you had a severe mental or physical impairment during the year, which markedly restricted you in all, or almost all, of the basic activities of daily living and/or your impairment was prolonged, which means it lasted or is expected to last at least 12 months.

The only persons that qualify to certify your impairment are doctors, optometrists, psychologists, occupational therapists, and audiologists.

9. Dependant Disability Credit

You may qualify to claim all or part of any disability amount for which a dependant (other than your spouse) qualifies.

You must have either claimed for that dependant

- an equivalent-to-spouse amount,
- infirm dependants amount, or
- a caregiver amount.

10. Spousal Transfer Credit

Your spouse can transfer to you any part of an age, disability, pension, or tuition and education credit that he or she qualifies for but that your spouse does not need to reduce federal income tax to zero.

Exactly which, if any, of these credits are applicable to you will depend on your particular situation and circumstances. But it is definitely worth while to look into the applicability of these credits to your situation; your financial adviser can also investigate on your behalf. After all, when it comes to tax credits, it pays to be informed.

Did You Know...

Your parent may qualify for additional benefits

- Canada's Old Age Security pays benefits to most people over 65.

- If your elder is 65 or over, with low or modest income, he or she may be entitled to the Guaranteed Income Supplement (GIS).

- If he or she is 60 to 64 and is the spouse or common-law partner of a GIS recipient, your parent may also be entitled to the same allowance.

- If your parent is 60 to 64 and widowed, he or she may be entitled to a benefit called the allowance for the survivor.

Want to Know More?

1-800 O-Canada (622-6232)

TTY/TDD devices: 1-800-464-7735

or visit the Web site www.hrdc-drhc.gc.ca/isp

Numbers to Note

Canada Pension Plan: 1-800-277-9914

Information on pension payments, transfers, benefits, etc. Have the person's SIN handy when you call.

Canadian Home Care Association: (613) 569-1585
Good starting point for accessing home-care resources across Canada.

Canadian Bankers Association: 1-800-263-0231
Information on rights and responsibilities when dealing with the bank.

Ontario Ministry of Consumer Relations:
1-800-268-1142, in Toronto (416) 326-8555
Provides useful information on protecting seniors from fraud and other crimes.

Protecting Your Parents from Fraud

Scammers target anyone. However, seniors are considered easier targets for a number of reasons. They are easy marks because

- They are often home during the day, which gives home repair or telemarketers prime access.

- Today's seniors were raised to be more trusting of others and are often lonely.

- Disposable income: Our parents and grandparents have more savings and assets than previous generations.

- Criminals know that some seniors are easy to intimidate and that widows are often good targets for home repair, maintenance, or financial swindles.

Protecting your elderly family member from fraud is not always easy. Reduce the chances by approaching the subject casually and reviewing these helpful questions with your elder:

Q. *Do you buy products over the phone or when people knock at the door?*

A. If the answer is yes, discourage them from paying in advance or on the spot for products. Remind your elders that it's not always safe to open the door to canvassers or salespeople.

Q. *Do you understand sweepstakes and prize notifications that ask you to call a 1-900 number?*

A. Be sure your parent knows that there is a telephone charge for all 900-calls. Remind him or her to get a second opinion before entering and to carefully read all the details and fine print.

Q. *Do you make spontaneous charitable donations?*

A. Con artists often hide behind false charities or pretend they are working for a recognized charity. Suggest that "giving on the spot" is a risky business. Recommend asking for head office contact information and making a donation through official channels (this way, a charitable receipt is also guaranteed).

Q. *Do you read contracts before signing them?*

A. Point out that there's no rush to sign, and being able to read the entire contract is a must (even if the language is difficult and the print is small). Most honest businesses and charities will not bully anyone into buying or signing right away. Encourage advice from a trusted friend before putting pen to paper.

Q. *Do you have most of your pension or other income deposited directly into your bank account?*

A. Criminals steal cheques, bank statements, and credit card information from mailboxes and assume the identity of an unsuspecting victim. With regard to personal finance, suggest reducing the paper trail as much as possible.

Q. *Do you talk to strangers or chat with telephone solicitors?*

A. Explain that friendly strangers are not always well-intentioned. Support the practice of never paying for items over the phone with a credit card or revealing any bank account or personal investment information.

Q: Do you feel comfortable arranging for home repairs and maintenance?

A. Offer to assist with the planning process. At the very least, encourage the homeowner to get at least three written estimates and check references for any home maintenance work to be done. The contractors should be recommended or known to be legitimate businesses. Watch for fraudulent home-repair people who offer unneeded repairs and charge double or triple what the job is worth.

Doug's Story

Doug is the only son of his widowed mother. She is in ill health, but it is Doug's hope for her to live with him as long as possible. She has a modest CPP pension, along with survivor benefits from her late husband, approximately $600 a month. She owns a small condominium worth $60,000. Doug has inquired about daytime home care, which will cost approximately $800 a month.

How can Doug provide care for his mother without depleting his savings and emergency funds?

In this case, Doug and his mother agreed to sell her home and place the proceeds of the sale into an annuity. Doug and his mother will use the growth on her annuity (using a conservative 7% rate), along with her CPP pensions, to pay for the daytime home care. By achieving more growth than expense, they hope they will not need to dip in to the savings and can leave it there for any unexpected expenses (e.g., home-care equipment, renovations, or residency in a long-term-care facility).

Doug has also spoken to his employer and is able to use some banked vacation pay to decrease his work schedule by a few hours a month. This will allow him more time with his mother and let him be around when the daytime home care is there.

Source: Solutions Magazine

Bob and Mary's Story

A retired married couple with two daughters, this pair faces a difficult financial decision. Mary requires daily help, a wheelchair, and renovations to the home if she is to continue to live there.

How can Bob and Mary continue to enjoy their life together, without depleting their retirement savings?

After seeking professional financial advice, Bob and Mary discuss the situation with their family. Their retirement income is such that they can provide for their daily needs, but not the expenses of renovations and equipment. Lump sums taken from their RRSPs would be taxable—depending on personal income for the calendar year—and decrease their savings for everyday living. They agree to take out a reverse mortgage, an option that unlocks the equity in their home. They choose not to repay it, as their income is not sufficient to do this.

The family agrees that if the home is no longer suitable for either Bob or Mary, they will sell it and pay back the reverse mortgage. The children are aware that this will decrease their inheritance. Their concern is the welfare of their parents and not that of money.

As well, the daughters and their family will gladly help Bob with the care of Mary, allowing him time for himself.

Source: Solutions Magazine

Sample Budget

MONTHLY INCOME

Wages/Salary (You) $_____

Wages/Salary (Spouse) $_____

Investment Income $_____

Government Benefits $_____

TOTAL MONEY IN $_____

MONTHLY SAVINGS & INVESTMENTS

Savings $_____

RRSP $_____

Spousal RRSP $_____

Education Fund $_____

Pension Plan Contributions $_____

Tax-sheltered Non-registered Investments $_____

SUBTOTAL $_____

MONTHLY FIXED LIVING EXPENSES

Mortgage $_____

Utilities

Heat $_____

Light $_____

Telephone $_____

Water $_____

Cable/Satellite $_____

Loan Payments $_____

Car Lease $_____

INSURANCE

Life	$_____
Disability	$_____
Critical Illness	$_____
Long-term Care	$_____
Car	$_____
Household	
(Contents, fire)	$_____
Child or Elder Care	$_____
Other	$_____
SUBTOTAL	$_____

VARIABLE MONTHLY LIVING EXPENSES

Transportation	$_____
Food	$_____
Clothing	$_____
Home Maintenance	$_____
Furnishings	$_____
Personal Care	$_____
Medical and Dental	$_____
Education/Self-Improvement	$_____
Vacations	$_____
Charitable Donations	$_____
Bank charges, Fees	$_____
Miscellaneous	$_____
SUBTOTAL	$_____
TOTAL MONEY OUT	$_____
MONTHLY EXCESS OR LOSS	$_____

Further Reading
Misplaced Trust
William (Bill) Hyde

Carlos DeSouza's father, Antonio, has been living in a retirement home for a number of years, ever since he developed dementia. To ensure he received the best care they could afford, Carlos and his wife supplemented Antonio's care by hiring a private-duty nurse.

Antonio's mail was delivered to him at the retirement home and the nurse was able to obtain a great deal of his personal financial information. Several GICs were coming due shortly and the nurse "counselled" Antonio to the effect that "the government would take 50% of his money unless he registered it jointly." The nurse volunteered to have her name put on the GICs as joint owner as they matured and were rolled over.

Antonio's health deteriorated and he died shortly after this happened. It was only then that the family discovered that the nurse had been able to get $60,000 of GICs registered jointly. Of course, on death, the money became hers and the family was ultimately unable to do anything to recover it.

It is a common myth that the elderly in Canada are poor. The generation now approaching retirement age is one of the wealthiest demographic cohorts in history. It is also generally accepted that as people age, their physical and mental competence will often decline.

This combination of wealth and declining mental competency is dangerous to the elderly and their families. Unfortunately, this combination frequently draws financial predators like iron filings to a magnet.

Many elderly in the early stages of dementia, because of declining short-term memory, tend to forget that they have a caring family that does visit regularly. They have a tendency to bond with other caregivers or "friends." This is commonly referred to as "transference of affection."

Families who find themselves in similar situations—with an aging parent with declining mental capacity—can take a number of simple steps to protect their loved ones and themselves from being victimized in this manner. (For more information, read "Protect Your Loved Ones" on page 191.)

The Canadian Institute of Chartered Accountants (CICA) maintains a registry of chartered accountants who have taken special training in eldercare and who are able to provide valuable advice and assistance in designing and carrying out a care plan for your elderly loved ones.

"The longer I live the more beautiful life becomes."
—Frank Lloyd Wright

William (Bill) Hyde is a chartered accountant and a certified financial planner. He has been a member of the AICPA/CICA Joint Task Force for the past five years.

Source: Solutions Magazine

Protect Your Loved Ones

- Do not wait too long to check up on and be ready to activate a valid power of attorney for property and medical issues. Once someone becomes incompetent, it is too late to start putting appropriate legal paperwork in place.

- As soon as it becomes evident that there are signs of dementia, the family should act quickly to ensure that all financial affairs are taken over by a trusted financial adviser or by a responsible family member.

Be very careful about selecting and trusting caregivers who have regular access to elderly family members. Keep financial matters as private as possible. Many elders are very vulnerable and need protection in much the way small children do.

Living Too Long...the Biggest Financial Risk of All
Cliff Oliver

The main problem with retirement planning is that the financial assumptions are based on averages. There are many of us who lie outside of the range of average life expectancy.

FACT: Failing to build your financial plan based on the assumption you will live long is a recipe for financial problems.

Consider an example of a woman age 55 who is attempting to determine how much capital she will require at age 65 to retire comfortably for the rest of her life. Let us assume that her projected annual expenses at age 65 will be $48,000 per year, and that she will receive $12,000 from government and other pensions. Hence her investments must produce $36,000 after tax plus the tax payable on the pension income. We will also assume an inflation rate of 2.5% and interest earnings on her capital of 6%.

If we assume that she will live to her life expectancy, which is to age 84 using current population mortality statistics, she will require a capital sum of $750,000 to provide the required income and cover inflation. The capital will be exhausted by age 84.

On the other hand, if we were more conservative and assumed that she would live to age 95, the capital sum required would be $1,050,000—40% more. Is she able and willing to set aside $1,050,000 of retirement capital by age 65? If this means selling the home and downsizing, is she willing? Many are not, and then pay the price later in terms of capital running out.

Wendy's Story

Somehow Wendy's father has survived to age 98 on capital of less than $400,000 for most of his retirement years. He is able to pay for a semi-private room in a nursing home, as well as hire a visitor to see him once a week. ("Now," Wendy notes, "he's a canny Scot, we can't forget that!") He lived in the same house for 50 years, always paid cash for his car or truck, and went to Florida every winter until he was in his early 80s. Like many retirees who operate small businesses doing what they love, he has an erratic income through his honey business, and that, combined with his capital, has been enough for him. The moral? Don't be scared by financial experts with big numbers—work out your own plan.

FACT: The assumption about how long we will live is by far the most important ingredient in the financial plan's model.

When problems arise, the first solution is to turn to capital assets that can be realized in cash. This would include the primary residence and any cottages or vacation homes. Capital gains tax becomes an issue on the sale of cottages and vacation homes, so this is not a desirable solution. Emotional attachment to the primary residence is a major problem in considering the sale of that asset. In summary, if neither of these solutions is palatable to the retiree, it is best to plan prudently and avoid these choices.

Another avenue is to rely on children for support. The baby boomers have done very well financially in their own right and often are capable of supporting parents financially. However, this does squeeze the finances of these families who are still paying for their children's education and are servicing high levels of debt and lifestyle expenses. Again this is not a desirable solution, although many end up in this position. Familial relationships suffer great strain when put to the test of financial aid.

Just ask Mel Goodman about a parent outliving normal life expectancy and having to deal with the financial consequences. His mother is 87 and in reasonable health. She lives at home but needs daily help. She has an assistant stay with her and help five days of each week. Mel helps bear the expenses because his mother's financial position could not bear the entire burden.

Or look at Barry Kagan's situation. His mother is in a nursing home. She is 85. Her capital ran out a few years ago, so Barry has to fund the lion's share of the nursing home cost. This creates a strain on Barry's financial position. While there is no question that he is willing and does help, the drain on his financial resources will affect his family's position now and in the future.

FACT: Nursing and home-care costs are not insignificant.

Nursing and home-care assistance is not cheap. Nursing home costs run from $3,000 to $6,000 monthly. (Publicly funded nursing home rates are subsidized—my mother pays just under $2,000 in Ontario.) This must be paid with after-tax dollars. Help in the home is not much cheaper. It can cost anywhere from $1,500 to $3,000 monthly and these costs are tax deductible.

It is best to go through the planning process early on and stare the various possibilities in the face, with potential courses of action for each possible outcome, rather than ignore the problem and then be faced with a crisis later on. Issues such as the possible need for private nursing care can and should be addressed through the purchase of long-term-care insurance, which is available as long as one buys it before age 80. How to invest monies, to achieve the required rate of return, and how to deal with illiquid assets such as the home, are issues that need to be addressed in the planning process. While not necessary in all cases, it is sometimes necessary to analyze the expense side of the equation and work out detailed budgets.

For the boomers themselves there is much they can do to avoid financial pitfalls in the future. One cannot emphasize sufficiently the importance of constantly reviewing the financial plan for retirement with a financial adviser. You should be alert to not only constantly changing personal circumstances, but also to the various assumptions in your financial model.

As more medical advances are realized and people continue to live longer, the need for long-term funding will be exacerbated. The only way we can ensure self-sufficiency from a financial viewpoint in light of this is to *plan* to live a long time. We do this in our minds anyway (humans are generally positive thinking beings), so why not carry the same logic through to financial affairs? You will be glad you did, if you get what you wish for—a long life.

Cliff Oliver is a fellow of the Canadian Institute of Actuaries and is president of Oliver Financial Services.

Source: Solutions Magazine

Legally Speaking: Legal and Estate Planning for Elders

It's never easy talking about uncomfortable subjects with an older, perhaps fragile relative like your mother or father. As hard as it may be, however, talking to your loved one about his or her estate planning is important. Many of us talk a lot about it jokingly or with veiled threats to come back and haunt someone, but few of us plan properly for our later years and estate assets.

While some facilities and financial institutions allow spouses to act for each other where assets and finances are involved, there is a potential for family conflict. Plans must be made in advance to avoid both distress and costs.

Estate Planning: An Overview

First things first—what's an estate? Simply put, an estate is an individual's total assets, debts, and interests that are left behind when he or she dies. Estate planning, then, is the means by which you can help your elders organize the estate with respect to business, legal, and tax affairs for peace of mind in a number of areas. Proper planning will mean that your parents' final wishes will be met. A lot of families seek professional advice in these matters from lawyers, accountants, and estate planners. Planning will also ensure that any of your parents' dependants will be cared for financially in case of death or disability and maximize your parents' assets in the estate to be distributed to any beneficiaries. Financially speaking, the object is to reduce the tax debt that your parents will incur and

"True healing has more to do with listening than with trying to fix people."
—Gerald Jampolsky, MD

have to pay before and after their death through their estate. Should your parents become incapacitated, smart planning will mean that all legal documentation is in place in advance and that you and your family will be able to deal with your parents' physical, emotional, and financial needs when they are unable to help themselves.

Two of the most important and powerful legal instruments you may have to deal with as a caregiver are powers of attorney (which can take a few different forms, serving different purposes) and the final will and testament. Each plays a distinct role in your parent's well-being. A will comes into force upon a person's death, while powers of attorney come into force as soon as they are signed and will cease effect upon a person's death.

When There's a Will

People often say, "I'm not rich—do I really need a will?" The answer? Yes! Estate planning, of which a will is only one part (see "Estate Planning: An Overview"), can benefit anyone, at any stage of his or her life but in later years, it's a necessity. The goal of an estate plan is to protect a person's family and distribute the person's wealth the way he or she wants, without subjecting relatives and friends to unnecessary stress, avoidable taxes, and potentially costly legal battles.

The will is the most powerful tool in ensuring that assets pass to the chosen beneficiaries as quickly and tax-effectively as possible. Without a will, state-imposed rules dictate "who gets what" when a person dies, and the results may come as surprise. For example, when a person who is married with two children dies, the spouse does not automatically receive all the assets. Likewise, in the case of a common-law spouse or a same-sex partner, that person will not automatically receive all assets if there is no will. By making a will, however, you can ensure that those you care about are provided for in the way you want.

It is possible to address the family's specific circumstances in a will. For example, in the case of someone with a disability, the person can be provided for without jeopardizing his or her government entitlement. If your parent is in a second marriage, he or she may want to provide for both the current spouse and the children from the first marriage. More recently, many entrepreneurs in Ontario who hold shares in private corporations have been taking advantage of the tax and fee savings in preparing multiple wills. This is an estate-planning technique that allows a person to pass shares in private corporations to beneficiaries without having to pay Ontario probate taxes on those assets.

A regular review of the will is essential. Has anyone named in the will died or moved to another jurisdiction since it was drawn up? Remember, the will that your elder prepared when he or she was 30 years old probably will not address the family's needs when your elder is 65.

What If There's No Will?

Should a person die intestate (without any will), the government takes control and distributes the assets according to a specific, legislated formula. This formula may not always be amenable to the family's wishes. If an individual has no will, spouse, or children, all assets may go to the provincial government. Therefore, a final will and testament is essential to ensure that all interests of the deceased and all beneficiaries are protected. A will is also the means by which legal guardians are named for any minors or dependants.

Executors

Certain individuals play a critical role in drafting a person's will. These include executor, legal professionals, trustees, and guardians. These crucial members of your support team are not to be appointed lightly or without a great deal of thought. The executor plays a pivotal role in estate planning. Executors (liquidators in Quebec and estate trustees in Ontario) are individuals or organizations who are directed by the will to "execute" or carry out the last wishes of the deceased. These individuals should be, first and foremost, trustworthy. An executor does not have to be a family member and is often a lawyer, accountant, or trust company. This tends to give some objectivity in the case of conflict should any arise.

Trustees

If the will creates any trusts, a trustee must be appointed. Trusts are, generally, monies held until minor children attain a certain age. For any minors or dependants who were under your parents' care, a legal guardian should also be appointed.

Powers of Attorney

A will comes into effect only when a person dies. What you really need is a will and two powers of attorney, one for medical, the other for financial, purposes. Understanding how these instruments work is the first step toward sound estate planning. The value of these powers of attorney becomes apparent when a person suffers a massive stroke or becomes virtually incapacitated by the advanced stages of a disease like Alzheimer's. These powers of attorney should be in place for both parents. (P.S. Put yours in place now, too!) Powers of attorney are governed by provincial law, so any lawyer within your province should be able to give you advice about preparing and drafting these documents.

In a medical power of attorney, people can select the individual they want to make personal decisions for them if they become mentally incapable of making decisions regarding such things as medical treatment or long-term care.

In a financial power of attorney, the person can name whom they wish to make financial decisions. Unlike medical powers of attorney, financial powers of attorney need not be restricted to a person's incapacity. Financial powers of attorney can be general or limited to a specific bank account or to a specific time period. Business travellers and snowbirds often prepare general financial powers of attorney, which allow named individuals to take care of certain financial transactions while they are out of the country.

Similarly, living wills or other health-care directives ensure that the wishes of an adult are communicated to family and medical personnel in end-of-life circumstances. All the instructions may, in fact, be combined in one document usually called the enduring/continuing power of attorney (or, as it is called in Quebec, a mandate in case of incapacity). Generally, however, they are separated to maintain confidentiality. You would not want, for example, the details of your complete power of attorney to be read by a third-party hospital when all they want or need to know about are your health-care wishes.

It is important to discuss with your loved one his or her wishes should your elder become terminally ill or incapacitated and unable to communicate. The living will is your elder's voice when the person may not have one as to the nature or extent of medical care and "heroic measures" that your elder wishes in case of an emergency. These vital documents can save unnecessary, unwanted, and expensive medical treatments.

> "Happiness is not something you experience: it is something you remember."
> —Oscar Levant

While there are no fixed rules or laws as to the content of these planning devices, the hallmarks of such instruments are that the adult—the "principal"—must have the requisite mental capacity to execute the instrument. It must be signed before two witnesses, each of whom must sign in the presence of the principal, and it should be properly prepared with the assistance of legal counsel.

A word about do-it-yourself will kits: Although they have their place, particularly in extremely simple wills, there are good reasons why people use lawyers. If a will is not in the correct legal language, is ambiguous or contentious, or fails to provide for certain circumstances, it may not be considered legally binding. Under these circumstances, the administration of the estate may be delayed and family members may have to go to court in order to have the will interpreted. This is both time-consuming and potentially costly.

Estate-planning professionals can also help to ensure that your will is flexible enough to deal with unforeseen contingencies, including marriage breakdown, the birth of more children or grandchildren, or the death of any named beneficiaries or executors.

Additionally, it is recommended that, where there is any potential for conflict, the principal have one person to represent his or her personal affairs and another person for property or financial affairs. How the financial "attorney" manages the principal's assets should be monitored and reported upon periodically to the "attorney" who is responsible for the personal affairs. To best represent the wishes of the principal, these documents and similar planning instruments may be the most important legal instruments a person may ever execute.

Other Considerations

Depending on circumstances, you may wish to talk about other estate-planning options. Disability insurance will provide income if the person is unable to work. Life insurance can provide a lump sum to pay immediate expenses, tax liabilities, and large debts, such as the mortgage on the family home.

If there is life insurance, RRSPs, or RRIFs, it is important to ensure that there is a designated beneficiary of those proceeds. By designating a beneficiary, the person can ensure that the proceeds are distributed outside of the estate and are not subject to provincial probate taxes. In addition, tax savings are available where the spouse is designated as a beneficiary of a registered retirement plan.

There's Been a Health Crisis: A Legal Checklist

The following should be on any family's checklist if a relative becomes ill or disabled.

✓ **Get solid financial and legal advice from professionals you know and trust.** Contact, consult, and get advice from bankers, lawyers, accountants, insurance agents, or financial planners your family has dealt with in the past. Let them know of your situation and your problems.

✓ **Consider working with lawyers and financial advisers who specialize in helping the ill or elderly.** These include lawyers and financial planners who regularly handle estate planning, health insurance issues and claims, fraud cases, and other legal affairs affecting the elderly.

✓ **Take advantage of free or low-cost assistance programs.** Many lawyers, financial advisers, and other professionals offer free initial consultations. For ongoing assistance at little or no cost, consider the services available from private organizations and government agencies in your city or province.

✓ **Closely review your relative's insurance coverage and government benefits.** Often, a disability insurance policy covers more than just wages, but might also cover physical therapy and other services. A life insurance policy might also have cash value (sometimes even an option, in dire situations, to receive an advance payment of some of the policy's death benefit).

✓ **Respect your relative's opinions and desire for autonomy.** Caregivers may be well meaning, but out of their own anxiety and guilt become overly protective. This can mean making decisions of which your elder is fully capable. Although your elder may be frail physically, the care recipient must make his or her own financial decisions.

✓ **Share financial decisions with the family.** If you must assume full responsibility for a relative's finances, share information with other family members openly and honestly. This will save any future surprises. Hold family meetings to discuss finances and to keep everyone current on spending and income. Also keep records of key discussions you have had with family members and any action taken.

✓ **Share duties with family and friends.** Some regular responsibilities, such as bill paying or deposit making, might be done most efficiently by one person. But don't be shy about asking family, neighbours, and old friends to help out where appropriate, from occasional banking matters to basic errands, phone calls, and letters. Those with legal, health-care, or financial training can be particularly helpful with certain tasks. If help is available on a regular basis, that's even better. You'll need a break occasionally.

✓ **Be aware of your potential liability.** A caregiver may become a joint owner of a chequing or savings account, serve as a legal representative (through a power of attorney) or become someone's trustee or guardian. Make sure you get at least a second legal opinion from a qualified professional before signing any documents or powers of attorney.

✓ **Be prepared for out-of-pocket expenses.** Caregivers don't get paid, often don't get thanked, and frequently don't get reimbursed for long-distance phone calls, travel, groceries, medications, personal care items, or other purchases. This doesn't include "hidden" costs, such as unpaid leave from work. Of course, as a caregiver your main concerns are to help someone who's helped you in the past, and to know that this person is being well cared for.

CHAPTER 13

Holidays Family Style

Planning holidays and mini-getaways can be fun and quite necessary for stress relief and relaxation. Maybe you're game to venture away for a week or two if everyone has time. We've discovered a number of special getaways, hotels, inns, and spas that are senior friendly, tourism destinations that want your business, and fabulous spa and fitness resorts with health and wellness packages that will cater to you.

Relaxation and fun is what you need. Perhaps all it takes is a little time away from daily routines. Whether it's for you alone, to rest, rebuild, and refresh, or a family vacation that you'd like to take with kids or parents, a little planning makes all the difference in the quality of your getaway experience. Not only do you deserve it; you'll be a happier, healthier person because of your time away.

For many members of the "sandwich generation," family vacation plans may need a slight adjustment to include our elders. What about Mom? She's alone now since Dad died and you are basically looking after her. Couldn't she benefit from some time away? If both parents are still alive, they could enjoy spending time with their grandchildren. With a little bit of common sense and some creative thinking, you can plan a senior-friendly family holiday that's full of fun and pleasant memories for the whole family. Here's some practical advice to get you on your way.

> "If the shoe fits, you're not allowing room for growth."
> —*Robert Coons*

Where Do You Want to Go?

Consider what each person might be looking for and any limitations that will affect the trip. Think physical, think stamina, think agitation, think noise, think diet, think stress, think safety. Is budgeting a concern (who's paying? is there a budget?)? Is timing an issue (school, work, medical appointments)? Is medical care an issue? Do any physical limitations come into play?

Look for a destination or place that offers something for everyone. Perhaps there is somewhere your older travelling companion has always wanted to go or would like to return to. Is there an activity some of you would like to try? Safety is a consideration, as are climate and distance from home and medical care.

Planning for Various Fitness Levels

You'll need to find a spot that won't hamper you because of your elder's physical or cognitive limitations. Will you need on-site medical care, for example? Whatever the destination or type of trip, you are usually more active on holiday. Whether it's strolling on the beach or visiting museums, you will likely be doing more walking than you are used to. Even long walks between airport terminals can be a strain. Plan accordingly. Consider the temporary use of manual wheelchairs, and try to plan journey lengths so there's not too much waiting in airport terminals, bus terminals, car rental agencies, and so forth.

How Will You Be Travelling and Where Will You Stay?

Whether by car, train, plane, or ship, watch for potential obstacles. For example, seasickness is an issue that must be addressed if planning a cruise (and it can be overcome, with appropriate medications and therapies). Some people have a fear of flying that should be carefully considered before booking a flight! Carrying bags is difficult at the best of times, and with an elder it's not an option. Take into account ground transfers between planes or terminals and the time you have to wait between flights. Choosing the right form of transportation—and a suitable hotel—makes all the difference.

Our Top 5 Family Vacations

1. **Cruises:** The fastest-growing segment of the travel industry, cruises offer a wide choice of destinations and itineraries. Some lines specialize in senior travel, while others try to accommodate the whole family with a range of activities. Be sure to explain your needs to your travel agent and the crew on board.

2. **Train trips:** The romance of the rails still holds special appeal. Via Rail and private companies offer a range of short and long train excursions across North America, including accommodation and meals. Trips through the Rockies or to the East Coast are particularly popular.

3. **Spa breaks:** Consider a spa getaway and pamper yourself and your family. It's a chance to focus on health and well-being together. Choices range from health resorts, spas set amid stunning scenery, and hotels with spas on-site. Plan treatments carefully, especially when medical conditions are a concern.

4. **Coach tours:** Escorted tours in modern, comfortable coaches through North America and Europe remain a good alternative and can be surprisingly affordable. Sit back and enjoy the sights as someone else does the driving, carries your bags, and takes care of the details.

5. **All-inclusive resorts:** The ideal, one-stop destination. Many resorts offer enticing packages that appeal to everyone—golfing for Dad or Granddad, a poolside spa for Gran and Mom, and organized activities for the kids. Ask about healthy meals, exercise programs, and educational lectures.

Will You Be Travelling or Staying in One Location?

If you're travelling with companions who have low energy or need routine and familiar surroundings, select an accessible home base for the entire vacation. Once you're sure your elder is comfortable, plan day trips that are easy to join or take turns escorting other family members to more active activities.

Meeting Special Needs

Is on-site medical care a consideration? Don't be put off or discouraged by mobility restrictions. If mobility is an issue, take note of how daily activities are accomplished at home and come up with a list of questions about and requirements for any prospective destination or travel agent.

Find a travel professional who specializes in planning vacations for people with special needs and be clear about current daily activities and abilities. Come up with a list of requirements and conditions that need addressing. For example, the guest will be using a walker or wheelchair, so wheelchair-accessible hotels are essential; the guest is frail; the guest has diabetes. Put everything in writing—you can use fax or e-mail to speed things up—but do not rely on verbal responses. Confirm all your requirements and the responses in writing. An experienced professional will source and question destinations about their ability to meet your needs, make arrangements for dietary requirements, and even arrange for equipment rentals.

Did You Know...

Age and restricted mobility need not stop you from enjoying a family vacation. Buses and trains offer comfortable, affordable alternatives for travelling with older family members.

Bus companies such as Greyhound offer senior discounts (10%), smoke-free travel, wide spacious seats, wheelchair-accessible coaches, and "kneeling" buses. Most drivers have first aid and CPR knowledge and are able to assist if there are any problems.

Trains have the benefit of sleeper compartments for those family members who can't sit for extended periods of time. Via Rail also offers senior discounts (10%), wheelchair lifts, tie-downs (these lock down the wheels of your elder's chair so that the chair won't roll during travel), and grab bars. Food areas and washrooms are wheelchair-accessible throughout most trains. On-board attendants are also available to assist passengers with medical, diabetic, or vegetarian needs.

For more information visit www.travelcanada.ca, or call Greyhound at 1-800-661-8747 or Via Rail at 1-888-842-7245.

Source: Canadian Tourism Commission

Getting Ready to Travel

Some time may have passed since your elder has been on a holiday. Make sure that you encourage them to do a little pre-vacation "training and prep" work. Get them involved in some research (we asked Mom and Dad to look into day trips that might be fun).

Encourage your elderly travelling partners to start walking and exercising before the trip. A good pair of comfortable walking shoes is essential. These should be broken in before you leave on your trip. There are many exercise alternatives to choose from, such as mall-walking programs, formal exercise programs, or walking the dog. With a bit of luck, holiday exercising will set the stage for a light, regular fitness routine.

It's advisable to make a visit to the family doctor well before the departure date, especially if you are thinking of travelling abroad. The doctor can discuss any medical concerns or issues regarding immunizations, climactic conditions, flying, etc., and reassure you and your elder that this trip is a good, safe idea. Bring up the subject of medications and make sure prescriptions are renewed in time to take and to be in good supply for the first week of your return. Ask about customs and security regulations. Often written prescriptions are required for any medication carried and all drugs must be in their original container. Syringes must have their needle guard in place and be packed with the medications. In addition, some airlines and airports will not even allow syringes in carry-on luggage. Your pharmacist may also be able to help.

Think about whether you'll need extra supplies such as extra batteries for hearing aids and pacemakers and a spare pair of glasses. If a wheelchair is needed, make arrangements in advance. Airports and airlines and train personnel are very accommodating and usually have all the procedures and services ready if they know ahead of time. Arrive a little early so there's time to board ahead of the rest of the passengers, and allow staff the opportunity to fix any problems that have arisen.

For tips and advice on insurance, see the section "Don't Leave Home Without It" below.

Don't Leave Home Without It: Buying Travel Insurance

There are two essential things Canadians need to know about travel insurance.

First, never travel without it. Your provincial insurance no longer offers unlimited coverage. Medical treatment outside of Canada is exorbitantly expensive, often reaching thousands of dollars a day.

Second, know your coverage. Make no assumptions. Read the policy and ask for clarification of anything you do not understand.

Ask the following questions for yourself and elders:

- Do you have enough coverage or do you need to purchase additional coverage? You might be covered under a work or group plan and/or by your credit cards. If so, find out exactly what the benefits and exclusions are for everyone.

- Do you need to book the trip with your credit card in order for the coverage to be effective? Are there any restrictions on health, trip duration, age, and/or the benefit amount? Once you know that any preexisting conditions are not covered under your credit card, you may shop elsewhere for a plan that will cover them.

- Are you covered for the full amount of time when you're away and do you have cancellation or return travel coverage? Are all family members covered?

- Will you be reimbursed or will the plan pay directly? How long will reimbursements take?

- Be upfront about medical conditions when applying. Non-disclosure is one of the top reasons for claim denial—something you can't afford to consider if you've got an elder with you.

- Always call the insurer's assistance hotline. Sometimes claims are denied because the treatment received was either not covered or deemed unnecessary by the insurer.

Source: Association of Mature Canadians

Maximizing Enjoyment

Don't be too ambitious about holiday plans, and stay flexible. Just because you've planned to go somewhere today doesn't mean you have to do it. Don't take unnecessary risks, and recognize when your elder needs down time or relaxation. Pace yourselves. Make health a priority. Be sure energy levels are at their peak for the key activities by picking the time of day when they'll feel the best. Avoid long line-ups and waiting times by planning schedules carefully. Often if you have someone who has special needs or is in a wheelchair, you can scoot into a special lineup or pre-book your entry time.

Maintain the same at-home diet or schedule, especially if your loved one is on any medications. Carry healthy snacks such as fruits and vegetables and bottled water while sight-seeing. People have more energy if they have several small, healthy meals rather than a few large ones.

> "Always do right. This will gratify some and astonish the rest."
> —Mark Twain

You Deserve a Break

Give yourself a treat—many spas offer the basics at reasonable prices. Check out those that offer nutritious spa cuisine, hands-on wellness seminars, and fitness activities. Not only is a spa meant for relaxation, but many offer health, fitness, and skin-care education too. Many treatments have real medical benefits, like massages designed to ease muscle pain, improve circulation, promote relaxation, and even aid digestion.

Go Spa-ing Guilt-free

Indulgence and excess, this isn't. Experts agree you function better when you take a real break mentally and physically and find a time when the focus is on you. Reestablishing your work-life balance, destressing, and being in the company of those who are focused on health and well-being is a great feeling.

For those looking for respite, taking a few hours or days away from the routines and stress may just be the ticket. Whether it's a "Ya Ya Sisterhood" package, good friends for old time's sake, or a men's package to destress, time at a well-run spa—be it a destination or day spa—is time well spent.

Try reflexology, the ancient healing art practiced by the Chinese, Indians, and Egyptians. It is founded on the principle that the foot mirrors the makeup of the body. If there is tension or distress in a certain part of the body, such as the stomach, massaging the area of the foot representing the stomach will relieve stress and tension in the stomach. Treating the foot can have a therapeutic effect on the whole body.

A few of our body parts often go unappreciated as we rush through life. If it weren't for those poor tired feet, where would we be? Foot care is a priority. Your sore, callused, or cracked tootsies deserve a pedicure with a soak or scrub. Add a paraffin manicure for those dried-out hands.

Thinking of Spa-ing with Mom?

- Call ahead. Explain your needs and situation and stick to simple services or treatments.

- Ask your specialist or family doctor if it's okay for her to go, or have the doctor suggest a specific treatment.

- Depending on your circumstances, ask a friend or support worker to come along. It eases the burden on you, giving you time to sneak in a few treatments.

- Space treatments out throughout the day and leave time to lounge and enjoy.

- Bring appropriate attire, comfortable sandals or slippers, casual clothing, a bathing suit, and hair tie.

- Drink as much water as you can throughout your spa day to replace the water lost when you have a wrap or use a steam room, sauna, or hot tub.

Experienced practitioners can customize treatments specific to your needs, but they should ask about medical conditions to avoid risk. Their goal is the same as yours: a refreshed, revived you.

My Story: Mother-Daughter Getaway

Nine months post-stroke, Mom and I desperately needed to "shut down" just for a day. We needed to find a positive, non-clinical, wheelchair-accessible, and private spot where we could feel special, safe, and pampered. The well-trained team at the spa came through for us, with their focus on customer service and willingness to go the extra mile. While the step-by-step logistics weren't always the easiest, Mom and I managed to have a special day to remember.

Our massages were followed by a lovely lunch in the bright, casually elegant dining room. (It was Mom's first try eating with her left hand only, in public—she did us proud!) Manicures and pedicures for us both, and boy, just putting on those all-day bathrobes felt wonderfully decadent.

CHAPTER 14

Taking Care of Yourself

Your dad has Alzheimer's and you don't know which way to turn. Your mom, who lives with you, had a stroke and is now wheelchair bound, but you have wall-to-wall plush carpets. It's time for skilled nursing care but you feel guilty so you quit your job. You're feeling tired and run down. You need help. Where do you go from here?

The way you start and spend your day does make a difference. Begin by doing things you take pleasure in, and your stamina increases. Take some time off to relax and refocus and, somehow, things seem to fall more neatly into place. Downtime and simple pleasures are not a luxury. Research shows that besides being fun, they also help you to live longer.

As an honest-to-goodness member of the "sandwich generation," you won't find it easy to set aside personal time, keep up energy levels, and stay well balanced between work, family, and caregiving. As many of you know, it takes a bit of juggling.

Burnout Blues

It can happen to anyone. Put the kibosh on burnout with just a few adjustments. Here's a test our friends at Veterans Affairs Canada suggest you take to identify your risk.

True/False   I am always tired.

True/False   I get sick more often than I used to.

True/False   I have gained/lost weight unintentionally.

True/False	I suffer from back pain and headaches, and often feel depressed.
True/False	I don't have time for myself anymore.
True/False	I have recently given up hobbies and lost contact with friends.
True/False	I experience irrational outbursts.
True/False	I worry about not having enough money.
True/False	I feel I don't have enough knowledge or experience to give proper care.

If you answered "true" to a significant number of these questions, you are probably close to experiencing caregiver burnout. It's time to seek some help. Turn to your family doctor, friends and family, day spas, and caregiver respite services to get yourself some "time out."

Balance Your Time to Reduce Stress

Just helping a family member with simple daily tasks such as bathing or dressing can take nine hours per week. Add that to your other responsibilities and it's clear that effective time management and evaluating weekly priorities are essential. Since there are still only 24 hours in every day and you can never increase them, the only option is to change things. That's easier said than done, but be open to doing things differently at different times. Find a system that helps you channel your energy toward accomplishing the most important tasks. Divide tasks into what you (and only you) can do, rather than what you need to do and want to do, then delegate accordingly.

If you fail to plan and keep records, the chaos will get you down, so make notes of all discussions concerning care coordination, and be sure to keep track of care-related expenses, including dates and results of medical appointments and tests. Friends, neighbours, and siblings may be willing to help with household chores, pet care, property care, errands, or childcare. Experts recommend building an eldercare telephone and e-mail directory with a list of neighbours and contacts at the local provincial health office.

Get Up and Go!

- **Best practice**: Work out at least three times a week, ideally to a personalized exercise program or a set video workout.

- **Book an appointment with yourself**: Put your exercise time in your daily diary or Palm Pilot and treat your commitment to yourself like a business meeting—in other words, not to be missed!

- **Best foot forward**: Take a walk at the same time every day—for example, at lunch or an hour after dinner. If you feel guilty about spending the time on yourself (and you shouldn't), take along the kids or even your parents (if they are up to it).

- **Getting there**: If your parents' home is close by, walk there. If they live in an apartment, take the stairs when you get there.

- **On the job**: Learn to do some simple at-work exercises and stretches. These can be done for five minutes, twice in the morning, twice in the afternoon.

- **Family affair**: Do some simple exercises with your parents. Try rotations of the hands, feet, shoulders, and neck. Tense and relax muscles such as biceps, chest, calves, and shoulder blades.

- **Good morning**: Make a first-thing-in-the-morning appointment with yourself. You're less likely to cancel in the morning. Wake up half an hour before the rest of the family (or at least the kids) and do some simple crunches, stretches, and exercises.

- **Chill out**: Sign up for a yoga, fitness, meditation, or Tai Chi class with a friend, or even a parent, if he or she is fit enough.

Lean on Me: Caregiver Support Groups

Support groups exist across Canada, providing caregivers with a sense of community and a feeling that they are not alone. They help to deal with the negative emotions—from guilt to fear, to isolation, to frustration—shared by many individuals who find themselves in a caregiving situation. Members have no preconceived notions of who others are or what kind of care they are giving an elderly parent. It is a safe haven where the goal is to create a feeling of openness and a lifeline to others willing to offer support in difficult times.

If you can, choose a support group that provides a variety of services, from practical seminars and workshops with guest speakers to weekly discussion forums, which allow caregivers to share their feelings and experiences with others in a similar situation. In many cases, an educational component serves as an introduction, followed by more hands-on group sessions. Sessions tend to be informal. Many are led by a caregiver with special training and direct experience—an approach that works. Caregiver support groups seldom follow an agenda; topics vary and discussion always arises through the members' input. The group size tends to be

My Story: Setting Limits

Since Mom's stroke, a typical day involves frequent scheduling challenges and emotional highs and lows. My desk is sometimes overflowing and I've sometimes missed dinner or pushed a deadline or two. But believe it or not, I'm learning to cope and find a few quiet moments for myself once in a while. I'm getting much better at setting my limits and looking after myself. I've also made it a priority to head off for a rejuvenating massage or a quick reenergizing swim at my friend's pool to keep myself well grounded. While I'm not physically there every day—in fact, I live one and a half hours away from where Mom resides—I'm in touch regularly and on top of her progress. Because Mom's eager to be active, I visit and take her out as often as I can. Many times it's just a quiet walk or a simple meal at a local restaurant that gives us both a break in routine.

A recent special time for both of us came when we were invited to spend a day—and who could resist—at a well-known spa. Admittedly, I was nervous about the logistics of how a 76-year-old, post-stroke senior in a wheelchair might manage. However, the friendly therapists soon waylaid my concerns, accommodating and assisting us in the most unobtrusive, caring way possible. They even arranged a special caregiver to help with Mom to give me a break to enjoy my services.

We both left feeling massaged, pampered, reenergized, and ready to go back to the challenges of our daily lives. I'm glad we were brave enough to push the envelope and try the spa—it's an outing we can enjoy together in the future. And it's a way of sharing some quiet, pleasurable time away from the bustle of everyday care.

small to ensure that everyone has a chance to discuss what is important to them. You can talk about a problem you are having or ask others to suggest what they have tried.

Finding a support group in your area can usually be done through local chapters of organizations that have a mandate to educate and share knowledge on a particular medical condition (e.g., Heart and Stroke Foundation or Parkinson's Society). Ask local religious groups, other caregivers, and hospital discharge planners and social workers for recommendations.

Check the back of this book for resources that can also help to point you in the right direction.

Too Close to the Edge

As helpful as caregiver support groups are, many experts believe that they are underutilized. Part of the challenge for people is admitting that they are, in fact, caregivers. Care providers often turn to support groups as a last resort rather than as a tool for helping them to understand, plan, and flourish along the way.

"A truly happy person is one who can enjoy the scenery on a detour."
—Anonymous

Imagine caring for a mother who needs kidney dialysis and a brother with Alzheimer's. This caregiver didn't make a move to getting help until her own health began to fail. "I am all my mother has—I am all my brother has—I am all I have," she says. "I couldn't risk burning out." Or think of this 60-year-old man struggling by himself to care for a bedridden wife. At the end of each day, when his wife was comfortably asleep, the man, overwhelmed by the loneliness and the situation, would move silently in the dark to the end of the bed and cry. Eventually, close to breaking down, he found the courage to seek help.

It's at these low points that action often happens. Prior to desperation, people are often ashamed to admit that they need help. The feeling of being isolated, caught up with difficult decisions, and full of turbulent feelings are what eventually lead most caregivers to seek aid. It's no longer about simply coping from day to day, but it's about personal survival.

The open discussion provided by support groups helps caregivers work through the emotions of providing care, including the sense of failure. One support facilitator told me the group takes anger and frustration and makes it productive. Talking it out helps channel the negative emotions away from the caregiver and the person they are looking after. Many participants, even after the first session, find that this openness helps.

Caregiving, like life, is a cycle with its ups and downs. Regardless of the family size, people find themselves in the caregiving situation several times in their adult lives. Depending on the relationships and the severity of the care needed, some caregivers worry about care becoming a permanent stage in their lives. The performance may be repeated as another relative ages simultaneously or within a short period of time. Support groups not only prevent burnout, but also help caregivers think more clearly about present and future challenges in a neutral environment with sensitive support.

Thankfully, support doesn't end when the session is over. In many groups that click, there is an ongoing bond, and the group informally continues discussions, meetings, and educational or social events. One professional woman who cares for her mother-in-law who has Alzheimer's enjoyed meeting with her group once a week for six weeks. After the formal sessions ended, she and her group decided to continue and now meet once a month. "Just talking regularly really helps me out," she says. "Group members make suggestions that I never would have thought of."

My Story: I'm Not the Only One

When Mom was first placed in the nursing home, I felt so alone and like such a failure that I couldn't manage her on my own—physically or financially. She was angry and weepy each time I left, and my guilt ran high.

I've found meeting with other family caregivers who have relatives in nursing homes has helped me tremendously. They come and go like I do, we follow similar routines, and we share our experiences and "how-tos." I learned the ropes quite quickly, and other families have become supportive and friendly. People who live close by and visit more frequently even watch out for Mom when I'm not there.

Other groups continue through one-on-one phone counselling. The Alzheimer Society of Toronto, for example, offers most of its support over the telephone. It's easier for people to join in and participate without going anywhere—it's super for those who prefer to remain anonymous.

Something for Everyone

New caregivers tend to use support groups more than workshops or seminars. But this doesn't mean that support sessions are only for beginners. Everyone is at a different stage. Attendees range from someone whose father was recently diagnosed with dementia to someone who has been caring for an aunt with cancer or even caring for a person with a disability. Experienced caregivers, who know specifically what they need, sometimes prefer personal counselling, while some newcomers like the support and community of the group.

The variety of attendees is what makes the support groups so helpful. In fact, members will continue to meet with groups even though the loved one they are caring for is no longer at home or has died. But beyond the experiences, stories, and shared frustrations a bond forms among members. That first phone call is the most difficult. Once you've made it, you're on your way. "Take the plunge regardless of your fears," said one caregiver. "After all, part of caring is being cared for."

Caregiving is an emotional roller-coaster ride, ranging from calm periods where everything seems under control to periods of crisis and chaos. How do you cope? Each of us does so in different ways, but one thing that we all have in common is the occasional (or sometimes frequent) need for support along the way.

Belonging to a support group helps some provide better care and allows them to live an easier and more enjoyable life. Self-help groups can be the source of some of a caregiver's best support and advice regarding what to expect and where to get help. Caregivers are the first to champion the needs of their care recipients and often the last to take care of themselves. Support groups encourage caregivers to take time out and utilize respite care—because caregivers need care, too.

Self-help mutual support discussion groups emphasize "sharing" and "caring" with the underlying messages "You are not alone" and "You must take care of you."

Ready to Start Your Own Group?

Support groups were initially led by professionals and focused on education and the need to normalize feelings and set limits of caregiving, but many groups have evolved into peer-led self-help support groups. Success depends on the individuals involved and the planning and effort put into the development of the group. Support groups can be quite specific in defining their membership—for example, focusing on those caring for a person with cancer. Sometimes even older grandchildren attend the meetings.

Usually a group will be quite informal and flexible—confidentiality is essential, as is respect. A group size of between 10 and 12 members is small enough to allow time for everyone to share, listen, and ask questions.

The first meeting sets the tone and scene. The group is expected to reach a consensus of the most convenient time for meetings and with the help of a social worker or counsellor discuss guidelines, establish a format for the agenda, and encourage the shared ownership of the group by its members. A caregiver group exists only for the members and every attempt should be made to meet their needs.

For new members, begin with everyone providing a brief synopsis of their own caregiving situations. Next suggest that the newcomer is given an opportunity to share his or her experiences and describe how and why the person is there. The meeting then continues with updates of upcoming events that may interest the group, such as speakers, presentations, etc. There should also be an opportunity to discuss pertinent articles, issues raised by members, news, and other items of interest for future meetings.

Monthly meetings often offer respite for many family caregivers so an element of humour or fun is always welcome. Refreshments or healthy snacks can add to the social feel of the meeting.

The success of most support groups can be credited to devoted facilitators, all of whom have personal experience as family caregivers. These brave individuals create an inviting, trusting, and helpful environment for members. It goes without saying, however, that the ultimate success of any support group occurs because it has developed out of a real need, and because sometimes the best people to help others cope with a difficult situation are those who have been through the same situation themselves.

Technology can be your best friend when trying to find support. Web sites for existing groups, on-line discussions, and newsgroups are excellent ways to find and share information. This is especially beneficial for people who live in remote areas who might have trouble getting in to a town or live in such a small place that their situation is unique.

Caregiver Hint: Make sure that your conversations don't get off track. Keep discussions focused on the daily issues of caregiving and helping to reduce the stresses of caregiving. In fairness to the group, arrange to meet others at different times if you strike up a friendship or find interests in other areas.

What You Can Take Away from a Support Group

- Feeling less isolated knowing others share similar problems

- Ideas and effective ways to cope

- A new sense of control over your life

- Information about the best community resources, care alternatives, etc.

- Networking connections

- The opportunity to joke and laugh about your circumstances with people who really understand and won't judge you

- A chance to cry and complain without others making you feel guilty about your own needs and pain

- Time to focus on just you

- Respite from caregiving tasks

- Help to brainstorm solutions to your problems

- Hope as you listen to how others have coped

- Stress relief through emotional ventilation

- Validation by affirming your valued role and identity

- Easier acceptance of institutional placement of the care recipient

- Comfort during the grieving process

Workplace Warning Call

Are you coping? Take this quick test to see if your workplace productivity and advancement are being interrupted by your eldercare responsibilities.

❏ Taking extra personal phone calls related to your parents?

❏ Not completing or decreasing the quality of your work?

❑ Unwilling to work overtime or handle business travel?

❑ Calling in sick or taking time off to provide support or care?

❑ Being late or adjusting work time without notice?

❑ Rearranging your schedule to accommodate other responsibilities?

❑ Unable to accept extra projects or new assignments?

❑ Requesting reduced hours when work is busy?

❑ Having to turn down a promotion or relocation opportunity?

❑ Avoiding issues at work because you're worn out?

❑ Feeling depressed or tense?

❑ Distracted and therefore at risk of on-the-job injury?

Have more than five checkmarks? Before you burn out, speak to your employer about implementing some of the creative options discussed in this chapter. Having a supportive work environment will allow you to become a better caregiver while making you more productive at work.

If you are currently balancing eldercare and career responsibilities at the same time, fear not. Many employers are beginning to recognize the challenges of eldercare and the loss of productivity it can cause. Just as employers launched childcare initiatives a few short years ago, some attractive eldercare programs have begun to pop up. Expect more. Take a leadership role in sniffing out new opportunities and pioneering programs that will help both you and your co-workers. Statistics show that one in five employees is facing the same thing you are.

Be creative, be open, be ready to flex, and you just may be able to work out a solution that will keep both you and your employer happy. Hint: Don't hide your eldercare needs; there's nothing worse than the office rumour mill for spreading the wrong story. Check into some of the following:

Caregiver leave: This type of leave is similar to maternity leave. A number of leading-edge companies already allow a six-to-eight-week family or extended leave that can be used to provide short-term care for elderly family members. Based on recent public opinion research, the federal government has introduced a compassionate caregiver leave of absence program.

Flexible work arrangements: Think about flextime, a compressed workweek, a shorter workday, or job sharing. Sometimes, depending on the nature of your job, an employer may be willing to accept the option of working at home on occasion.

Special compensation plans: Additional services may be available through your benefit programs and there may be "items on the menu" that you have never noticed before. Check them out and ask about employee assistance programs that are at your disposal. Family and personal days off are also great ways to cover time off that you need to care for Mom or Dad.

Workplace wellness: The stats are in: Research has shown that a company would realize a possible $3:$1 return on their direct costs in work-life programs. Simply put, when your company invests in helping you to manage your eldercare issues, they are investing to

- reduce absenteeism,

- cap employee turnover,

- reduce your stress and health-care costs,

- save lost performance time.

You owe it to yourself to investigate programs in the workplace that promote health, reduce stress, and provide access to caregiving resources. Some corporations encourage caregiver support groups and "lunch and learns." Remember you are not alone. In 2000, 77% of employees were bearing some type of responsibility for elderly relatives according to the Conference Board of Canada. Many companies are even developing education materials and providing copies of *Solutions* magazine (a Canadian magazine written for family caregivers) to employees to help them more easily understand options and make arrangements.

Smile Away Your Stress

It's no coincidence that comedians like George Burns, Bob Hope, and Sid Caesar lived long healthy lives. The expression "laughter is the best medicine" is more than a cliché. In fact, the healing power of humour has been scientifically validated.

"A clown is like an aspirin, only he works twice as fast."
—*Groucho Marx*

Laughter has been shown to have a positive effect on your health, and if you think about it, it can also be a helpful method of helping a parent or loved one cope with the onset of age or a disabling illness. Latest research demonstrates that laughter has positive physiological and psychological benefits:

Cardiac health: Experts compare the effect of laughter to "internal jogging." It can provide good cardiac conditioning, especially for those who are unable to perform physical exercises.

Blood pressure: Regular laughter helps regulate blood flow. For some reason, women seem to benefit more than men in lowering the risks of hypertension.

Respiratory function: Laughter empties the lungs of more air than it takes in. The result is a cleansing effect similar to deep breathing. It's especially beneficial for people suffering from emphysema and other respiratory ailments.

Gastrointestinal health: Laughter triggers the release of an enzyme that helps digestion.

Pain reduction: Humour allows a person to forget about the aches and pains, even for a short time.

Muscle tone: When you laugh, the stomach muscles not involved relax. Once you finish laughing, those muscles involved in the laughter start to relax. This alternating workout helps strengthen muscles.

Find a Funny and Share It

Studies have shown that there is a connection between a sense of humour and the overall ability to cope with what life dishes out. People are less likely to succumb to feelings of depression and helplessness if they are able to laugh at their circumstances. It cheers people up, and their improved emotional state, in turn, further boosts the immune system. Laughter can also help you function better as a caregiver. Finding humour in a situation and being willing to laugh freely with others is a powerful coping mechanism when you are facing a serious crisis.

Share a Joke

Maintaining a sense of humour gives a sense of perspective on problems, while providing an opportunity to release those uncomfortable emotions that, if held inside, can cause harmful distress. Sure, it is sometimes difficult to force a laugh when things are tense. But that's just when you need it. So, next time the pressures of caregiving begin to build, find ways to have fun. Tune into a sit-com, read a funny, or call a buddy to share a joke. Laughter is therapeutic. And, to top it all off, it's free, you don't need a prescription, and there are no known negative side effects. As Bill Cosby says, "If you can laugh at it, you can survive it."

The Lighter Side of Caregiving

The troubles of caring for and dealing with aging parents has provided ample fodder over the years. Next time the going gets tough, try out one or two of these movies and books for a funny pick-me-up.

Movie Madness

Think your parent is difficult to deal with? Check out *Throw Momma from the Train*. Once you stop laughing at what Danny DeVito's character has to go through, you won't feel so hard done by. You (and your parents) might identify with—and get a kick out of—Jack Lemmon and Walter Matthau in *Grumpy Old Men*. It's a hilarious look at the eccentricities and challenges of old age. Matthau also stars in *Hanging Up*, a comedy about three yuppie sisters (Meg Ryan, Lisa Kudrow, and Diane Keaton) dealing with their dad's sudden illness. For a funny male perspective, watch *Mother*, with Albert Brooks moving back home with his older mother, played by Debbie Reynolds.

Books

Erma Bombeck's books, such as *Family-Ties That Bind...and Gag*, deal with the adventures and misadventures of life, including caregiving. Guys may identify with the baby boomer author's trials and tribulations in *Dave Barry Turns 50*. For a funny and off-the-wall in-depth look at caregiving, check out *Elder Rage—or Take My Father, Please!* by Jacqueline Marcell. Her touching story of caring for her aging parents is filled with laughs as well as practical advice.

Television

Single caregivers, especially, might get a weekly chuckle from *Frasier*, as he struggles with the demands of his retired, disabled father while trying to keep his life under control. Or for a really irreverent, but hilarious, take on aging, tune into *The Simpsons* and the ongoing adventures of Grandpa at the Springfield Retirement Castle.

Fighting Fatigue

Conserving your precious energy can be a challenge in our rush, rush world of trying to do many things at once. When you are called upon to go to extra appointments, lug around equipment, and help with mobility and personal care activities, caregiving can be physically draining. While there is no quick fix, one potential solution is to eat well and practice energy management. Women especially feel tired and run down. If you can't head for a once-a-month getaway at a quiet spot, occupational therapists have some advice, outlined below, for those with busy schedules. These practices will help reduce stress levels and preserve valuable energy. Some may also be great to share with other families.

Reduce fatigue by sitting. Energy consumption is reduced by 25% when you are not standing. Taking regular breaks and sitting down for five minutes at a time will increase your overall endurance. Practice good posture. Poor posture can drain energy. Posture can be improved in a number of little ways. For example, carry two small bags of groceries—one in each hand—rather than one large heavy bag.

Manage your time by dividing tiring activities. Instead of doing all the big things at once, try spreading them out during the week. And pace yourself. Alternate light and heavy tasks and rest when tired.

Keep your home organized. Unnecessary clutter can tire you out mentally and physically. For example, think of the time and energy wasted searching for car keys or a pair of glasses. Create a comfortable environment, because a pleasant relaxed atmosphere will do wonders for your energy levels. Make sure your surroundings are well lit with subtle colours and your favourite music playing.

Plan outings. It's not the event but your perception of it that makes all the difference. Stay calm, make a list, and schedule your errands in a logical manner. Follow a route that eliminates extra travel, traffic, and extra trips. Travel sensibly. When you pack, do so in the same order each time. You might start with items you need in the morning, then clothes, then accessories.

Source: www.otworks.com

Research Roundup

Even moderate exercise, like brisk walking, can do a caregiver good.

Stanford University researchers followed 100 female caregivers who participated in either an exercise program or a nutrition program. The exercise group performed moderate physical activity (brisk walking, stationary cycling, working out to fitness videos, etc.) for at least 30 minutes, four times a week. At the end of the study, the exercise group had less stress and better sleep quality compared to the nutrition group. Blood pressure levels also improved in the exercise group.

Source: Journal of Gerontology

Ten Steps to Getting a Better Night's Sleep

Work, kids, parents, social life—it can add up to a hectic juggling act and sleep often becomes a low priority. Studies show that the average adult needs to avoid late nights and irregular bedtimes to get seven to eight hours of sleep a night, yet more than 15% of us suffer from sleep disorders while an astonishing 50% of us experience sleeping problems at some point in our lives. Skip the exercise program that you thought you'd do before going to bed. Experts suggest that you need to unwind for a few hours prior to bedtime instead of getting all cranked up by a late-night aerobics class.

Eating or drinking just before bedtime, especially spicy foods or large meals, can cause wakeful indigestion or late-night trips to the bathroom. Avoid caffeine, nicotine, and alcohol before bedtime. All of these contain chemicals that adversely affect sleeping habits. Watching TV is also a no-no, according to the experts, but some people swear that it's the thing that gets them ready for bed. "TV puts me into that real couch potato relaxation mode," says one overworked editor.

Create a comfortable sleeping environment. Set the tone with a bedroom that's quiet, dark, and cool. (Environments that are too warm tend to discourage consistent, restful sleep.) You'll also want a comfortable mattress and pillow. Try not to over-sleep. Research on sleeping has shown that the extra sleep tends to be fragmented and unrefreshing. Avoid catnaps. Sleeping for even brief periods of time during the day will disrupt your nocturnal snoozing patterns. If you must nap, limit the time to 20 minutes or less.

Avoid regular use of sleeping pills. They should only be used infrequently and only when recommended by your physician. He or she will diagnose your condition to ensure that no serious, underlying disorders exist and refer you to the appropriate treatment.

Best of all, try to relax and calm down before bedtime. Don't sweat the small stuff when it's time to sleep. Worrying about things will not help the cause. Instead, if you want to be bright-eyed and bushy-tailed in the morning, plan to slow down and do something that you find relaxing (such as reading or writing).

Just How Do You Take a Break?

According to author and family caregiver Bart Mindszenthy, respite and time away are key elements in your journey as a caregiver for your aging parents. His advice for planned down time is to focus on something totally different to escape the pressures of eldercare. "Make it your goal to turn off your mind for a set period of time and activate your body to give a physical outlet to the mental stress." His list of activities to try sounds like fun and welcome respite.

Golf: Helps you focus on all parts of your body and gets you outdoors.

Tennis, squash, or badminton: Each calls for focus, coordination, speed, and good reflexes.

Drawing or painting: Excellent ways to practice concentration and focus and test your perceptual skills.

Reading: Allow yourself to delve deeply into a good story and turn off all other intrusions.

Gardening: Simple, yet satisfying work with tangible results.

Woodworking: Exacting and difficult tasks exercise concentration and produce visible results.

Plays, concerts, ballet: A change of pace and sheer entertainment will offer temporary and welcome mental relief.

Your bottom line: Identify things you'd like to do—regularly. The key is to set aside escape time, so that you can find a period of solace and comfort away from the tensions of the busy day. This will help you to remain strong and put you and your family in a much better position to tackle your regular responsibilities.

CHAPTER 15

In the
End...

Gradually, as adult children, we'll all be faced with the fact that, despite best efforts of both doctors and family members, our elders will not be around much longer.

For most of us, death is too awkward to talk about and painful to think about. But, as Dr. Sherwin Nuland says in How We Die, *"Death belongs to the dying and to those who love them. This doesn't mean your parent shouldn't be in hospital or be cared for by a doctor, rather it means that it is you, your parent and your family who have control over where he or she dies, which treatments are preferred and which will be refused and the type of palliative care provided."*

End-of-Life and Palliative Care Explained

When a patient's health team determines that the disease can no longer be controlled, medical testing and treatment stop but the patient care continues. The care, now called palliative, is focused at this point on making the patient as comfortable as possible. Medications are given to manage pain and treat other symptoms such as shortness of breath, nausea, and constipation. Some people choose to stay home at this time while others enter a hospice or a hospital. Wherever your elderly relative is, there is generally help available to families to support medical care as well as psychological and spiritual issues concerned with dying. Active total care is offered to patients with progressive disease and their families when it is recognized that the illness is no longer curable, in order to concentrate on the quality of life and the alleviation of distressing symptoms in the framework of a coordinated service.

The focus of palliative care is neither to hasten nor postpone death. It provides relief from pain and other distressing symptoms and integrates the psychological and spiritual aspects of care. Furthermore it offers a support system to help relatives and friends cope during the patient's illness and the survivors' bereavement. The great majority of patients seen by most palliative care programs have advanced or terminal cancer. Current trends also show that patients with other terminal illnesses such as AIDS, amyotrophic lateral sclerosis, and multiple sclerosis may have special needs that require a palliative approach.

Advanced Care Directives

A living will is a form of advance directive that outlines, in writing, what kinds of treatment are and are not wanted and other details that involve last wishes.

Generally, advance directives are written documents meant to make explicit the conditions under which individuals wish to receive certain treatment or to refuse or discontinue life-sustaining treatment, in the event that they are no longer legally competent to make their own decisions.

It's your role as a caregiver to be sure that advanced care directives are communicated and followed as your loved one would have wanted.

Hospice Helps

Based on the belief that death is a natural and inevitable part of life, hospice services are often sought at the point when all concerned feel that, rather than battling illness and trying to ward off death, the time has come to focus on enhancing whatever life remains. Hospice services are delivered 24 hours a day by qualified teams with a medical director, nurses, home health aides, social workers, nutritionists, speech therapists, physiotherapists, and volunteers, all working as needed with the patient and his or her family. These services can be delivered on a residential basis or as part of home care and as respite. Temporary respite care that provides relief for family caregivers is a godsend for many families. With help from hospice personnel, a person who is not going to get better can be removed from the bustle and machinery of the hospital to die in peace.

To qualify for care, some organizations require a doctor to determine, as much as is possible, that the patient has less than six months to live. For a referral, talk to your loved one's doctor; this service is sometimes presented as part of palliative care.

"A strong positive mental attitude will create more miracles than any wonder drug."
—*Patricia Neal*

Positive Things a Caregiver Can Do

Here are eight things you can do whether your parent is dying at home or in a hospital or nursing home:

1. **Make the most of the days**. Be aware as the days go by of your loved one's mental and spiritual health by offering a chance for your parent to talk to a chaplain, counsellor, or social worker. Think of positive things to do if he or she is able, even for a little while. Watch a favourite TV show, look at pictures, go outside in the gardens, visit with a family pet.... Make sure the room smells nice. Fresh linens and flowers are uplifting for both the patient and visitors. Keep things clean and the patient changed regularly. If there is a choice, choose the side of the room with a window—there's less traffic and generally a better view. Open a window if you can for a few minutes each day.

2. **Give lots of affection and personalized time**. Just a simple touch or a held hand can be a big comfort in the long hours. Stay the night if you can so that your loved one isn't frightened and knows you're there if he or she needs you. Maintain a gentle, respectful, and dignified approach. Preserve what's left of your parent's privacy when grooming, washing, and toileting. Be discreet and caring. Keep the curtains drawn and ask visitors to leave the room during this time. Ask for permission when you work with private areas.

3. **Keep things as familiar as possible**. Often an elder's last days are full of equipment and tubing as well as a lot of caregivers coming and going. Try to have people around that your parent knows and bring items from home or other parts of the house close enough for them to see.

4. **Alleviate suffering**. Do your best to keep your parent comfortable and pain-free. I had a friend who brought her mother earplugs and a sleep mask so that it would be easier for her to sleep in the hospital. Whatever else you do, make sure that the doctor is willing to administer whatever medications are available to provide relief. Think about requesting a do-not-resuscitate order before a person is in that situation (this should be part of the advance care directive). If possible, discuss your elder's wishes. And determine how much medical intervention you would like toward the end of the person's life.

5. **Watch for painful bedsores**. With prolonged inactivity, a patient may experience bedsores either from being in the bed with pressure on the same parts of the body or from sitting too long in a wheelchair or a tilt-and-recline seating system without pressure relief. Ensure that good seating and positioning equipment are available and that professional advice is given for repositioning and turning. Make sure health professionals are performing regular checks, and if bedsores are present, be sure to ask questions to understand how pain is managed and treated. Check bony spots such as elbows and heels, as well as the back of the head and buttocks.

6. **Be there**. Talk through the process of what is happening with your loved one. Before procedures, tell the patient what to expect. If it's going to be uncomfortable, let the patient know how long the procedure and discomfort will last. Whether you say it out loud or not, your parent likely knows that he ir she is receiving palliative care and is getting ready to die. Don't be afraid to broach the subject—be ready to share your feelings, fears, and memories. (I've had quite a few people tell me lately about amazing last weeks with one of their parents when they shared, loved, grieved, and felt very blessed to have had that special time.) Hearing is the last sense to go. Be quiet when necessary but add interest with soothing music or reading aloud. Avoid excessive noise or third-party conversations. (Boomers, put your office cellphones away!)

7. **Wash your hands often**. Do it before, during, and after visits. Ask visitors to wash their hands as they enter and leave the

house and avoid letting people who have colds or the flu near the patient. Spray disinfectant on doorknobs, telephone receivers, etc. Make hygiene and cleanliness a priority for yourself and your loved one. And, when things get really yucky, reach for disposable gloves and breathe through your mouth.

8. **Know who to call for help and what to say**. Make sure that you have all the necessary contact information for health team members, medical records, insurance papers, prescription information, and legal papers, including health cards, advanced directives, and living wills, in a safe but easy-to-access spot. When things are not going well, the last thing you want to be doing is rummaging around looking for the papers and/or information that you need. Doctors frequently over-treat dying patients and ignore requests to withhold life support. Remember, they are trained to treat, not give in. Also, remember to treat paid caregivers, doctors, and volunteers calmly and with respect in a crisis and on an everyday basis. If you lose your cool or get overanxious, make sure you apologize when things are settled down again.

End-of-Life-Care Questions and Answers

The National Cancer Institutes Web site presents some common questions and answers they receive. With their permission, we reproduce some of these questions and their answers from the site's update of October 10, 2002.

The following information can help answer some of the questions that many patients, their family members, and caregivers have about the end of life.

Q. *How long is the patient expected to live?*

A. Patients and their family members often want to know how long a person is going to live. This is a hard question for doctors to answer for fear of instilling false hope or destroying a person's hope. In the case of cancer, factors like where the cancer is located and whether the patient has other illnesses can affect what will happen.

Q. *When should a family caregiver call for professional help?*

A. If you are caring for a patient at home ask for help when

- the patient is in pain that is not relieved by the prescribed dose of pain medications

- the patient shows discomfort such as grimacing and moaning

- the patient has trouble breathing and seems upset

- the patient cannot urinate or empty the bowels

- the patient has fallen

- the patient is very depressed

- the caregiver has difficulty giving medication or is overwhelmed or scared by the situation

Q. *What are some ways that caregivers can provide emotional comfort to their family member?*

A. Common to most dying patients are the fear of abandonment and the fear of being a burden. They also have concerns about loss of dignity and control. You might consider providing comfort by

- keeping the person company—talk, watch movies, read, or just be with them

- allow the person to talk and express fears about leaving others behind

- reminisce about the person's life if he or she wishes

- respect privacy and need for peace and quiet

- reassure the patient that you will honour advance directives such as living wills

Q. *What are the signs that death is approaching and what should a caregiver do?*

A. Certain signs and symptoms can help a caregiver anticipate when death is near. Not everyone experiences each of the signs and symptoms and the presence of one or more doesn't mean that death is close. To be better informed, check with a member of your loved one's health care team.

Here are some suggestions for what to expect and how to manage:

- **Symptom**: Drowsiness, increased sleep and/or unresponsiveness (caused by changes in the patient's metabolism)

  Manage by: Planning visits and activities when the patient is alert. Speak directly to the patient and talk as if he or she can hear you even if there is no response. Most patients are still able to hear even if they can no longer speak. Do not shake the person to try and wake him or her.

- **Symptom**: Confusion about time, place, and/or identity of loved ones; restlessness, visions of people and places that are not present and pulling at bed linens or clothing

  Manage by: Gently reminding the patient of the time, date, and people who are with him or her. If your loved one is agitated do not attempt to restrain the patient. Be calm and reassuring. Speaking calmly may help to re-orient the person.

- **Symptom**: Decreased need for food and fluids and loss of appetite (caused by the body's need to conserve energy and its decreasing ability to use food and fluids properly)

  Manage by: Allowing the patient to choose if and when to eat or drink. Ice chips, water, or juice may be refreshing if the patient can swallow. Try and keep the patient's mouth and lips moist with products such as glycerin swabs and lip balm.

- **Symptom**: Loss of bladder or bowel control (caused by the relaxing of muscles in the pelvic area)

  Manage by: Keeping the patient as clean and dry and comfortable as possible. Place disposable pads on the bed beneath the patient and remove them when they become soiled.

- **Symptom**: Darkened urine or decreased amount of urine (caused by slowing of kidney function and/or decreased fluid intake)

Manage by: Consulting with a member of the health care team about the need to insert a catheter to avoid blockage. You can learn how to take care of the catheter from a team member if one is needed.

- **Symptom**: Skin becomes cool to the touch, particularly the hands and feet; skin may become bluish in colour, especially on the underside of the body (caused by decreased circulation to the extremities)

  Manage by: Using blankets to warm the patient. Although the skin may be cool, patients are usually not aware of feeling cold. Caregivers should avoid warming the patient with electric blankets or heating pads, which can cause burns.

- **Symptom**: Rattling or gurgling sounds while breathing, which may be loud; breathing that is irregular and shallow; decreased number of breaths per minute; breathing that alternates between rapid and slow (caused by congestion from decreased fluid consumption, a buildup of waste products in the body, and/or a decrease in circulation to the organs)

  Manage by: Making breathing easier by turning the patient on his or her side and placing pillows beneath the head and behind the back. Although laboured breathing can sound very distressing to the caregiver, gurgling and rattling sounds do not cause discomfort to the patient. An external source of oxygen may be of benefit. If the patient is able to swallow, ice chips may also help as well as a cool mist humidifier.

- **Symptom**: Turning head toward a light source (caused by decreasing vision)

  Manage by: Leaving soft, indirect lights on in the room

Q. What are signs that the patient has died?

A. There is no breathing or pulse. Eyes do not move or blink and the pupils are enlarged. Eyelids may be slightly open.

Body fluids are released. The jaw is relaxed and the mouth is slightly open and the patient doesn't respond to being touched or spoken to.

Q. When the patient has died, what do we do?

A. Place the body on its back with one pillow under the head. Caregivers may wish to put the patient's dentures or other artificial parts in place (i.e., toupées, limbs). Follow the guidelines from the hospice program, which may suggest that a nurse verify the patient's death. Contact the patient's doctor and the funeral home and call other family members, clergy, and friends. Don't ignore the need to obtain emotional support for yourself and other family members from team members and friends. However prepared we are, it's still a shock and an emotional time. It's ok to cry. It's also important for surviving parents to see their adult children cry. It confirms that they are not alone in their grief and that the spouse they loved was loved by others.

Illness or Death of a Spouse

Older parents have often not really prepared themselves for the death of a spouse and find themselves faced with grief, traumatic decision-making, and the reality of their own mortality. Spouses may find it hard to discuss the subject, even though they both know that one of them is dying. Often, there is a sudden wish by the parents to discuss death with their children and ask for, or expect, help. This is when words like "terminal," "hospice," or "funeral" are usually danced around by kids and parents alike. It's as if by using the words, it's really going to make it happen. Be patient and try to be there when they need you during the illness and to help make appropriate after-death arrangements.

Expect the surviving parent to have plenty of new needs. After all, many couples have been together for 30 or 40 years. Aside from loneliness, consider all the things that the deceased spouse did for the survivor. Did one parent take care of the finances and write all the cheques? Was the deceased spouse the one who did most of the driving and shopping? Who kept track of the medicines?

Caregiver Hint. Offer lots of support. Stay in close contact and encourage outings. Perhaps to fill the gap there are some things that you as the adult child can take over, at least in the interim to help bridge the loss.

My Story: A Sudden Change

After my father, Ralph, passed away suddenly in his mid-60s, my mother was lost and lonely. Dad had always paid all the bills and made all the car and household maintenance arrangements.

Friends who were couples disappeared, and Mom decided to move and try to start her life again. It was painful to watch her struggle but she was fiercely independent and wanted very little help and advice. Without Dad, she became a different woman, one who wasn't interested in family or grandchildren. Mom refused to cook for just one and snacked her way to gaining almost 100 pounds. She seemed like a stranger to us for a while. It took a couple of years of chaos, several moves, and quite a bit of extra expense before she was able to settle down in her own house and manage most of her affairs.

Expecting Visitors

The timing is not always perfect for friends to drop by, so don't hesitate to send them away if your loved one isn't up to a visit. But, if you can manage it, it's best for all concerned to try a brief visit. Here are a few simple hints:

- Ask people not to bring large gifts or send huge flower arrangements. Many of us feel like the funeral is already underway if the room is too flower-laden.

- Be mindful of and facilitate cultural and religious traditions that your loved one and the person's friends may wish to uphold. Prayers, blessings, and rituals are often comforting.

- Accept gifts of food and offers of help. Don't try to do everything yourself. When people come over, they're often more than willing to help out with a few things around the house instead of just sitting.

- Don't be afraid to laugh together and share some humorous stories with the patient. This doesn't have to be a solemn, boring time.

- Keep a supply of paper plates and other disposables for snacks or treats that guests may bring. (The last thing you need right now is dishes.)

Accept the Challenges

- Keep to a routine. It helps to get the job done when you are feeling down.

- Keep in touch with those who want to help you. Make a point of regularly calling, visiting, or writing to those who are closest to you.

- Admit that there are times when you feel down. Really think about what it is you are missing. Plan new ways of making up for that loss and getting help where you need it.

- Avoid loneliness. Care for needs of others—neighbours, children, pets. You are a person who is needed. You have a background and skills that can be used through voluntary work as well as paid employment.

- Look for support and help when you need it. It can come from many community sources if they know of your need. Have a talk with your minister or volunteer coordinator.

- You may have some free time that you have not been used to having. Think about taking up new activities. Are there hobbies from the past that might be picked up again?

Source: OT Works

Good Grief

After an illness, the death of an older person can be a relief. Grief is a normal reaction to a death or loss in a person's life but it can be hard, stressful, and tiring. According to counsellors, there are a number of stages of grief that may be experienced to help us let go of the past and adjust to a new life without the person who died.

Each person's reaction to the loss will be different and highly personal and he or she will grieve differently. Generally there is a shock or denial accompanied by a sense of numbness or disbelief. First reactions are a sense that this didn't happen and there is for many a kind of detached, disoriented feeling. Some caregivers or family members are unable to do much and feel extremely tired while others set about cleaning up and getting on with what needs to be done. People who are grieving may cry a lot, blame others, have upset stomachs and headaches, and have problems sleeping or resting, eating, or doing small tasks.

Whatever the grief response, this is a stressful time and experts suggest that most people would do better taking a bit of time off work and spending time with friends and family until they feel more balanced.

Five Stages of Mourning

Understanding the process of mourning will help comfort you and make you aware of what to expect as you pass through its five stages.

1. **Denial:** Sometimes it can be difficult to accept reality.

2. **Anger:** Perhaps you feel upset with yourself, a loved one, or the doctor.

3. **Bargaining or guilt:** Exploring the "what if..." and "If only I had..." scenarios is quite common.

4. **Depression:** You have finally recognized the loss.

5. **Acceptance:** You realize that it's not your fault and that you must go on with your life.

Source: www.seniorwellness.com

Caregiver Hint: Encourage your surviving parent to visit the doctor regularly to take care of his or her physical health. If you're the survivor, take this advice for yourself. Poor health makes you more susceptible to depression and illness.

Extreme Loss

In the weeks after the condolences and casseroles are gone, you may find yourself visiting the grave, yearning for days gone by, and even dreaming about the lost parent or loved one. Some adults often adopt the behaviours, habits, and mannerisms of the one who has passed, even to the extreme of displaying symptoms of the illness in a number of reported cases. People who are grieving find that grief goes on much longer than they imagined and that there are no quick fixes. Each person has to work through his or her grief, and it's not always easy for others to help. In fact, if time to grieve is not allowed, and it is not dealt with, it may come up later as a mental or physical illness. Be prepared for other losses in life to come to the surface again. And if issues were unresolved or conflict reigned in the person's relationship with the person who died, there will be some sorting out to do. You may need help to let go. If the confusion continues, consider a support group, psychotherapy, or counselling.

> "Happiness comes through doors you didn't even know you left open."
> —*Anonymous*

No Regrets

Once a parent or loved one has died, there is no longer a chance to do more or do things a different way, and many people feel guilt over this. Perhaps you didn't visit as often as you might have, maybe you were impatient or angry or disgruntled with your parent's indecisiveness toward the end. Maybe you even wished that your parent would hurry up and die!

Don't be too hard on yourself. First, any thoughts you had about your parent's death didn't speed up the process. Try to remember all that you did for your parent, how glad he or she was to see you in good times. Think of the hours of calls, care, worry, and commitment you gave. Now this time is over—don't feel guilty about a lack of sorrow or a feeling of relief. Your grieving time may just be over if your parent had been ill for a while. Your role as a caregiver is finished and with it perhaps a sense of purpose. When your only surviving parent passes away, you become an orphan. That may leave you feeling rootless and very alone.

A parent's death removes your buffer against the future. You'll be forced to deal with your own wrinkles and white hair…your own raison d'être. This face-to-face time with your future can be depressing, but if you choose, it can be re-energizing. Slowing down, re-establishing ties, and finding worthwhile tasks with meaning may take time. Remember that others have been through this before. Think positively. Soon, all things will pass and new things will come to be. Decisions about the future are yours to make. You'll never forget your caregiving journeys but when the time is right you'll be ready to move on.

Celebrating and Remembering Life

Don't lose touch with your past just because there's illness, the death of a close family member, or the loss of a good friend. Find ways to keep good memories alive. Remember all the helpful things your parents taught you… their wisdom, their funny quirks, their patience or impatience with some of your nonsense as a teenager. I'm sure you can come up with some funny stories. I have a few of my own, like the time Dad fell in the water while he was trying to feed the ducks, or the time we found out my mother had been a guest at a nudist camp. Continue to mark down their birthdays and wedding anniversaries in your day planner, even though it's hard because things will never be the same.

Keep traditions for festive holidays that will remind you of the way they did things and how much you enjoyed it as a child. We celebrate Christmas in the hospital with Mom and now we always take Thanksgiving and Easter dinners into the nursing home for her.

Pass what you can on to your children to keep memories alive. Our daughter Ashleigh went off happily to McGill University with more pots, pans, utensils, and china than any student would ever need—fresh from Grandma's house Now that she's graduating, she plans to save them for her younger sister Elise to use as she sets up her own digs in a couple of years (we call it Grandma's University Starter Kit).

My Story: Savour the Memories

My father was a jazz lover and a part-time radio show host in Penticton, British Columbia. After he died, I had the job of clearing out tapes that stored hours of his jazz programs. At the time, I just wanted to get rid of them but thankfully my husband and brother insisted on keeping a few. Nearly 14 years later, my daughter, who was only two at the time of her grandpa's death, enjoys listening to those tapes with him hosting his twice-weekly show and playing his favourites on air.

Take an afternoon to sort through and label old photos and home movies so that you can keep their memories alive through pictures and words. Most of us have digital capabilities. Now is the time to empty out the drawers and catalogue those family pictures. But most of all is allowing yourself to stop for a moment and be thankful that you have been able to be such a significant part of an elder's life as he or she entered the final years. Celebrate the fact that you are or were fortunate enough to be able to care for and about your parent.

Hold your head high and be proud.

And, remember, be nice to your kids...it's they who'll be choosing your nursing home!

Further Reading

Mum's Last Requests: Good Caregiving Also Means Planning for the Inevitable

Barbara Carter

As a family caregiver, you must accept the fact that preparing for the inevitable is essential. The more you know, and the better you prepare, the easier it will be for you and your family when the time comes, as it often does.

Here are some of the lessons that've been shared over the years. Many aren't pleasant, but they're real:

Legally Deceased

A doctor is required to officially declare that a person has died. Paramedics have to work at reviving until they can get through to the doctors by phone. Once they've connected they are legally allowed to stop the treatment. (I've heard of situations where this has taken close to an hour.)

This is extremely sad and difficult for the family members present, who know the reality of the situation but must stand by and witness futile attempts at revival.

When someone dies in their own home it is considered a possible crime until the appropriate authorities agree that it is not. Paramedics, the police and ultimately the coroner, arrive within a few hours and interview all family members.

24/7...Just Call

Funeral parlours are open 24 hours a day. It's best if you've preselected (I had the dreadful task of making a choice of funeral parlour via the Yellow Pages from the hospital pay phone when my father died). Friends who've been at home when a parent died have had to call for pick-up of the body. (This usually happens within a few hours.)

What Do We Do Next?

We talked and visited the funeral parlour the next morning. Then we called the church minister and somehow, a number of friends. Gradually, we planned a funeral—with music...my father's favourite..."When the Saints Come Marching In,"...and little sandwiches from the ladies at the church.

[After my mother died] it wasn't until five days later that we found Mum's "little blue book." Mum had written explicit instructions on what to do should she pass away. While my mother was great at writing a will, setting up powers of attorney, and we had talked to her about these, we had never discussed her funeral plans. And she never told us about the little blue book.

So we didn't know until after the fact that...

- Mum wanted a party at the local Naval Club. (We held a fussy, expensive funeral service.)

- Mum wanted her body donated to science to help new doctors learn. (We had her cremated.)

- Mum wanted donations made to the Seaman's Mission. (We chose the Epilepsy Society.)

- Mum had a favourite poem she wanted read during her eulogy. (I wrote a story about friends and her grandkids.)

Some of my siblings felt badly that we had not done everything as Mum would have wished. I think we did a pretty good job anyway given what we knew at the time. But, it would have been nice to try and fulfill Mum's simple final wishes.

Preparing for the Worst

Although you can never be totally prepared, I think it would have been better if I'd followed these six tips:

1. **Keep track of the will**. Make sure your loved one has an up-to-date will and that copies have been given to the appropriate people. Often times there are several versions floating around. Many times it is uncomfortable to ask for a copy but, along with powers of attorney, this document is vital.

2. **Share responsibilities**. Taking a role helps everybody to heal.

3. **Keep cash on hand**. Life insurance policies are just not accessible in a hurry. Your parents' assets are often invested or money is tied up in the family house. Bank accounts can become temporarily frozen at this time. I had to use my money and credit lines for funeral and emergency expenses in the months after Dad died.

4. **Choose a good executor**. Think about the executor of the will. Is this person detail-oriented, well-organized, and able to deal with the emotional trauma of a close death? Does everyone in the family trust this person? Will there be arguments? Can he or she quell the waters without massive legal bills and delays?

Caregiver Hint: Choose an executor who is ready, willing, and available!

Wendy's Story

Some years ago, Wendy's dad had changed his bank account so it was a joint one. Gradually, she began to pay all his bills and administer all his finances. All his money was paid into the account...Wendy didn't contribute anything, and he paid tax on the interest. The idea was that this was to be Wendy's money on her father's death. When she informed the bank that her dad had died, the account was frozen! This was in spite of the fact that he had deliberately not ticked the box not conferring survivorship rights—in other words, it was clear he wanted Wendy to have access to the money immediately. What bothers Wendy is that if she'd realized his death was imminent (he was quite ill but she didn't realize that he would go so quickly—"He was 98, after all so I should have known," she says) she could have moved all the money into her own account.

To complicate matters, there were two banks involved, the one he had banked at for over 50 years and the branch they used in Toronto. After meetings and phone calls, Wendy finally got them to unfreeze the main account—the one with most of the money in it—and was able to write cheques. But it was a dreadful shock.

5. **Preplan the funeral**. It's much easier on family members if the funeral is preplanned. It's a not-so-many-decisions-at-a-difficult-time approach to leaving your house in order. All choices are made ahead of time and the bills are discreetly prepaid. (No discussions about the size and quality of the coffins...no wondering about burial or cremation plans.) The funeral director professionally handles everything according to the deceased's wishes.

6. **Just the facts**. Get a record book and take down the basics. Knowing where to look makes all the difference. Whether you're getting left bills or assets, there's still a good amount of administrative work to do when a loved one dies. Do the work now while you can still ask questions.

Caregiver Hint: Avoid last-minute trauma. Make arrangements and pay funeral costs ahead of time.

Source: Solutions Magazine

Veterans Affairs:
Lest We Forget

If your parent is a veteran, he or she may well qualify for any of a wide number of benefits and services provided by Veterans Affairs Canada (VAC). Depending on eligibility, these programs may be able to provide assistance with household maintenance, home care, medical services and supplies, transportation, and other areas of eldercare.

What Is Veterans Affairs?

Canadians owe their veterans and peacekeepers a debt of gratitude and should honour those who have served their country and continue to defend all that Canada stands for.

The Department of Veterans Affairs Canada is run by our federal government. Its mandate is to provide exemplary, client-centred services and benefits that respond to the needs of veterans and other clients and their families in recognition of their achievements and sacrifices for Canada.

Caregiver Hint: Visit www.vac-acc.gc.ca, the Web site of Veterans Affairs Canada. It has a variety of archived and current material for veterans and their families. Of particular interest is the innovative Youth and Educators program, which can involve a veteran family member in a meaningful way, and a number of activities and games.

Do They Qualify?

In general, only soldiers who served during World War II or who served in Korea during the Korean War are eligible for health benefits. However, anyone receiving a disability pension from

Veterans Affairs Canada (including retired RCMP and armed forces officers) is also eligible for health benefits. Spouses of veterans are not entitled to health benefits; however, certain benefits under the Veterans Independence Program, which will be outlined below, may be transferred to a widow after the passing of their veteran spouse.

Veterans Affairs Canada distinguishes between two groups of clients eligible for their Health Benefits program. Clients in the first group, Group "A," are eligible only for benefits directly related to a condition for which they receive a disability pension, while Group "B" clients are eligible for more extensive benefits based on health needs that are not met by provincial or private health coverage. All clients are issued with a VAC Health identification card that clearly identifies which programs and benefits they are eligible for.

Group "A" clients include the following:

- Veterans and civilians, including retired members of the Canadian Forces and Royal Canadian Mounted Police as well as regular serving civilian members of the RCMP who have been granted a disability pension by Veterans Affairs Canada.

Group "B" clients include the following:

- Income-qualified veterans and civilians, including Civilian and War Veteran Allowance recipients.

- Veteran, civilian, and special duty area pensioners who are receiving services under the Veterans Independence Program.

- Canada Service Veterans receiving services under the Veterans Independence Program.

- Veteran pensioners or Overseas Service Veterans receiving care in a departmental or contract care facility.

- Seriously disabled pensioners, meaning anyone in receipt of a combined total of 78% disability pension or above.

What Services Could Be Covered?

Veterans Affairs Canada provides two main programs to support qualified veterans and civilians: Health Benefits and the Veterans

Independence Program. Most eligible veterans are entitled to benefits under the Health Benefits program, while the Veterans Independence Program (VIP) is provided only for clients with extensive health-care needs or those with insufficient income to cover the cost of home or long-term care. Both programs are outlined below.

Health Benefits—Programs of Choice

The Health Benefits program offers a wide range of benefits ranging from the provision of certain medical aids and assistive devices to dental care. If your elder qualifies for any health benefits through VAC, he or she will almost certainly be receiving benefits under this program, although your elder may also be able to apply for the VIP. Below is a listing of the services that qualified veterans will be eligible for to varying degrees, depending on their status with VAC.

1. Aids for Daily Living

This program provides devices and accessories, including necessary repairs, designed to assist the activities of daily living.

Examples of covered devices and accessories:

- walking aids such as canes and walkers
- self-help aids for dressing and/or feeding
- bedroom aids such as foot boards or over-bed tables
- bathroom aids such as raised toilet seats or bath benches

2. Ambulance and Medical Travel Services

Ambulance: This program covers ambulance services to or from a medical facility when it is required due to an emergency or medical condition.

Some services require a prescription from a physician. You should verify these requirements with the appropriate provider or VAC before the service is provided.

Medical Travel Services: This program covers travel costs incurred in order to receive certain treatment benefits.

3. Audio (Hearing) Services

This program offers benefits to compensate for hearing impairment.
Examples of covered benefits:

- analog hearing aids

- basic digital hearing aids

- basic programmable analog aids

- telephone amplifiers and infrared devices

- hearing accessories

- dispensing and fitting fees

Special authorization is required for non-standard hearing aids such as:

- multi-channel programmable analog and digital aids

- completely-in-the-canal aids

4. Dental Services

This program offers basic dental care and preauthorized comprehensive dental services. Those eligible are also entitled to receive dentures from their dentist or, in those provinces where they are licensed to practice, their denturist.
Examples of covered benefits:

- annual basic treatment (cleanings and fluoride treatments)

- fillings

Examples of excluded benefits:

- implants

- equilibrated, custom, or semi-precision dentures

Examples of treatment requiring predetermination:

- any annual basic treatment exceeding $600 or

- crowns

- bridgework

- specialist treatment (referral required)

The frequency of treatment is also an issue that should be clarified as the recipient may be compensated for only a certain number of treatments. To find out about dental benefits, contact the toll-free enquiries line at 1-800-565-9670.

5. Hospital Services

This program offers benefits for treatment services provided in an acute-care, chronic-care, or rehabilitative-care hospital. It includes both inpatient and outpatient services provided to a veteran.

Costs for private or semi-private rooms are not normally covered by Veterans Affairs Canada.

6. Medical Services

In the case of a VAC disability pensioner, this program offers medical services provided by a licensed physician. The costs of medical examinations, treatment, or reports specifically requested by VAC are also covered by this program. For most VAC clients, physicians' services are the responsibility of the provincial health-care programs and are not normally paid under this program.

7. Medical Supplies

This program offers medical and surgical equipment and supplies normally used by an individual in a non-hospital setting.

Examples of covered medical and surgical equipment:

- inhalers

- bandages

- incontinence supplies

8. Nursing Services

This program offers services provided by a registered nurse or coverage for basic foot hygiene by a registered nurse or a qualified licensed or certified nursing assistant.

Examples of covered services:

- administering of medications
- application of dressings
- counselling veterans or caregivers in the use of medical supplies and health care
- foot care

Examples of excluded services:

- continuous nursing (i.e., ongoing care of more than two hours per day by a registered nurse)
- private nursing provided in a long-term-care facility

9. Oxygen Therapy

This program offers oxygen and accessories, as well as the rental or purchase of other supplies and equipment for respiratory conditions.
Examples of covered benefits:

- oxygen concentrators
- compressors
- oxygen gas

10. Prescription Drugs

This program provides drug products and other benefits dispensed by a pharmacist.
Examples of covered benefits:

- prescription drugs
- some over-the-counter medications
- some medical supplies

Pharmaceutical products that VAC does not generally cover:

- Talwin
- Rogaine

- Glucosamine

- Dextronex

- Visudyne Kit

- Xenical caps

11. Prosthetics and Orthotics

This program provides necessary prosthetics or orthotics in addition to accessories and repairs for these aids.

Examples of covered benefits:

- prosthetic and orthotic appliances

- custom-built footwear

- modifications to regular footwear

    Example of excluded benefits:

- off-the-shelf footwear

12. Related Health Services

This program offers alternative benefits and services from health professionals.

Examples of covered services (directly obtained services):

- chiropractors

- massage therapy

- physiotherapy

- acupuncture

    Examples of covered services (requiring referral by physician):

- occupational therapists

- physiotherapists

- hearing and speech therapists

- psychological counselling

Examples of excluded services:

- homeopathic services
- naturopathic medicines and therapies

13. Special Equipment

This program provides special equipment required for the care and treatment of disabled VAC clients.

These benefits must be prescribed by a doctor, and in many cases, they must also be supported by the recommendation of another health professional.

Examples of covered benefits:

- hospital beds
- lifts
- home adaptations
- wheelchairs
- driving aids

Examples of excluded benefits:

- mattresses for a regular bed
- Craftmatic-type adjustable beds

14. Vision (Eye) Care

This program offers lenses, frames, and accessories to correct sight impairments, as well as low-vision aids available from the Canadian National Institute for the Blind.

Examples of covered benefits:

- basic single or bifocal lenses
- frames
- eye examinations

Examples of excluded benefits:

- no "two pair of glasses" option

- sunglasses

Veterans Independence Program (VIP)

The Veterans Independence Program is the second health-related program offered by VAC. As mentioned above, the benefits and services provided through this program are more extensive than those provided through the Health Benefits program. Accordingly, the program is offered to a more limited number of veterans. Canada service veterans, those who fall under the War Veterans Allowance Programs, and people receiving VAC disability pensions may be eligible for the VIP in addition to health benefits if they meet the eligibility requirements.

Who Is Eligible?

The following individuals may be eligible for VIP services:

- veterans whose income is insufficient to cover the cost of home care or long-term care

- disability pensioners who require home care or long-term care due to limitations directly related to their pensioned condition

- veterans with exceptional health needs

- seriously disabled pensioners, meaning anyone in receipt of an income consisting of 78% disability pension, with any of the listed circumstances

Determination of VIP Services

District Office Area Counsellors visit the veteran to carry out a comprehensive assessment to determine the person's health and social needs. Their acceptance will be decided on the basis of their needs.

It should be noted that the VIP is not intended to duplicate or replace existing provincial or community services. However, when provincial or local services are not sufficient to meet the veteran's needs, VIP services may be approved to complement or top up the services provided by the province or local agency.

Based on the health assessment, the veteran's area counsellor will work with him or her to determine the services to be provided and the amount to be paid. After the application has been processed, the veteran will be provided with a letter outlining the VIP services and dollar amounts approved.

VIP Elements

The Veterans Independence Program is designed to assist with the costs of certain services provided at the veteran's home such as the following:

Grounds Maintenance: Grounds maintenance includes work regularly required to maintain the grounds immediately surrounding the client's principal residence.

Examples of covered services:

- snow removal from steps, walkways, and driveways to allow safe access to the principal residence

- snow and ice removal from roofs and eavestroughs when such conditions pose a threat to safety and access

- lawn mowing and raking

    Examples of excluded services:

- lawn planting or seeding

- material and labour costs for spraying and fertilizing

- pruning trees not posing a threat to safety and access

Housekeeping: Housekeeping services are routine tasks or domestic chores required to support the client in remaining self-sufficient at the principal residence. Certain non-routine tasks or domestic chores may also be covered, with pre-authorization by VAC, if they are required as a result of the client's health and safety being at risk.

Housekeeping and grounds maintenance are the only two services offered by Veterans Affairs that may be transferred to the widow of a veteran after the veteran's death. However, this will happen only in cases where there remains a clear need for the service.

Examples of covered services:

- laundry, including ironing and mending
- vacuuming
- cleaning floors (sweeping, washing, waxing, etc.)
- dusting and general picking up
- meal preparation

Personal Care: Personal-care services are approved services provided by individuals other than those defined as health-care professionals (i.e., attendant as opposed to nurse). These services include assistance in the performance of the activities of daily living and supervision required by clients who cannot be left unattended.

Examples of covered services:

- eating/feeding
- dressing
- washing
- grooming
- adjusting prosthetic appliances
- attending to toileting
- ambulation
- respite care

Examples of excluded services:

- advanced foot care
- administration of medication
- any services beyond those identified as covered services

Home Adaptations: Home adaptations can be made to a client's principal residence. For example, bathrooms, kitchens, and doorways can be modified to provide access for basic everyday activities such as food preparation, personal hygiene, and sleep. Home adaptations do not include general renovations or repairs.

Examples of covered services:

- handrails on stairways
- ramps

Examples of excluded services:

- general renovations or repairs
- additions

Nutrition Services: Access to nutrition services is aimed at ensuring that clients access nutritional food, whether it is delivered to the client's principal residence, offered in the community, or served at a local restaurant.

Examples of covered services:

- the cost of delivering food to the home (i.e., Meals on Wheels)
- transportation cost to bring the client to a local restaurant or community facility to obtain meals (i.e., Wheels to Meals, taxi to restaurant)

Examples of excluded services:

- services of professional dietitians or nutritionists
- meal service as the result of the terms and conditions of a rental agreement
- cost of the meal itself

Health and Support Services Provided by Health Professionals: Health and support services are health assessments and diagnostic services, care, maintenance, and related personal care provided by health professionals and approved by VAC. These can be provided only when they are not insured services under a professional health-care system or available to clients as residents of a province.

Ambulatory Health Care: Ambulatory health care covers certain health and social services provided outside the home such as adult daycare and travel costs to access these services.

Intermediate Care Services: Intermediate care services may be provided when living at home is no longer practical and a greater level of nursing and personal assistance are needed.

Social Transportation: Transportation service may be approved to allow clients to participate in social activities, in response to the clients' basic social, recreational, or personal needs. These may include transportation to church services, occasional visits to friends and relatives, community centres, banks, and grocery stores, when transportation is not otherwise available.

How to Obtain Benefits

There are two options for obtaining and paying for benefits under the Health Benefits program:

Receiving Care from VAC/Blue Cross Provider: If your parent receives benefits from a provider who is a participant of the VAC/Blue Cross system, your parent can simply present the VAC health identification card, along with the necessary prescription, to the health-care provider. The provider will supply the benefit and send the bill to Blue Cross for payment. Some benefits must be pre-authorized by VAC before they can be issued by the provider.

If you don't know of any participating providers, be sure to call the client information number on your parent's VAC health-care identification card next to CLIENT INFO.

Reimbursement for Care Received from a Non-Registered Provider: If you and your parent opt to obtain a benefit from a provider who is not a participant of the VAC/Blue Cross system, you will be required to pay for the item and be reimbursed later. Be sure to call the client information number before obtaining the benefit to ensure that it is a benefit that will be paid for by VAC. After you have paid for the benefit, get an itemized receipt and submit it, along with the prescription, to the Treatment Authorization Centre at the VAC office location nearest you. For dental and pharmacy claims, use the following address:

Treatment Authorization Centre
Veterans Affairs Canada
Daniel J. MacDonald Bldg.
161 Grafton Street
P.O. Box 7700
Charlottetown PEI C1A 8M9

Whom to Contact in Your Region

To enquire about eligibility, making claims, or for any additional information about Veterans Affairs Canada programs, contact the regional office nearest to you:

Atlantic Region
Alderney Gate
40 Alderney Drive
Dartmouth, NS B2Y 2N5
(902) 426-6448
1-800-565-1528 (NS, NB, PEI)
1-800-563-9623 (NF)

Quebec Region
4545, ch. Queen-Mary
Montréal, QC H3W 1W4
1-800-291-0471

Ontario Region
145 Government Rd. W.
Kirkland Lake, ON P2N 2E8
Mailing Address:
Bag Service 4000
Kirkland Lake, ON P2N 3P4
(705) 568-4371
1-800-387-0930 (English)
1-877-678-4711 (French)

Prairie Region
610-234 Donald St.
P.O. Box 6050
Winnipeg, MB R3C 4G5
(204) 983-7040
1-800-665-3420

Pacific Region
900-605 Robson St.
P.O. Box 5600
Vancouver, BC V6B 5G4
(604) 666-7942
1-800-647-1822

Did You Know...

During the first half of this century, some 1.5 million Canadians were called upon to defend peace and freedom around the world during the First World War, the Second World War, and the Korean War. Following these terrible conflicts, Canada began looking for ways to prevent wars. Contemporary peacekeeping is a natural extension of Canada's long-standing commitment to the principles of peace and freedom.

Questions and Answers

Ask us…answers to some of your most frequently asked questions regarding home care (Excerpted from Solutions Magazine *with special thanks to* We Care Home Health Care Services *and other contributors.)*

On Home Care

Q. *My 74-year-old aunt lives alone. I don't think she needs a nurse, but she could definitely use some help at times. Are there other kinds of assistance available?*

A. There are a variety of non-medical services available to help your aging aunt to live independently and safely within her home. Among the types of help available are personal support workers. These individuals can provide help with bathing, house cleaning, meal preparation, and similar activities. There are also companions, who can help with daily activities such as shopping or light housework, or can just sit and spend time with your aunt.

  Your local government home-care authority, such as a Community Care Access Centre (CCAC) in Ontario, should be able to assist you in finding qualified help for your aunt. Private agencies also provide similar services.

Q. *When I arrive home after work to care for my mother, I can't tell if the nurse has been visiting and if she has helped my mom that day. (My mom has had a stroke and has trouble communicating.) Can I see the nursing records to determine the level of care she is receiving?*

A. All client health records are confidential legal documents. The health-care company providing the nursing services would need your mother's permission before you could access the files. Once this process is completed, then records could be obtained.

    The client health record contains nursing visit dates with time and duration of visit. The record includes the care plan that defines the client activities being carried out. On each visit the nurse documents the health status of the client and the care performed during that visit. Each visit documentation is also signed by the nurse who provided the client care.

Q. *My father-in-law has recently lost a considerable degree of mobility and now requires toileting, bathing, and dressing assistance. How can we help him retain his dignity?*

A. The first thing to keep in mind is that your father-in-law's mobility is impaired, not his cognitive ability. In order to maintain his dignity, it is his spiritual, emotional, and physical needs that must be met. He may feel strongly about maintaining his personal privacy and feel resentful about his loss of control in daily living. He will need to feel a sense of control over his routine and support services to preserve his dignity.

    Every effort should be made to include him in the decision-making process about his care and any adaptations to the home environment. Give him the opportunity to voice his concerns or objections.

    Changing things too rapidly without his consent may cause your father-in-law more distress rather than give any benefit.

Q. *My mother and her hired caregiver have become close friends during their time together. I'm worried that my mother will be devastated when the caregiver leaves (she plans to move next year). What can I do?*

A. It can definitely be a challenge for caregivers to avoid personal bonding when they are with their clients. Many care agencies advise their staff at orientations not to talk of their home life or give out their phone numbers. They generally stress the need for caregivers to keep their professional lives separate, both for their safety and for the well-being of the client.

One thing you might do is to ask your local agency to rec-ommend gradually introducing a new staff member to your mother in order to help ease the coming transition.

Q. *I've been washing my parents' laundry ever since Mom's operation. Now that my work schedule has increased, I've decided to look for help. Should I hire a cleaning lady or a home-care worker?*

A. First off, you should contact some cleaning ladies to find out if they will agree to wash clothing as many will not wash per-sonal items. This option may be less demanding financially.

On the other hand, if you hire a worker through an agency, you will have the reassurance that the worker is bonded and screened (by means of a criminal reference check). When you think about a stranger coming into your home, sometimes paying a few extra dollars to have peace of mind is more than worthwhile.

Q. *When looking for a home-care nurse, should I be checking refer-ences?*

A. Whether you are planning to hire someone to work for you pri-vately or through an agency, reference checking is an essential step. If you are considering help acquired through a home-care or nursing agency, it is likely that a reference check was part of their own hiring process. You can confirm this by asking the agency what their hiring process is.

The standard process should include three key things: (1) a criminal background check, (2) checking at least two profes-sional references, and (3) validation of nursing licence (or cer-tificate for non-nursing caregivers). If these three things are not included as part of the hiring process, you really can't be sure that a thorough check has been carried out on their staff.

Hiring privately can often be less expensive than hiring through an agency, but there are several things that you will now have to be responsible for, including this screening process.

The person you are considering hiring should be responsi-ble for his or her own criminal background check through the local police department—the person may have to pay a small fee. Be sure to see an original copy of the report. With regard to references, it is important to call previous employers and not personal friends or associates for a reference because you will need this information to validate the person's ability to do the job. References can also provide information on reliability, attendance, and performance with previous employers. Also be sure to see the person's original nursing licence or professional accreditation to ensure its validity.

Q. A home-care nurse visits my dad regularly while we are at work. However, when I ask him what she said, or if she left any special instructions, he always says, "I don't remember" or "I'm not sure." How can I be sure we are getting any important information?

A. One of the best ways to make sure that important information gets to you and other family members is to establish a means of written communication. This can be as simple as keeping a spiral notebook for the nurse to refer to. She can use it to answer any questions you have left for her, and to jot down any instructions for your father's care. It's a good idea to set up the pages with headings such as date, questions, instructions, etc.

Discuss the book with the home-care nurse first to ensure her participation and understanding of its purpose.

Q. The home-care nurse who visits my mother is very capable and professional. However, she and my mother simply don't get on well. I am worried that this may somehow hamper the care my mother is receiving. What should I do?

A. Discuss the situation with the nurse as soon as possible. Make her aware of your mother's feelings and ask her for input on what is going on. She might not even be aware that your mother feels that way. Often, when issues like this are discussed out in the open, they can be easily resolved.

However, if this does not resolve the problem, or if you don't have a comfort level in talking to the nurse directly, speak to the manager or supervisor at the nursing agency. Most agencies recognize the importance of a good match between a client and a caregiver and will make every effort to provide a different nurse if necessary.

Q. *I keep hearing the term "Community Care Access Centres" used when talking about home care. What exactly are these?*

A. Community Care Access Centres, or CCACs, are local government-approved organizations in Ontario that coordinate services for seniors, people with disabilities, and people who need health-care services. Their mandate is to help these people continue to live independently in their own homes for as long as possible and to assist, when needed, with admission to long-term-care centres.

CCACs provide information and a variety of services, including professional care (that is, nursing, therapy, social work services, nutrition, and speech), personal support services, and homemaking. Approved services are provided free of charge. There are 43 CCACs located throughout Ontario and accessible to all Ontario residents. You will find the number for your centre in the local government section of the phone book or in the health section of the Yellow Pages. For more information, contact the Ministry of Health INFOline at 1-800-268-1154, TTY: 1-800-387-5559.

Other provinces have their own equivalents offering services similar to CCACs. In Quebec, these are called Centres Locaux de Service Communitaires. In B.C., Alberta, and Manitoba, services are coordinated by Regional Health Authorities. In Saskatchewan, P.E.I., and Newfoundland, Regional or District Health Boards are responsible for home-care services. In New Brunswick, services are handled by Regional Hospital Corporations and in Nova Scotia by the Department of Health.

Source: Jocelyn Jones, past President of the Ontario Case Managers' Association

Q. *My mother refuses to let her care provider bathe her. Just when she begins to get comfortable with the person attending to her personal needs, the agency sends someone new and we have to start all over again! What can I do to improve the situation?*

A. It is very common for elderly people receiving personal care to be concerned about protecting their privacy. It is always difficult to expose oneself to a stranger, and having to do it over and over again makes it even harder.

Although services agencies realize that continuity is extremely important for their clients, the lack of continuity with home-care services providers is still a significant problem. Funding is often a major issue as government-paid or subsidized services are not always able to attract a stable, high-quality work force.

One suggestion would be to work out an exchange of tasks with the provider agency. Perhaps you or your family members could be responsible for bathing while the agency covered other chores that would normally be the responsibility of the family.

Another option could be to hire a private homemaker to bathe your mother. This would cost money, but it may provide the chance for your mother and the rest of your family to relax as she becomes used to a single person. You could consider asking relatives not directly involved in regular care to put up the money. You could also enquire about the service from a not-for-profit agency, which would be likely to have lower client fees.

Source: Marja Cope, Community Care Access Centre

Q. *A home-care nurse comes three times a week to assist us with the care of my elderly mother. Unfortunately, the nurse's time is limited to one hour on each visit. How can we make sure that we get the most out of each visit?*

A. The overall goal of home care is to meet the needs and expectations of clients as well as their families. As such, ensuring each home visit is as useful and productive as possible is as important to the nurse as it is to the client and his or her family. During each visit the nurse assesses, plans, and delivers the person's care and treatments. To ensure all your questions or comments are addressed in a timely fashion, here are some tips on how to prepare for and maximize the nurse's visit.

Keep a notebook handy and jot down questions, concerns, or issues that arise between the nurse's visits. Discuss the use of the notebook with the nurse. Ask him or her to review any new notations at the beginning of each visit—especially if you can't be there. Discuss where and how you can get quick answers to your more serious questions in the nurse's absence.

Keep the nurse's phone number(s) with you, as well as close to the phone, where they can be easily accessed as needed.

Q. *I'm thinking about arranging an in-home assessment for my elderly father. What exactly would it involve?*

A. An assessment is a way of helping to look at a person's needs and how these needs can be met. During the assessment, your father would be guided by the health-care professional providing the assessment. Only the areas of difficulty would be discussed; for example, coping with personal hygiene needs, coping with household tasks, or getting around both inside and outside of the home.

The health-care professional will look at ways of meeting your father's needs and discuss a care plan with all involved.

Q. *How can we determine the level of care someone might need to help him or her live as independently as possible?*

A. A key factor in assessing if someone can live in his or her own home independently is family support.

- Is there a network of support from family and friends?
- Does the individual live alone, with a spouse, or with a family member?
- Is there a family member to help with personal care or with meal preparation and housekeeping?

Another aspect to consider is to identify the needs of the individual. How able is the person to perform the activities of daily living, including grooming, ambulation, hygiene, dressing, and bladder and bowel control? Can the elder manage diet and medications?

Also, depending on location, there may be a variety of resources in the community that will help to maintain the individual in his or her own home for as long as possible. These services are provided by organizations such as the Canadian Cancer Society, the Heart and Stroke Foundation, Meals on Wheels, and Seniors Helping Seniors.

On Health and Safety

Q. *After four o'clock in the afternoon, my mother and her gentleman friend insist on pre-dinner cocktails. They continue to have drinks with dinner. I'm concerned about the mix of medication and martinis.*

A. People don't often realize the implications of mixing alcohol and medication, and they do need to be made aware. For many, the habit of the cocktail-hour drink has become such a part of their routine and who they are that it is difficult to stop.

It's very important that you let your mother's doctor be aware of the fact that she is drinking. Encourage her to talk with her doctor or pharmacist to ensure that it is safe to consume alcohol with the medications she is taking.

Q. *My father still has his licence, but I know that he should not be driving, due to his deteriorating health and signs of dementia. I know he doesn't want to lose his sense of independence, but I want him to be safe. How can I prevent him from driving?*

A. Taking away a parent's driving privilege, or any privilege, for that matter, can be a very difficult thing to do. The last thing any elder wants to do is depend on anyone else for help! Before you share your concerns, have a plan in place that will be easy and simple to follow, one that won't interfere with his normal routine too much.

Get a prescription from his family doctor that states "no driving" and show this to your father if he insists on getting behind the wheel. Think about selling or removing the car.

You should also think about making a list of the places he drives to on a regular basis. Check out available alternatives for transportation. Many communities are starting to address this issue with specialized services for seniors. Depending on where you live, this service could be as comprehensive as special senior buses or as informal as a list of volunteer drivers. Check with your local community agencies to see what might be available in the area.

Remember to present your case firmly, but lovingly. After all, you are only trying to protect him.

Q. *My mom and dad live independently in their own home. I know they need help coping but they refuse to admit it. How can I be sure they are safe?*

A. One thing you could do is to spend a few days, or even a week, with your parents. Observe them and note how they cope with daily tasks. Pay particular attention to areas involving personal safety. For example, do they remember to lock up the house securely at night? Are there areas of the home that they are having physical trouble with (e.g., climbing stairs)? Are there places in disrepair that might cause a safety hazard (e.g., loose carpets, bare electrical wires)?

If your list of potential problems is extensive, sit down with your parents and go over it. Point out that you are only thinking of their safety, and how terrible it would be for each of them if the other one got injured. If things are really bad, suggest a home assessment by a qualified occupational therapist or other professional. Investing a little time and money in making their home safe now is far better than the consequences of an accident.

Check out these resources for tips on how you might "senior-proof" their home:

- The Safe Living Guide, available by calling 1-800-622-6232 or (613) 952-7606

- Canada Safety Council: Tel. (613) 739-1535, Fax (613) 739-1566, Web site www.safety-council.org

- Health Canada Web site: www.seniors.gc.ca

Q. *Our elderly neighbour lives alone and is quite independent, but we have noticed that she is losing weight. She says that she can't be bothered to cook for one person. Are there any suggestions to help her get proper nutrition?*

A. One option may be Meals on Wheels, a program offered to the community that provides a serving of one hot meal every day during the lunch hour. The cost is very reasonable, but does vary from one community to another.

There may also be other meal plans available from within your community. For example, some cultural centres also provide hot meal delivery service to seniors at a minimum cost.

Another alternative could be to have a personal support worker (PSW) visit her home to assist with meal preparation and creating a grocery list. Nowadays, many grocery stores will take a telephone order and even have the food delivered.

Q. *My mother is recovering from a stroke and will be coming home soon from the hospital. Are there any special things I need to know about her diet?*

A. The stroke rehab team at the hospital will assess your mother's ability to swallow and eat. It's particularly important that she be seen by a speech pathologist if she has a swallowing problem. You should find out whether she was on a special diet at the hospital because she may have to continue to follow that diet, at least in the short term.

Talk with the stroke rehab team about the sorts of food that she should eat. In general, it is important that your mother have a balanced, healthy diet that is reduced in fat and salt and high in dietary fibre. Sometimes, small, frequent meals are easier for a stroke survivor to eat. Some stroke survivors experience stomach upset if they eat spiced or seasoned foods or high-fat fried foods. Another concern after a stroke is the risk of constipation due to inactivity, so ensure that her diet is high in fibre and fluids!

Source: Heart and Stroke Foundation of Canada (with some material from We Care)

Q. *Dad has trouble with stairs and we can't afford a lifting device. What do you recommend to promote safe, easier access?*

A. First, you need to find out why he is having difficulty. Is there a challenge with strength and conditioning? Is his eyesight failing? How is his balance? Aside from having these questions addressed by a physician, there are a number of things that may help. Arrange a visit by a client care manager for a fall and risk assessment and consider involving an occupational therapist. Try these tips:

- Be sure your dad's footwear is appropriate. The shoe should support the foot and have soles that provide adequate (but not too much) grip. Heel height should compensate for any muscle weakness in the lower leg.

- Check for good lighting in the area.

- Ensure the handrail is secure and extends past the bottom step.

- Your father should avoid using the stairs on his own. Try to modify the environment so that everything he needs is on one level.

- General strengthening exercises may improve or maintain his current ability.

- Check to see if he has extended health or Veterans Affairs coverage that may assist with funding for a lifting device.

Q. *I know my mother's sight is getting worse, but she insists everything is okay. How can I encourage her to visit an optometrist?*

A. Our parents can certainly be stubborn at times! In this case, the refusal to admit failing eyesight could be due to many reasons: from a reluctance to admitting to growing old to the simple fact that the decline in eyesight has been so gradual as to be barely noticeable to her. Here are three ways to encourage your mother to see an optometrist:

1. Schedule an appointment for yourself at the same time so that you can go together.

2. Explain the importance of an annual checkup. Tell her it is something that everyone should have—at any age.

3. If she is agreeable about going to the family doctor, have the doctor conduct an eye test or remind her that she needs to see the optometrist.

Explain that you want her to remain safe in her house.

Source: Becky Russell, BSc(OT), Community Therapists Inc., Vancouver, BC

Q. *My dad doesn't answer the phone and avoids making calls. He says he just can't be bothered, but we all know it's because he can't hear as well as he used to. What should we do?*

A. Age-related hearing loss (presbycusis) is very common, but many people are reluctant to admit there is a problem. The first thing to do is to try to gently encourage your dad to have his hearing checked by his family doctor or a hearing clinic (many clinics will waive the testing charge for seniors). One of the many new styles of discreet, comfortable hearing aids may make all the difference.

If you are having trouble persuading him, try enlisting the help of a trusted health professional, like his home-care nurse if he has one, or the local pharmacist, to subtly raise the issue.

In the meantime, there are phones especially designed for seniors and people with hearing problems. These include models that have extra-large numbers or lights that flash when the phone rings and, of course, adjustable ring tones and volumes. Some have an especially great range of volume. Many large phone retailers will allow you to test a phone and return it if it is not suitable.

Q. *My 70-year-old mother is having problems seeing clearly, even with her new glasses on. She describes her vision as blurry or foggy. Is this a serious problem?*

A. Your mother may be developing cataracts in one or both eyes. A cataract is an opacity, or cloudiness, that develops in the lens of the eye diminishing or distorting vision. It is a common problem in the elderly. While some special-prescription glasses or medications may help slightly, they won't solve the problem.

The recommended treatment for cataracts is a surgical procedure that replaces the lens with a plastic or silicone lens. This operation is simple and safe—usually done under local anesthetic with no hospital stay required—and the vision improvement can be dramatic.

You should take your mother to an optometrist or ophthalmologist for a checkup, and if cataracts are the problem, he or she will let you know the next steps.

Source: Tom Evans, OD, Optometrist, Don Mills, Ont.

Q. *My father-in-law is 78 and during the last few months has started to act out of character. He has become more aggressive and at times uses abusive and foul language that he's never used before. Is this a normal part of aging?*

A. No, the behaviour you describe is not a normal part of the aging process. Under normal circumstances, people's characters do not change dramatically as they grow older. What you are describing may be early signs of a cognitive disease, such as Alzheimer's. However, neither you nor any other non-qualified individual should jump to conclusions or make a diagnosis without consultation.

Your father-in-law should have a thorough examination by his family physician and if his doctor feels it necessary, a further examination by a specialist in geriatrics and/or a neurologist. Be sure that the doctor is aware of all the unusual behaviours you have noticed, as your father-in-law may not even be aware that he is acting that way. This examination will likely include a series of tests to determine his cognitive awareness.

Once the reasons for your father-in-law's behavior are determined, you will be told what you can do and given more advice on how to handle the situation.

Q. *Can my mother's nurse recommend over-the-counter drugs?*

A. To be safe about medications, your mother's physician or pharmacist should be consulted. Consideration needs to be given to her medical history and other medications she may be taking. Be aware that herbal remedies can have negative interactions and side effects. A nurse can make recommendations about nutrition and lifestyle changes. It may be helpful to have the nurse share his or her assessment findings as they relate to the need for over-the-counter medications with your mom's physician.

Q. *My husband has Alzheimer's. He is restless at night and will get up and wander. I am concerned about his safety. I am also not getting enough sleep and finding it harder to cope with my day!*

A. Offer your husband lots of opportunity for physical exercise during the day and try to avoid going to bed too early. In the evening, start a regular routine of a warm drink of milk and soothing music. Avoid stimulating activities in the evening. This might help to calm him down to get him ready for bed.

Many older people take an afternoon nap; try to avoid lengthy naps in the day or, if possible, schedule them early in the afternoon. To help you relax and get some sleep, try using a room monitor or an inexpensive "musical welcome mat" to let you know that he is out of bed. You can also push his bed against the wall or place a piece of furniture across the end of the bed so that he has fewer ways to get out of bed.

Source: Hilary Drummond, Occupational Therapist, President of Creative Therapy Consultants, Penticton, B.C.

Q. *My mother recently had a stroke. Right now she can't see on the left side. Will her vision come back, and what can I do to help her?*

A. This is a common problem after a stroke. If your mother has a true visual field deficit, it will not spontaneously return. Your mother can, however, learn to compensate for her loss of vision.

The best strategy is to teach your mother to physically turn her head to the left, exaggerating the movement more than usual. You can help by reminding her to stop and turn her head when walking. Sit to the left of your mother, reinforcing her awareness of that side. When doing activities with her, place objects slightly to her left and gradually increase the distance to the left as she learns to compensate. Keep your reminders short to make them easier for her to remember, such as "Turn your head" and "Look to the left." Repetition is the key. And be patient—this process will take time.

Source: Lisa Kristalovich, BMR (OT), Community Therapists Inc., Vancouver, B.C.

Q. *Because of my husband's heart condition, I need to check his blood pressure at home. I've noticed that the readings sometimes vary for no apparent reason. Am I doing something wrong?*

A. Many factors, including the specific equipment or technique you are using, and your husband's condition at the time of the measurement, can affect blood pressure readings. An irregular heart rate can cause apparent changes in blood pressure readings, and even experienced professionals may have to take several measurements with manual equipment to obtain a good blood pressure assessment.

For the best results, use a blood pressure measuring device of high quality and ensure it is properly calibrated. Your husband's arm should always be supported, relaxed, and positioned according to the directions that came with your device.

Your husband should be prepared in advance for each reading. Here are some things to keep in mind:

- Clothing should not restrict blood flow or placement of the cuff.

- Have him avoid caffeine and nicotine before the test.

- Eating, heavy physical activity, exposure to cold, emotional extremes, and bowel and bladder fullness can affect readings.

- Age may also be a factor. As you get older, eating has a longer-lasting effect and may cause a drop in blood pressure.

- During the readings, your husband should be relaxed, but not talking.

- Finally, if you have any problems, talk with the pharmacist or home health-care dealer who sold you the equipment.

Source: Dr. Donald W. McKay, cardiologist and member of the Executive of the Canadian Coalition for High Blood Pressure Prevention and Control

Q. My elderly mother is active and loves to cook, but tends to be forgetful. Are there ways to make her kitchen safer?

A. One of the simplest and most effective safety devices for the kitchen is timers, especially those with loud buzzers that do not stop until someone turns them off. Some stoves come equipped with timers. But if not, or if these aren't effective, there are a number of timers on the market with large easy-to-read numbers and easy-turn dials that are ideal for seniors.

    Both stove-top and oven controls should be well lit so that it is always clear when they are on. You can also color-code the temperature settings of the dials (using coloured stick-on dots) so they are easy to read.

Source: Ruth Mallin, Occupational Therapist and President of the Independent Needs Centre, Toronto, Ont.

Q. My father-in-law is recovering from a stroke. Apart from this condition, he is in good physical shape. How can we help him keep fit during his recovery?

A. As your father-in-law is in good physical shape and his condition is stabilized, his recovery should progress well. However, factors such as the side of his body that is affected, and if he was left-handed or right-handed previously, will affect the impact the stroke has on his abilities. In order to encourage mobility, get him to use a cane or a walker, or make modifications to his residence (e.g., a ramp).

    Work with your father-in-law and his health professionals to develop a daily exercise plan—monitor his progress and make changes to the plan as needed. Make sure that the plan allows for sufficient rest and that it fits in with his normal daily routine. Exercise can be done either actively by your father-in-law or passively by a caregiver. Consider using equipment like sponge balls to improve hand strength or pulleys to work on arm strength. Good supportive shoes and a companion for encouragement are essential!

On Caring from a Distance

Q. *My mom is in a long-term-care facility. Family meetings and discussions are usually held during the day when I'm at work. How do I stay in touch?*

A. A lot of facilities have meetings that include all members of the care team. This may include the physician, the dietitian, the chaplain, the nurse in charge, and the health-care aide who is most likely to be the usual care provider.

One way that you could be involved would be to set up a conference call between the team members and yourself during the care meeting. This would allow you to hear what is being said, ask questions, and contribute to the discussion. Another way, although not interactive, would be for you to request a copy of the minutes following the meeting.

In any event, the staff should always be available by phone to answer questions and can usually suggest the best days and/or times to contact specific members of the care team.

Source: Carol Shaw, past administrator, Golden Plough Lodge, Northumberland, Ont.

Q. *My uncle, who receives home care, recently gave up driving due to health issues. However, he desperately misses being on the road. I wish I could take him around town for an hour during the day; however, I'm at my full-time job. Is it possible to have a paid caregiver take him out?*

A. This depends on the nursing agency. If the caregiver is approved to drive and is using your uncle's vehicle, the agency may have insurance to cover potential accidents or may require the release of liability. If your uncle no longer has his vehicle, it may be possible to use the agency's or caregiver's car—again providing that it is adequately insured. However, don't expect anyone to agree: many caregivers use their personal car for transportation to and from jobs and may feel uncomfortable transporting others in their car.

Source: Stephanie Schlosser, Visiting Angels Living Assistance Services, Langley, B.C.

Q. *My mother broke her hip and has been placed in a nursing home. It breaks my heart to see her there and I dread every visit! She cries and asks me to take her home as soon as I see her—but I can't. What should I do?*

A. Deciding to place your mother in a nursing home must have been a tough decision, but it reflects the fact that you were being realistic about your caregiving abilities. Here are some things to think about as you continue to visit and be a caregiver:

Before you go, sit down, take a deep breath, and picture the visit with your mother. You know you are likely to feel sad and guilty when she cries. Also realize that the adjustment to a nursing home could take weeks and even months.

When visiting, also remember that when your mother asks you to take her home she could be expressing feelings of fear, sadness, and anger about the change in her situation. Try to find out from the nursing home staff how your mother is adjusting. Does she participate? Has she made any friends? Hopefully, this could give you ideas for action. Be sure to attend activities with your mother when you can and send messages often. If you can, try to find a caregiver support group. Hopefully, this will make the visits easier for you.

Source: Marja Cope, Community Care Access Centre

Q. *Dad's nursing home is five hours away and I can't always visit. What can I do besides call him?*

A. Few things can brighten a resident's day more than receiving mail. Whether you use it to stay in touch with a family member between visits or simply can't visit as often as you'd like, don't ignore the therapeutic benefits of regular letters and notes to your family member.

- Start small. A bright and cheerful greeting card can be as welcome as a long letter—sometimes better. A simple, short note is better than nothing; the importance of mail is the connection, not necessarily the content.

- Take note of special occasions like Valentine's Day, holidays, family birthdays, and anniversaries. Relay children's news regarding school, vacations, Scouts, and Little League.

- Since mail can double as decoration for your family member's room, select bright, colourful note cards, scenic postcards, or page-a-day calendars that he or she will enjoy seeing on the walls.

Source: Extendicare (Canada) Inc., Markham, Ont.

On Family, Lifestyle, and Other Concerns

Q. *I'm the only caregiver for my mother. When I'm not around she gets depressed. I've heard that pets can help relieve depression. Can one really help my mother?*

A. Pets can definitely make people healthier and happier. Animal companionship has special value for seniors, especially those who are ill or isolated. Studies have shown that pets can lower blood pressure and reduce tension and stress levels. A pet's unconditional love can have positive psychological benefits for those who are lonely or withdrawn. Having another living thing to care for helps fulfill a person's need to nurture. Be aware, however, that owning a pet means making a firm commitment to its care and welfare!

Before selecting a pet, consider the commitment it will require and whether your mother is willing and able to care for it. Can your mother handle the responsibilities independently or will other arrangements be required? If considering a dog, take into account the type or breed that will fit with her lifestyle. Would she be able to provide daily walks for a dog that requires outdoor exercise or would a lapdog be more appropriate? Puppies and younger dogs require a great deal of training and patience; perhaps a mature dog would be a better choice.

Source: Darlene R. McDonnell, Director, Pet Therapy Society of Northern Alberta

Q. *My father is a widower who lives alone. He is quite active and would love something to keep him busy and provide a challenge. How can he connect with appropriate groups that need volunteers?*

A. Volunteering is an excellent way to stay active and contribute. You could start by calling places in the area that he may have an interest in, such as the local hospital, food bank, or public library. In addition, Volunteer Canada operates the Canada-wide Volunteer Opportunities Exchange, which has an excellent Web site designed specifically to match potential volunteers (by interests, skills, etc.) with relevant local organizations that may need their help.

   You can access the VOE site at www.voe-reb.org or call 1-800-670-0401 for more information.

Q. *My 83-year-old aunt insists on walking to the grocery store each day and wobbling home with heavy bags. Should we be intervening?*

A. It is important to help your aunt maintain this level of independence, as it is directly related to her well-being. People need to have a sense of control in their lives regardless of age or level of functioning.

   However, you have to think about your aunt's safety and the risk of falls or muscle strains. Having a professional or volunteer caregiver assist your aunt with her shopping and some household tasks may be an excellent way for her to maintain her independence longer in her own home.

   You can sell this idea by discussing scenarios with your aunt. For example, if she sustains an injury while carrying grocery bags, the possibility of not being able to do any shopping at all becomes very real.

   If she has someone help with the shopping and heavier tasks around her home, however, she can still have independence, input, and choice and stay at home longer.

   When choosing a caregiving company, be sure to ask questions about policies related to shopping, handling clients' money, and taking clients out of their homes. Ensure that the company carefully screens their employees and that they are well trained for whatever needs to be done.

Q. My mother is in a nursing home and I desperately want my two young children to visit her, but they are reluctant. How can I encourage them to visit their grandmother?

A. Family visits, especially from grandchildren, contribute significantly to an elder's sense of well-being. However, in some cases, children may be reluctant to visit. Here are a few things you can try: Listen to their concerns and perceptions. Acknowledge their difficulties and fears. Separate the visiting experience into several components. Tackle each part separately and see where change is possible.

Young children can easily learn to respect, care for, and build a connection with their elderly family members when encouraged. Being honest and open in your communication with your children shows respect for them, their feelings, and what they have to offer within the family.

Source: Ruth Goodman, MSW, Social Services Division, Baycrest Centre for Geriatric Care, Excerpted from Visiting with Elders: A Guidebook for Family and Friends

Q. My company's HR department is advertising eldercare seminars. I'm not exactly looking after my parents yet, but they are getting older. Should I attend?

A. As the saying goes, you're never too old to learn—and in the case of eldercare, you're also never too young. Many of the more progressive companies are beginning to invest in eldercare training for employees. It teaches them how to manage caring for parents more efficiently and balance it with their own lives and career commitments. This training also covers important subjects such as stress management and looking after yourself. After all, good self-care is the foundation for caring for others.

For your company, these seminars are a "win-win" situation. By helping employees to better manage eldercare and prevent stress, they can reduce absenteeism and increase productivity.

As to whether you should attend your work's eldercare courses or not: If you are over 35 and have parents or in-laws in your life, the answer is a definite "yes"! You'll have to face eldercare issues sooner or later. The more you know, the better it will be.

Q. *What exercises or exercise classes could my aging mother and I do together to help us bond and get a good workout at the same time?*

A. There are so many benefits to exercising regularly. Quality of life is improved in many ways, and it is an enjoyable way to spend more time with your mother. Many fitness facilities can provide a fitness assessment and develop a program for you that fits into your and your mother's lives.

Depending on your ages and physical well-being, some activities will be more appropriate than others. The important components of fitness that you will want to consider are flexibility, strength, and aerobic fitness. As we age, we tend to lose flexibility. Stretching exercises are important. We also lose muscle mass and need to keep what is left as strong as possible. Light weights can be used to increase strength. Aerobic exercises, including swimming, walking, or other activities that increase heart rate, may be a good starting point. Remember to consult your physician before beginning any exercise program.

Source: Elizabeth Chapman, Past President, Ontario Kinesiology Association

Q. *Before my mother had a stroke, she loved dining out. Now that she's in a wheelchair, she worries about being in a restaurant (taking up space, getting to and from the table). How do I plan so that her experience is a more enjoyable one?*

A. Offering convenient space allowing a person in a wheelchair to get to her table and offering a high enough table so that she is comfortable should be minimum requirements to expect from any restaurant. One thing you can do is to ask the restaurant to ensure that there is enough space between your party and other guests to prevent anyone being disturbed.

Source: Marie-Pierre Gervais, Director of Public Relations, Fairmont Tremblant

Q. I want my children to have a relationship with my mother, but her hearing loss makes communication very difficult. Any tips?

A. A referral from your mother's doctor for a hearing evaluation would be the first step to better communication with her grand-children. She will receive information about the latest hearing aids and assisted listening devices that can help the whole family enjoy a closer relationship. Meanwhile, the following tips may assist with communication:

- Face her directly so that she can read lips and take cues from facial expression and body language.

- Speak slowly and clearly, avoiding exaggerated lip move-ments and shouting.

- Do not obscure your face and mouth with your hands, and eliminate distractions such as eating or gum chewing.

- If you have to repeat yourself several times, try rephrasing your sentence.

- Be aware of the environment—large, crowded rooms are difficult settings for the hearing impaired. Turn off the TV and radio to reduce background noise.

Q. My parents often ask me to drive them to medical appointments. I know that seeing their doctors is vital to their health, yet I can't take so much time off work (I work 60-plus hours per week). Help!

A. Caring for parents and meeting work obligations can be very demanding. Explain the situation to your parents and tell them that you are exploring alternative ways of getting them to their appointments. Ask them for suggestions.

Whenever possible, arrange appointments to accommo-date your work. If you can, enlist help from family and friends. Could your parents go together by taxi? Would a community service group provide this service? You could also consider hiring a companion through an agency to accompany them.

Common Health Concerns of Older Adults

Heart Disease and Stroke

Heart disease and stroke are two major health concerns for the elderly in North America. In fact, the number of deaths from these and other diseases of the circulatory system combined is higher than the number of deaths from even cancer for the over-65 age group.

Although men are more at risk for heart disease than women, the incidence of heart disease increases with age for both men and women. Many risk factors, including smoking, poor diet, obesity, diabetes, high blood pressure, and high blood cholesterol, are linked to heart disease. In general, healthy eating, adequate physical activity, not smoking, and regularly having one's cholesterol levels measured are considered as ways to ward off encroaching heart disease.

Once we reach 55, the risk of having a stroke doubles every 10 years. And while stroke is a major risk for both older men and women, women account for 60% of all stroke cases, in part due to the fact that women live longer than men and thus have more opportunity to experience a stroke. High blood pressure, or hypertension, is the most significant risk factor for stroke. But many of the same factors that increase risk for heart disease, such as high blood cholesterol, inactivity, and smoking, are also important factors for stroke as is excessive alcohol consumption.

For more information, contact the Heart and Stroke Foundation:

Heart and Stroke Foundation of Canada
222 Queen Street, Suite 1402
Ottawa, ON K1P 5V9
Tel: (613) 569-4361
Fax: (613) 569-3278
Visit: **www.heartandstroke.ca**

Cancer

Even though cancer ranks as the second leading cause of death for both men and women over the age of 65 in Canada, it still remains the leading cause of death for adult Canadians over all. In fact, a startling 38% of Canadian women and 41% of Canadian men will develop cancer over their lifetimes. While prostate and breast cancer are significant concerns for men and women, respectively, for both men and women, lung cancer poses the greatest risk of death. Colorectal cancer is found predominantly among older adults and is also a major concern.

Cancer is caused by abnormal cell growth that leads to the formation of malignant tumours that invade surrounding cells and body tissue as they spread. Radiation therapy, chemotherapy (full body treatment with medications), and surgery are the three primary methods used in an attempt to treat cancer, though their success is not guaranteed.

While smoking is the major risk factor associated with lung cancer (it's the cause of 80 to 90% of cases!), poor diet, lack of exercise, overexposure to sunlight, and a family history of cancer are also risk factors associated with various cancers. Early detection generally increases the success of cancer treatment, but screening tests vary from cancer to cancer and some types of cancer can't be screened at all.

Your doctor will be able to talk to you more about your personal risk for cancer. Be sure to seek medical advice if your family has had a specific type of cancer in its background.

For more information, contact the Canadian Cancer Society:

Canadian Cancer Society
National Office
Suite 200, 10 Alcorn Avenue
Toronto, ON M4V 3B1
Tel: (416) 961-7223
Fax: (416) 961-4189
E-mail: ccs@cancer.ca
Visit: **www.cancer.ca**

Alzheimer's Disease

Alzheimer's disease is a degenerative brain disorder, the most common type of dementia occurring in elderly adults. Alzheimer's disease leads to the shrinkage or disappearance of brain cells. As the disease affects different parts of the brain, it can affect a person's moods, behaviours, and mental abilities—most notably, their memory.

According to the Alzheimer Society of Canada, one in 13 Canadians over the age of 65 has Alzheimer's disease or a related dementia, and more than half of all Canadians know someone with the disease. As such, Alzheimer's disease is an important concern for many of us. Many people incorrectly associate memory loss, mood changes, and difficulty in performing daily tasks with the aging process, but if you know someone experiencing these symptoms, you should contact your doctor as they can be warning signs for Alzheimer's disease.

Scientists are exploring the areas of family history and both internal and external environmental conditions for clues as to the cause of Alzheimer's disease, but unfortunately, to date, researchers still do not understand how it is caused. While there is no cure for Alzheimer's disease, medications and other treatment approaches may have some effect on its symptoms.

For more information contact:

Alzheimer Society of Canada
20 Eglinton Ave. W., Ste. 1200
Toronto, ON M4R 1K8
Tel: (416) 488-8772 or 1-800-616-8816
Fax: (416) 488-3778
E-mail: info@alzheimer.ca
Visit: **www.alzheimer.ca**

Arthritis

Arthritis, or joint inflammation, is actually made up of over a hundred related conditions and is a leading cause of disability. Up to half of adults over 65 are afflicted with some form of arthritis. And while a person's arthritis may cause just a little bit of joint pain, conditions like rheumatoid arthritis can seriously affect the entire body.

Osteoarthritis is the most common form of arthritis older adults experience, and like other forms, is triggered by the wearing down of cartilage that normally cushions bones. Age, excess weight, and past injuries are the major risk factors for arthritis, and exercise to maintain healthy weight levels is generally suggested for arthritis prevention. While men and women are at almost equal risk for developing arthritis, men tend to have symptoms in the hips, wrists, and spine while women are more likely to have symptoms in the hands, knees, ankles, and feet.

Although the causes of arthritis are not known, most forms of arthritis can be managed to some extent—particularly if they are detected early on. While pain from arthritis can sometimes be managed with over-the-counter pain medications, more extensive treatments may be required depending on the specific type of arthritis a person has—surgery is performed in some cases to diminish the pain in certain joint areas. Contact your doctor if you or someone you know may have symptoms of arthritis or could use some advice on how to manage the condition.

For more information about arthritis, contact the Arthritis Society:

The Arthritis Society
National Office
393 University Avenue, Suite 1700
Toronto, ON M5G 1E6
Tel: (416) 979-7228
Fax: (416) 979-8366
E-mail: info@arthritis.ca
Visit: **www.arthritis.ca**

Parkinson's Disease

Parkinson's disease is a neurodegenerative disease classified as a movement disorder, and its primary symptoms are tremors of the limbs, hands, and face; rigidity in the limbs and trunk; slowness of movement; and impaired balance. Parkinson's disease occurs when the brain is not able to produce enough dopamine due to the increased death rate of dopamine-producing cells.

The Parkinson Society of Canada advises that one in 300 people in Canada has Parkinson's and the average age of onset is 60, so the disease is a significant concern among older adults. As there are no simple x-rays or tests that can diagnose Parkinson's disease, diagnosis must be made by a neurologist.

Although there is no cure for Parkinson's, many patients are treated with medication and also receive some sort of physical therapy or occupational therapy, in addition to exercising. In a few patients, surgery is sometimes required.

Contact your doctor, who may refer you to a neurologist, if you have concerns that you or someone you are caring for has Parkinson's. For more information, you can also contact the Parkinson Society of Canada.

Parkinson Society of Canada
4211 Yonge Street, Suite 316
Toronto, ON M2P 2A9
Tel : 416-227-9700 or 1-800-565-3000
Fax: 416-227-9600
E-mail: General.info@parkinson.ca
Visit: **www.parkinson.ca**

Diabetes

Diabetes occurs when the body either cannot produce enough insulin (Type 1) or is unable to use the insulin that it produces (Type 2). According to Health Canada, 10% of people over the age of 65 in Canada have diabetes. Diabetes is especially significant for seniors as the complications of diabetes include heart disease and stroke, high blood pressure, vision loss, kidney disease, and limb amputations.

The overwhelming majority of diabetes cases in Canada are Type 2, which is closely linked to two main risk factors—lack of physical activity and obesity. So maintaining a healthy weight and exercising can potentially prevent or delay the onset of Type 2 diabetes; however, currently there are no known means to prevent Type 1.

For seniors with diabetes, education and attaining access to good-quality treatment are key. So, if you are caring for an older person with diabetes, be sure that you and the patient are aware of what needs to be done to control blood glucose levels, blood pressure, and cholesterol. Also be sure to be in regular communication with the elder's health-care providers and let them know of any changes in the person's condition.

For additional information, you may want to contact the Canadian Diabetes Association:

Canadian Diabetes Association
15 Toronto St., Suite 800
Toronto, ON M5C 2E3
Tel: 416-363-3373 or 1-800-226-8464
Fax: 416-363-3393
E-mail: info@diabetes.ca
Visit: **www.diabetes.ca**

Osteoporosis

Osteoporosis causes a thinning of bone tissue and puts people at much higher risk for back, hip, and wrist fractures. The Osteoporosis Society of Canada says that the probability of acquiring osteoporosis increases with age, and it is of particular concern for older women as the large majority of cases occur in women—one in four women over the age of 50 has osteoporosis.

Bone loss can occur for years before causing direct symptoms of osteoporosis, so diagnosis of the condition is quite difficult. Major risk factors for osteoporosis include fractures, family history, tendency, and early menopause (before the age of 45). If you and your physician feel that you may be at risk for osteoporosis, a Bone Mineral Density (BMD) test can be arranged for you. It can diagnose the condition or indicate your likelihood of acquiring it.

Hormone replacement therapy is often used as a means of treatment and prevention of osteoporosis in women. Treatment and prevention are generally focused on the maintenance of bone density. Calcium, vitamin D, and magnesium supplements are often recommended to that end, as is weight-bearing exercise, which can prevent the deterioration of bone mass.

For more information, contact the Osteoporosis Society of Canada:

Osteoporosis Society of Canada
33 Laird Drive
Toronto, ON M4G 3S9
Tel: 416-696-2663 or 1-800-463-6842
Fax: 416-696-2673
E-mail: osc@osteoporosis.ca
Visit: **www.osteoporosis.ca**

Tips and Tests

1. Your Planning Cheat Sheet—Our Top 10 Tips

2. Caring from Afar—Top 20 Warning Signs to Stick on the Fridge

3. Home Helpers—Discover Your New Best Friend

4. Questions to Ask When Housing Becomes an Issue—Ten Things You Need to Know

5. Home Safety Checklist—The 30 Best Ways to Help Your Parent Stay at Home

6. Family Life—Are You a Great Relative?

7. How Smart Are You?—Test Your Caregiving IQ

1. Your Planning Cheat Sheet—Our Top 10 Tips

Top down, these are the top 10 areas that are sure to need attention. Provide your answers to this quick list and you'll be on to next steps.

1. **Medical issues:** What are your elder's medical needs? What resources and skills will be needed to deal with them? Are you well trained enough?

2. **Legal and financial issues:** This includes who is going to be responsible for what. Do you have powers of attorney and wills close by?

3. **Day-to-day activities:** How is the person coping now, what will change, and what needs to be done to keep things going day by day?

4. **Mobility:** How will your elder get around? Is there a need for a cane, crutches, walker, scooter, or wheelchair?

5. **Environment:** You will need to review living arrangements and plan for adjustments as necessary. Stay at home or move? With support or not?

6. **Community:** Take a look at what community resources may be needed, and how they can be accessed, including home care, nursing care, long-term care facility, and retirement living.

7. **Safety:** Look for hazards in the home (present and future). Things to consider include the risk of falling, fire hazards, and security issues. Are your relatives safe?

8. **Work and family:** Can you afford time off work, both financially and from a career perspective? Have you spoken to your boss and discussed with your spouse and kids what's "coming down"? Is everyone supportive or is there resistance?

9. **Volunteering:** Do you have current commitments that'll need to be cancelled or cut back? Will you have time to help out in the community where your parents live?

10. **Caregiver:** Don't forget yourself. Look at ways to ensure you stay strong, healthy, and able to provide the care that is needed. Take a break before stress and responsibility put you over the edge.

2. Caring from Afar—Top 20 Warning Signs to Stick on the Fridge

Calling in once a week is tricky at best. You'd better put your ear to the ground and do some detective work if you or concerned others have noticed any of the following changes in a loved one:

1. Declining physical or mental health

2. Loss of appetite or missing meals

3. Wandering or confusion

4. Malnutrition

5. Incontinence

6. Unsafe or unsanitary living conditions

7. Accumulating clutter (even multiple pets)

8. Trouble remembering

9. Depression and mood swings

10. Reduced judgment and decision-making ability

11. Decreased listening skills

12. Unclear on telephone or with instructions

13. Limited mobility, frailty, or loss of balance

14. Unsafe driving

15. Limited access to transportation

16. Recently cut off from social network

17. Deteriorating personal hygiene and grooming

18. Unpaid bills or disorganized records

19. Lack of confidence to venture out

20. Fear of living alone or social situations

My Story: Check the Fridge!

After weeks of Sunday visits and friendly telephone calls during which my mother told me everything was okay, I finally discovered the evidence to the contrary in the refrigerator. To my surprise, I found cutlery, unfinished meals, spoiled food, and enough mess and dirt to alarm the public health department—all behind a conveniently closed door. The moral of the story: Ask for a glass of milk and get it yourself next time you're visiting.

3. Home Helpers—Discover Your New Best Friend

These days, technology introduces a multitude of clever devices to make your life easier and maintain independence. Some will literally make a jar easier to open or a knob easier to turn. Here are some worth investigating:

- Lever handles can be operated with the touch of a finger.

- Shower seats come in a variety of styles and provide more stability when climbing in and out of the tub or shower.

- Raised toilet seats—designed to fit over existing toilet bowl, they raise the seat 6 to 8 inches (15 to 20 cm) and can be purchased with side railings for easy use.

- Jar openers, usually under-the-counter mounted and accommodating a variety of lid sizes.

- Long-handled shoehorns—with a little practice, these can hold shoes in place for easier dressing if bending is an issue.

- Easy grip items—check out easy-to-use thicker handles on knives, utensils, toothbrushes, and other kitchen and grooming implements.

Your Home Helper Shopping List

Bedroom
Adjustable bed
Night-light
Grab bars, transfer poles
Stocking and sock aids
Air filtration system

Bathroom
Non-slip mats
Grab bars
Shower seats
Raised toilet seats
Bath lifts

Kitchen
Plastic utensils
Long-handled reachers
Easy-grab cupboard handles

- Lift chairs designed to make getting in and out of chairs a smoother process.

- Amplified phones—volume control on speaker phones is adjustable to make it easier to hear.

- Rocker or light touch switches.

- Keyholders that provide an easier grip on small, hard-to-turn keys.

- Bed extenders raise the bed a few inches to an easier height to sit on.

- Lightweight vacuums—easier to push and specially designed for those who can't handle the regular models.

Around the House
Magnifiers
Lift chairs
Railings
Environmental controls
Ramps
Transfer poles
Stairlift, elevators

All of these products can be found at your local home health-care centre or specialized pharmacy.

---

4. Questions to Ask When Housing Becomes an Issue—Ten Things You Need to Know

Often, when a parent is suddenly single or the family home is too much for Mom and Dad to handle, discussions lead to the possibility of a move. If you're in that position, check out our top 10!

- **Safety first:** Is the new housing clean, safe, and accessible for walkers, wheelchairs, etc.?

- **Where is it?** What is the proximity to family who will want to visit?

- **Dollars and sense:** Can your elder afford it and is maintenance manageable?

- **Timing and commitment:** When is the space available and do you understand the terms of the lease or monthly agreement?

- **Recreational facilities:** Are there adequate leisure or social activities available?

- **Convenience:** Are shops, banks, and churches easily accessible?

- **Four-season comfort:** How will it be in the winter—is it year-round accessible for walkers and wheelchairs?

- **Independent living:** Does it meet your loved one's need for privacy and independence?

- **Near doctor's office:** How far away is the family doctor's office and medical facilities?

- **Comforts of home:** Will your elder be able to bring or store household and personal items?

> ## My Story: Don't Go It Alone
>
> Be realistic. We went through a mix of emotions during these discussions, and an empty house for five months added to our stress and cost. Try to understand that downsizing and sorting will be a big part of what needs to be done. We did it all ourselves. If it ever happens again, I'll get external help to ease the discomfort and stop me from lots of musing and hoarding.

---

5. Home Safety Checklist—The 30 Best Ways to Help Your Parent Stay at Home

There are many reasons why older people tend to be more susceptible to falls and home accidents. Think:

- decreased vision or hearing

- gait changes or prosthetic equipment

- changes in blood pressure related to sudden movement or medical problems

- medical conditions requiring multiple medications

- slower reaction time

The good news: according to the experts, one-third to one-half of home accidents can be prevented by modification and repair. Open your eyes wide and see what you can do to make the family home safer:

- Clear the flight path. Prevent falls by making sure the way to and from the kitchen, bathroom, and bedroom are clutter-free.

- Telephone and electrical cords stretched across walkways could cause someone to trip. Furniture or rugs resting on cords may damage the cords, causing fire and shock hazards. Frayed or damaged cords, or overloaded extension cords, may cause a fire.

- Emergency numbers such as police, fire department, and poison-control centre should be posted by the phone. Also, at least one telephone should be accessible if your elder becomes unable to stand.

- Tripping over rugs and runners is a common cause of falls that can result in fatal injury for the elderly. Remove rugs that tend to slide; get rubber backing or secure them carefully to the floor.

- Install carbon-monoxide detectors and check smoke detectors. Make sure that you have at least one detector on every floor of your home. Do not place the detectors near air vents and ensure they are near the bedroom. Maintain the smoke detector according to manufacturer's directions.

- Bulbs that are too high a wattage for the fixture can cause overheating and may lead to a fire. Replace all such bulbs with the correct wattage for the fixture.

- If your outlets are unusually warm to the touch or have exposed wiring, they could present a shock or fire hazard. Unplug these outlets immediately and have an electrician check them as soon as possible.

- Examine space heaters for proper electrical grounding and adequate ventilation, and make sure that they are not placed in areas where they may cause you to trip. Improper venting of some heaters can cause carbon monoxide poisoning. Heaters that are improperly grounded may present a shock hazard.

- Do you have an emergency exit plan? Because a fire can spread rapidly, you will want to have an escape plan so your elder can avoid panic and confusion in the event of a fire. Establish a place away from the house where the family can safely meet.

- Be aware of the area around the stove. Be sure to keep towels and other flammable items away from the range to avoid the risk of fire. The elder should not wear loose clothing while cooking. Make sure that the ventilation system is working properly so that any vapours or smoke can be effectively cleared from the kitchen. Make sure that all electrical cords are located away from the range or sink.

- Low lighting can contribute to burns or cuts. Ensure there is adequate lighting, and select lighting fixtures that reduce glare. The elderly need three times as much light to see clearly. Consider "softer" lighting for areas with shiny floors to reduce glare.

- Standing on unstable stools and other items is a common cause of falls. Make sure that stools are stable and in good repair.

- Chimneys need to be cleaned regularly to remove the buildup of creosote inside the chimney. If neglected, this creosote buildup can cause a chimney fire. Make sure that the chimney is not blocked by leaves, birds' nests, etc.

- Check passageways. Put additional lights in hallways and stairwells to ensure all areas of the home are well lit and free of obstacles that could lead to a fall.

- Ensure the bathroom is safe. Make sure that the bathtub is equipped with a non-skid mat. If your elder is at all unsteady, install safety bars near the toilet and in the bathtub. Make sure that these are secured firmly to the wall. Lower the water temperature to 120°F (50°C) or less, to avoid scalding. Make sure that the bathroom has adequate lighting. Keep electrical appliances unplugged when not in use and away from water. An appliance that is plugged in and immersed in water can cause a lethal shock. You may want to install a ground-fault circuit interrupter in the bathroom if one doesn't already exist in order to protect against shock.

- Medications should always be stored in the package that they came in, and be clearly marked. Use childproof containers, if you have children visiting, to avoid accidental poisoning.

- Make sure lamps are located conveniently so that your elders can reach to turn on the lamp and get out of bed. Discourage sleeping on an electric heating pad, because it can cause burns even on the low setting. Make sure that the path to the bathroom and the exit are clear of obstacles.

- Watch for flammable and volatile liquids. Make sure that all flammable liquids are carefully capped and are stored away from heat and flame. If containers are not tightly closed, toxic vapors can escape from the container, posing a health hazard. Flammable liquids can burst into flame, even if placed several feet from a heat source.

- Put new locks on the entry doors. Make sure someone besides the elder has access; there have been instances in which a senior fell, but no one could get in to offer help. If entry doors have glass panes, replace them with solid doors for greater protection against break-ins.

- Install grab bars in bathrooms. These are easily nailed or screwed into the walls. Place them in areas where the senior might have balance problems, such as in and near the tub and near the toilet. Consider installing a raised toilet seat.

- Look for places where you can add handrails outside the home. Watch the elder coming and going and walking around inside the house. See where he or she naturally grabs for furniture or a wall, then put a handrail in those locations. Remember, these can be attractively designed, but they must be functional.

- Replace existing shaky or rusted handrails outside the home. If the senior is unable to climb stairs properly, consider installing a chair lift. They reduce risk of injury, and the cost is nominal given the long-term safety benefits.

- Other modifications might include putting a small stackable washer-dryer in the kitchen so basement stairs can be avoided, or renting a hospital bed and setting up a secondary bedroom on the first floor. Look for helpful assistive devices like telephones with big numbers or an emergency response or alarm system.

- Check stairs. Remove all loose rugs and coverings; ensure that the stairwell is well lit and has secure handrails to avoid falls.

- Avoid flimsy plastic chairs or chairs on wheels, as they can easily slip or tip under a person's weight.

- Talk to your pharmacist if your elder is taking medications. Some drugs can cause dizziness or drowsiness. The pharmacist can suggest precautions. Be especially alert if the person has high blood pressure. Standing up quickly can cause dizziness. Warn them to stand up slowly or help the person up.

- Be honest with the person—and yourself—if you think a mobility aid is needed. A simple cane, walking stick, or walker can make a tremendous difference.

---

6. Family Life—Are You a Great Relative?

It's more personal as we get involved in each other's daily lives during this tricky time. It's different than when we were kids. Be honest about yourself. Take this test to see if you've got what it takes to fit in and help out—or if there are one or two areas where you need to do some work.

❑ **Values communication:** Ideal relatives are good communicators; one of their greatest skills is the ability to listen. He or she does not pretend or talk over you, but truly listens.

❑ **Loves unconditionally:** The ideal family member loves you no matter what you do. If they have a problem with you, they talk about it instead of having opinions about it. Their love is constant and they are non-judgmental. Their unconditional love also extends to your spouse or partner and your kids.

❑ **Is accepting and respectful:** Ideal relatives recognize the unique characteristics of other family members and don't need you to be the same as they are. They understand that people will have differences of opinions, and they respect these opinions, even if they don't agree with them.

❑ **Offers support:** He or she will find out what support you need. They are respectful and considerate of other family members' feelings. They offer advice only when asked, knowing when to step back and allow you space, and yet they are there when you need them.

❑ **Is helpful:** They will help you when you're sick, pitch in when you're overwhelmed, provide guidance if you want them to, and coach you if you ask for direction. You trust them and count on them.

❑ **Keeps in touch:** They're there when you want them, not there when you don't. Ideal relatives take responsibility for your relationship. They make efforts to stay in touch with you in a way that values your time, relationships, and other commitments.

❑ **Is wise with money:** If they loan you money, they don't ask for it back right away. If they borrow money, they always repay it. If you're in need, they open their wallets, promptly forget they loaned you money, and then act surprised when you pay them back.

❑ **Is also a friend:** Because of mutual respect and support, a good relative is a good friend, to whom you happen to be related. As you each get older, the ideal relative looks to build common ground and nurture it.

❑ **Doesn't hold on to the past:** The ideal family member realizes that people evolve, so they don't limit their idea of you to the past. They don't keep reminding you of your mistakes or tell stories about your past that make you uncomfortable.

❏ **Is fun, optimistic, and a positive influence:** The ideal relative is someone you just want to be around because he or she makes you feel better about yourself. They lighten your emotional load instead of adding to it. You can go to them, concerned about something, and they smile, and let you know that everything will work out.

How did you do? For those areas you didn't check off, you now have an idea of what to personally work on. This will help you accomplish more than wishing your relative treated you better. If there's truth to the aphorism "We get what we give," then giving greatness should get you greatness in return.

Source: Excerpted with permission in Solutions Magazine *from* Dealing with Relatives (...even if you can't stand them). *McGraw-Hill, 2003.*

My Story: Brotherly Love

My brother and I are very different creatures who hadn't spent a lot of time together until Mom's stroke. While we don't always agree, he gets full marks in the fun, optimistic, and helpful categories. His caregiving jobs over time have included some funny events: buying extra-large underwear at Zellers for Mom because the nursing home called while I was away; spontaneously deciding to take Mom to the casino, wheelchair, diapers and all, on the way to his cottage for Christmas; and having her out to visit his new home during the largest power shut-down in years with no gas in his car. The lawn mower gas can sure came in handy that day!

---

7. How Smart Are You?—Test Your Caregiving IQ

Just to keep you honest, take this "smart" test to find out how well you're coping with the responsibilities of providing care.

For each of the following, pick a number from 0 to 3, with

0 = never   1 = sometimes   2 = most of the time   3 = always

____I try to schedule my caregiving activities along with the rest of my responsibilities.

____I realize that I can only do so much each day and don't try to do too much.

___Taking care of myself is still important to me, and I take time to eat well and exercise.

___I try to get at least seven hours sleep every night.

___I keep a care diary, which contains important information on medical visits, drugs, etc.

___I am open to suggestions on my role as a caregiver and seek out advice.

___I share my frustrations and challenges with family, friends, or a support group.

___I can rely on family members and others to do their part.

___I am not afraid to ask the doctor or health professional questions.

___I have investigated options, such as mobility aids and safety devices, that will make life easier for my loved one.

___I always involve my loved one in any caregiving decisions.

___I have taken the time to learn about my loved one's medical condition.

___I try to emphasize the positive and relish the good moments as they come.

___I am realistic about my loved one's condition.

___Every so often, I take some time to relax or pamper myself.

TOTAL:

0–15: Poor: You need to smarten up your caregiving skills now, before you burn out or do some harm to your loved one!

16–27: Not bad: You realize what you should be doing—now you need to work on doing it.

28–39: Pretty good: You are a smart caregiver and probably doing the best job you can.

40–45: Perfect: You should be giving lessons in caregiving!

Source: Solutions Magazine

Respite Caregiver Checklist

A respite-care worker provides the regular caregiver with some time off from duties (and the cost is sometimes covered by government or private health-care plans). But that does not mean that the respite-care caregiver has complete knowledge of the patient or knows the best way of treating the person. This is a useful checklist to share.

Caregiver Information

Primary   **Alternate**

Name _____   Name _____

Home Phone _____   Home Phone _____

Cellphone _____   Cellphone _____

Patient Information

Patient_____   Birth Date _____

SIN# _____   Health Card #_____

Physician Contact Information

Doctor & Specialty	Phone Number	Address
_____	_____	_____
_____	_____	_____

Hospital Information

Hospital	Phone Number	Medical Insurance Info.
_____	_____	_____
_____	_____	_____
_____	_____	_____

Home/Health/Hospice Information

Agency/Facility	Phone Number	Contact Name
_____	_____	_____
_____	_____	_____
_____	_____	_____

Diagnoses

For how long _____

Characteristics of diagnoses affecting care_____

_____

Current symptoms_____

Allergies _____

History of seizures? _____

Patient's general emotional state (shy, sense of humour, weepy, sudden outbursts, etc.)_____

_____

_____ Generally understands instructions

_____ May not understand instructions

_____ Vision limitations

Favourite distractions/Likes_____

Dislikes _____

Precautions / instructions can be found (state where): _____

_____

Vital Signs

_____ Don't need to take.   _____ Take every   _____ hours.

(Record date, time, and reading on separate sheet of paper)

_____ Pulse   _____ Blood Pressure   _____ Respirations   _____ Temperature

_____ Under Tongue   _____ Other

Medication	Dose	Time(s) to Be Given	Special Instructions (See Key Below)

Special Instructions Key

A. Give on empty stomach

B. Wake up patient to give medications

C. With food/liquid (circle)

D. Give (time) before eating

E. Give on patient request

F. Avoid _____

G. Document when given

H. Other _____

Medical Equipment

Equipment	When	Needs Assistance	Need to Know

Appointments (doctor's office, physical therapy, beauty/barber, visit friends, ball game, etc.)

To	Location	Phone	Date	Time

Personal Care and Comfort
(circle all that apply and attach instructions to this sheet)

Catheter care   Hearing aid   Shaving   Peri-care   Mouth/oral care

Bed sSores Foley bag   Dressings changed   Hair/skin/nail care Dentures

Moving Patient
(circle all that apply below)

Moves around unassisted   Transfers from bed to chair with assistance

Bedbound   Reposition   Requires special lift

Special Instructions: _____

_____

Walking/Transporting Patients
(circle below)

Unassisted   Cane   Walker   Wheelchair

Physical Therapies

1. Unassisted
2. Needs assistance
3. Range of motion _____ Frequency _____
4. Special exercises _____

Toileting
(circle below)

Unassisted   Bedpan   Urinal catheter

Colostomy   Bedside commode   Incontinent pads   Other

Bathing
circle below)

Bed bath   Shower   Tub   Needs assistance   _____ times per week

Equipment Needed

1. None
2. Transfer bench
3. Shower bench
4. Wheelchair

Bedroom Comfort

Bedtime _____   Wake time _____   Nap time(s) _____

Room   _____   Closed   _____   Prefers room _____
temperature   windows   dark

Change Bed

Pull sheet   Blankets(s)   Day_____ or night _____

Special bed items (sheepskin, egg crate mattress, extra pillows—attach sheet)

Food *(for meals/snacks or special instructions)*
(circle below and see attached list)

Needs assistance feeding   Needs to be fed   Has difficulty swallowing

Takes nothing by mouth   Tube feeding   Soft foods

Record liquid intake

Meal Times

Breakfast _____   Lunch   _____   Dinner _____

Snack(s)   _____

Entertainment Options/Preferences
(circle below)

TV   Radio   Reading or being read to   Cards   Other

Avoid _____

House Rules and Instructions

1. Locking doors

2. Don't smoke

3. Working stove

4. Fireplace

5. Gas shut-off valve

6. Fire extinguishers

7. Expected visitors

8. Pet care guidelines

9. Neighbours

Other information

_____

_____

_____

_____

_____

Emergency Preparedness

Discuss 911 preferences _____

DNR Order or Advanced Directives can be found _____

I'll return home on _____

I will be away from _____ to _____

Location _____

Phone (home and cell) _____

_____

Friends and relatives you can contact in an emergency

_____

_____

_____

_____

_____

_____

Who's Who
in Eldercare

Working through the maze of specialists, health-care profes-
sionals, and social services is time-consuming and demanding.
Whose help should you seek when? Who should you contact
first in a given situation? Here is a brief overview of some of
the cast of thousands you're likely to encounter as you make
your way through the world of eldercare.

Adult Day Centres

These innovative centres are the geriatric equivalent of a childcare centre. They provide stimulating social activities, nutritious lunches, transportation to doctors' appointments, and cost-effective, individualized nursing care for adults who need day-time supervision.

An alternative to paying for full-time home care, adult day programs allow families to keep their relatives actively engaged in an out-of-the-house community program. Ideal for family members who may be socially isolated or depressed, frail or confused, or suffering from dementia, and/or those who are dependent on you for care.

Family caregivers can help staff by providing a mini-biography and a current photograph of your elder.

Older adults may initially be reluctant to attend and you may also have a dreadful feeling of guilt when you drop off your elder. Our take: Drop Mom off in the morning with a smile on your face and go about your daily business. Just like your kids, she'll probably be fine and active shortly after you've turned the corner.

Some members settle into the program more easily than others. For example, people who were joiners throughout their lives take to the program routine more easily than people who always preferred a more solitary lifestyle. It may take a few visits before some people feel at ease with staff and fellow members. Some new members express a wish to call home to begin with. Staff members often respect this need. Check to see if the office phone is available and accessible.

Caregiver Hint: Affordable adult daycare centres are most easily found through your local Community Care Access Centre or equivalent.

Care Managers or Geriatric Care Managers

The term "geriatric care manager" is definitely more prevalent in the United States, but it's increasingly making its way into the Canadian eldercare lexicon. These hands-on health professionals go by many titles: social worker, discharge planner, and case manager, though there are some distinctions between case and care managers (see next entry). Regardless of title, these caring pros are usually an invaluable part of the care team during and after a stay in the hospital.

A care manager works with older adults and caregivers to identify risks, clarify needs, and evaluate options. They are usually qualified health professionals, such as registered nurses, and have extensive knowledge about the cost, quality, and availability of services in a community. They can conduct a personalized care-planning assessment to identify existing and potential problems (including safety, nutritional status, and mental state of the elderly individual) and they can also act as liaisons with the local health authorities or insurers to determine eligibility for assistance. Another primary function of a care manager is to talk over potential problems with their clients and their families, helping to look for realistic solutions. In essence, care managers can effectively assume the primary responsibility of the elder on behalf of the family. If you require identification of or advocacy with funding sources for your parent's caregiving needs, your care manager will also be an excellent resource.

Sometimes, the journey through the maze of hospital admission, treatment or rehab, and return home is sudden and stressful. Having an assigned support or resource person is truly a blessing and very helpful. Often, however, the family meetings take a while to arrange and decision-time is limited. A word to the wise: It's easy to merely accept their initial advice and recommendations as "must do's." You *can* say no, ask for other arrangements, or get a second opinion. Ask lots of questions, double-check everything, and advocate on behalf of what you think is best for your parent. More often than not, a care manager will point you in the right direction, but it's the squeaky wheel that gets the oil.

Where to Find

Though most geriatric care managers operate privately, look to your CCAC or family doctor for recommendations of trusted care managers in your area.

Case Managers (for Older Adults)

The role of case managers for older adults, sometimes called a geriatric case manager (see previous entry), definitely overlaps with that of geriatric care managers.

Case management is a very diverse profession, but it's possible to find some case managers who specialize in eldercare. While both case and geriatric care managers can help to manage and coordinate the care of elderly adults, the case manager's role is generally understood to be somewhat more limited. Though the distinction is fairly fuzzy in Canada, case managers are often reimbursed through public funding or insurance, whereas you will almost definitely have to pay for a care manager privately.

In the United States, case managers generally focus on healthcare issues only, while care managers are responsible for legal, financial, and household issues in addition to health care. A case manager can organize assessments to determine eligibility for assistance based on an individual's needs, coordinate medical services, and arrange for certain other health-related services that a patient might need.

Where to Find

Contact your local CCAC or Regional Health Authority for information on how to find a case manager for the older adult in your life.

Chiropractors

Chiropractors are medical professionals who diagnose and treat disorders of the musculoskeletal and nervous systems without prescribing medications or performing surgery. Utilizing traditional diagnostic testing methods such as x-rays, MRI, and lab work, along with specific techniques that involve hands-on manipulation of the articulations of the body, chiropractors work in the belief that one of the main causes of pain and disease is the misalignment of the vertebrae in the spinal column. Through the use of manual detection or palpation, carefully applied pressure, massage and manual manipulation of the vertebrae and joints (called adjustments), chiropractors relieve pressure and irritation on the nerves to restore joint mobility.

Some chiropractors dedicate their practices solely to locating and removing subluxations. However, most chiropractors, in addition to using manual adjustments, also offer other treatment modalities such as physiotherapy, massage, acupuncture, and herbal therapy.

As a result of recent research and changing attitudes, chiropractic has become more accepted, especially with older adults, and is now considered by many to be a part of benefits programs and mainstream Western medicine.

Caregiver Hint: These "spine guys" offer a drugless holistic approach that supports prevention and allows the body to best function and repair itself.

Where to Find

The Canadian Chiropractic Association
1396 Eglinton Ave. West
Toronto, ON M6C 2E4
Phone: (416) 781-5656
Fax: (416) 781-0923
E-mail: ccachiro@ccachiro.org
Visit: www.ccachiro.org

Dentists

Proper oral health is essential to any individual's overall health, especially in one's later years. Dentists are the knights of this crusade.

These professionals specialize in the lifelong treatment, care, and surgeries pertaining to dental and oral health.

Most provincial health plans do not cover dental work, even for seniors. Private or long-term-care insurance programs usually have coverage for some dental care.

Many dental offices are still neither senior-friendly nor accessible. Check first to make sure your dentist's clinic and equipment can accommodate your parent's changing needs and mobility limitations.

Dental clinics are universities where dental students, supervised by instructors, sometimes offer seniors a cost-effective alternative. There is generally a waiting list for these programs and fees are a percentage of the standard costs for the procedure.

For more information about contacting a dentist or setting up a dental plan, contact the Canadian Dental Association, a non-profit professional association that represents dentists in Canada. The CDA Web site provides news and general information about dental health care.

Where to Find

Canadian Dental Association
1815 Alta Vista Dr.
Ottawa, ON K1G 3Y6
Tel: (613) 523-1770
E-mail: reception@cda-adc.ca
Visit: www.cda-adc.ca

Dietitians

Whether your loved one has specific diet requirements linked to an on-going condition, or whether you think that your elder could just use a little help with eating habits, you may want to consider seeking the help of a dietitian. Registered dietitians are health professionals, and you can access a registered dietitian through a local community health centre, hospital, or branch of the department of health.

You can also arrange for a personal consultation with a dietitian. Dietitians may be able to provide help with planning meals for someone dealing with specific health issues. After assessing the needs involved, dietitians can help with drawing up grocery lists, coming up with practical and healthy recipes, and any other issues relating to diet and lifestyle. Most facilities have on-staff or consulting dietitians who monitor and provide individual recommendations and meal plans for residents.

Where to Find

If you have access to the Internet, the Dietitians of Canada Web site has an excellent searchable database of consulting dietitians across the country. Search for "Senior's Nutrition" under "Specialty."

Your family doctor or local hospital should also be able to put you in touch with a qualified dietitian in your area.

Dietitians of Canada
480 University Ave., Suite 604
Toronto, ON M5G 1V2
Phone: (416) 596-0857
Fax: (416) 596-0603
Visit: www.dietitians.ca

Eldercare Accountants

In response to the increase in dual-career households and situations where younger adults are away from their parents or unable to provide care, some accountants are now providing specialized services and support for the elderly.

Such services can assure clients that the financial, medical, and residential needs of clients or their parents or elderly relatives are met.

An eldercare accountant will offer a combination of consulting as well as direct support services to the elderly person living independently or in assisted-living facilities while offering the children and/or spouses or other responsible family members peace of mind that suitable standards are maintained.

With access to a network of expertise and services within their geographic areas, accountants with this specialty are qualified to help older adults and their families plan and review care options and costs. When looking for an accountant, contact the Canadian

Institute for Chartered Accountants, which has over 500 members who are designated as Eldercare Accountants.

Where to Find

The Canadian Institute of Chartered Accountants
277 Wellington St. W.
Toronto, ON M5V 3H2
Phone: (416) 977-3222
Fax: (416) 977-8585
Visit: www.cica.ca

Eldercare Lawyer / Attorney

As retirement living and health-care decisions are becoming increasingly complex, families and their seniors often find themselves searching for someone who specializes in areas of the law that are particularly relevant to themselves and their family members. Today, a number of lawyers are devoted to lending expertise and an especially sensitive ear with regard to issues including long-term-care planning, insurance, succession planning, public and private pensions, age discrimination, durable powers of attorney, guardianship, and elder abuse.

As a single point of contact for navigating the network of options and giving guidance that care is appropriate, an eldercare lawyer could be key for you and your family. The Canadian Law List's Web site has a searchable database of lawyers: search for "Elder Law" under area of specialty. Contact the Canadian Bar Association for more information about how to find a suitable lawyer for you and your family.

Where to Find

The Canadian Law List
Visit: www.canadianlawlist.com

The Canadian Bar Association
500-865 Carling Ave.
Ottawa, ON K1S 5S8
Phone: (613) 237-2925 or (613) 237-1988 or 1-800-267-8860

Fax: (613) 237-0185
E-mail: info@cba.org
Visit: www.cba.org

Eye Care: Ophthalmologists, Opticians, and Optometrists

Diminishing eyesight and varying eye conditions affect many people as they get older. If Mom's eyes are not quite what they used to be, consider asking your doctor if she could use a trip to one of these three "O"s!

Optometrists are qualified to diagnose, manage, and treat conditions and diseases of the human eye and visual system. Their practice consists of eye examinations, diagnosis of problems, and the prescription of corrective lenses and therapeutic drugs. Dispensing opticians fill the prescription that is written by an optometrist. They design, measure, fit, and adapt lenses and help select frames for their clients. Adjustments and repair of frames and lenses are often a necessity for older clients. An ophthalmologist, on the other hand, is a physician who diagnoses and treats eye disease. Ophthalmologists are also trained to administer medication and conduct surgery.

At the first sign of any eye trouble, contact your family doctor, who should be able to direct you to the appropriate eye specialist, if necessary.

Where to Find

Canadian Ophthalmological Society
610-1525 Carling Ave.
Ottawa, ON K1Z 8R9
Phone: (613) 729-6779
E-mail: cos@eyesite.ca
Visit: www.eyesite.ca

Opticians Association of Canada
2706-83 Garry St.
Winnipeg, MB R3C 4J9
Phone: 1-800-847-3155 or (204) 982-6060
Fax: (204) 947-2519

E-mail: canada@opticians.ca
Visit: www.opticians.ca

Canadian Association of Optometrists
234 Argyle Ave.
Ottawa, ON K2P 1B9
Phone: (613) 235-7924
Fax: (613) 235-2025
E-mail: reception@opto.ca
Visit: www.opto.ca

Family and General Practitioners

These docs, FPs and GPs for short, are the gatekeepers who are primarily responsible for the delivery of comprehensive health care to the general population, regardless of an individual's culture or age. Given their ability to recognize the impact of family factors in a patient's medical health and well-being, FPs play a pivotal role in eldercare, home care, and long-term care. It is your family doctor who will assist with diagnosis and treatment of conditions based on specialist's findings and recommendations. Doctors are intimately involved in long-term care and palliative care in the community. They're your point of entry into ongoing care. Take a look at Chapter 10, pertaining to the all-important relationship between an individual and the family physician.

Where to Find

The College of Family Physicians of Canada
2630 Skymark Ave.
Mississauga, ON L4W 5A4
Phone: (905) 629-0900 or 1-800-387-6197
Fax: (905) 629-0893
Visit: www.cfpc.ca

Foot Care: Podiatrists

Happy feet make happy people, so if you feel that your parent's feet aren't feeling as good and healthy as they could be, consider having them see a podiatrist.

A podiatrist is a physician who deals with the examination, diagnosis, prevention, and treatment of diseases and disorders of the foot and its related structures. Such treatment can be through surgery, medications, mechanics, and physical therapy. Many podiatrists perform surgery in their offices, although many also operate in hospitals. They can treat disorders such as walking problems, ankle injuries, broken bones, ingrown toenails, and foot infections.

Where to Find

Canadian Podiatric Medical Association
900-45 Sheppard Ave. E.
Toronto, ON M2N 5W9
Phone: (416) 322-5986 or 1-888-220-3338
Fax: (416) 733-2491
E-mail: info@podiatrycanada.org
Visit: www.podiatrycanada.org

Geriatric Care Managers (An Emerging Profession)

A geriatric care manager works with older adults and caregivers to identify risks, clarify needs, and evaluate options. Often health professionals such as registered nurses, they have extensive knowledge about the cost, quality, and availability of services in a community. They can capably conduct a personalized care-planning assessment to identify existing and potential problems (including safety, nutritional status, and mental state of the elderly individual). The details are communicated to the family in a written report. Care managers can also act as a liaison with the local health authorities or insurers to determine eligibility for assistance. In essence, care managers can effectively assume the primary responsibility of the elder on behalf of the family.

Recent good work has been done on behalf of out-of-town or working families to take care of even the minutest of eldercare needs. Expect help with hospital and doctors' visits, hiring and managing care providers, facilitation of household shopping and maintenance, personal and financial services, and wellness monitoring.

Where to find

Carol Edwards
c/o National Association of Professional Geriatric Care Managers
1604 N. Country Club Rd.
Tucson, AZ 85716-3102
Phone: (520) 881-8008
Fax: (520) 325-7925
or in Canada at CareAble: (416) 362-9176; careable@sympatico.ca

Hearing Health: Audiologists / Hearing-Aid Specialists

Many people experience hearing loss as they age. Sometimes, hearing loss may simply be due to the aging process, but it can also be caused by exposure to noise, certain medications, infections, illnesses, or hereditary factors.

An **audiologist** has a master's or doctoral degree in audiology, the science of hearing. He or she will perform an audiometric evaluation to determine the type and degree of hearing loss and conduct a thorough interview as well as visual inspection of the ear canals and eardrum. The audiologist can suggest medical or surgical alternatives for treating hearing problems. Many audiologists dispense the latest technology in digital hearing aids, which adjust automatically to different sound conditions, or the traditional less expensive analog versions. These professionals also assist in the purchase of related assistive listening devices for the telephone, TV, and other listening situations.

Hearing aid specialists have training in the assessment of patients who specifically seek rehabilitation for hearing loss. They are licensed to perform basic hearing tests and can sell and service hearing aids. The assessment and treatment of individuals with hearing loss and the fitting of suitable hearing aids are within the scope of practice of an audiologist.

Where to Find

Audiologists work in hospitals, schools clinics, rehab facilities, and private practice. Your family doctor should be able to put you in touch with an audiologist in your area who could in turn connect you with a hearing aid specialist. Also consider contacting the Canadian Association of Speech-Language Pathologists and Audiologists.

Canadian Association of Speech-Language Pathologists and Audiologists
401-200 Elgin St.
Ottawa, ON K2P 1L5
Tel: (613) 567-9968 or 1-800-259-8519
Fax: (613) 567-2859
E-mail: caslpa@caslpa.ca
Visit: www.caslpa.ca

Home Health–Care Retailers

Home health-care retailers are also referred to as dealers, medical supply stores, or pharmacy home health-care departments. These centres usually have qualified professionals on staff to assess, recommend, and provide a range of products and equipment from assistive devices to respiratory care products and mobility equipment.

While community health professionals and/or physicians can authorize funding support for a significant number of products, especially those requiring complex prescriptions, you should expect to pay for some equipment (especially if you want more than just the basics). However, if you qualify, funding may be available from many employee health-care or long-term-care insurance policies after your purchase. Simply process a claim for a refund.

Look for partial coverage for basics under most provincial health programs for products like walkers and wheelchairs when prescribed by an authorized health professional. For instance, the Assistive Devices Program in Ontario provides coverage for qualified individuals. (Note: Qualifying guidelines vary, may be quite rigorous, and may involve significant waiting time for approvals.) See our appendix section for information on what Veterans Affairs might cover.

Rentals and refurbished equipment also offer ways to accommodate short-term needs and provide significant savings.

Where to Find

Your doctor or occupational therapist or home-care nurse should be able to put you in touch with a specialty retailer in your area depending on what you're looking for.

Hospice Care

Hospice is a concept of care rather than a specific place. Choice is at the centre of this approach, which involves special, supportive services for the terminally ill and their families. These services include pain and symptom management, social services, and emotional and spiritual support. Hospice palliative care is usually provided in the patient's home or the home of a loved one where a patient can be surrounded by treasured possessions, family and friends so that the person may live out life in the comfort of familiar daily routines. Hospice services may also be provided in long-term-care centres or in patient residential settings.

A patient and family may turn to hospice care when the goals of the patient care have switched to comforting and encouraging as much independence and control as possible. The hospice objective is to preserve the life remaining for the patient and the entire family.

Where to Find

Canadian Hospice Palliative Care Association
43 Bruyère St., Suite 131C
Ottawa, ON K1N 5C8
Phone: (613) 241-3663 or 1-800-668-2785
Hospice Palliative Care Info Line: 1-877-203-4636
Fax: (613) 241-3986
E-mail: info@chpca.net
Visit: www.chpca.net

Hospice Association of Ontario
27 Carlton St., Suite 201
Toronto, ON, M5B 1L2
Phone: (416) 304-1477 or 1-800-349-3111

Fax: (416) 304-1479
E-mail: info@hospice.on.ca
Visit: www.hospice.on.ca

Massage Therapists

Every once in a while, we all could use a therapeutic massage. If your parents suffer from arthritis or any other conditions involving chronic muscular pain, regular massage therapy treatments may be just what the doctor orders!

Massage therapy focuses on decreasing bodily pain and inflammation and diminishing stress. However, massages can do more than just provide you with a bit of relaxation; massage also works to increase the range of motion of body parts while improving circulation and increasing flexibility.

Qualified massage therapists will have received training in massage theory, kinesiology, pathology, anatomy, physiology, and hydrotherapy. Each province has its own associations of massage therapists. To be sure that your therapist has an adequate amount of training, look for someone who is a member of the Canadian Massage Therapy Alliance (CMTA). CMTA members must complete a minimum of 2,200 hours of training.

Some extended health-care plans and benefits plans cover massage treatments, so be sure to check out that option and obtain receipts immediately after your appointment.

Where to Find

Your doctor should be able to put you in touch with a top-notch massage therapist, but you may wish to find one on your own. Below is a listing of the provincial massage therapy associations that adhere to the training requirements of the CMTA. You may also want to visit www.massage.ca for basic information about massage therapy and a searchable directory of therapists nationwide.

- Massage Therapist Association of Alberta 1-888-848-6822

- Massage Therapists' Association of British Columbia 1-888-413-4467

- The College of Massage Therapists of British Columbia
  (604) 736-3404

- Massage Therapy Association of Manitoba (204) 254-0406

- New Brunswick Massotherapy Association Inc.
  (506) 459-5788

- Newfoundland Massage Therapists' Association
  (709) 726-4006

- Massage Therapists' Association of Nova Scotia
  (902) 429-2190

- The College of Massage Therapists of Ontario (416) 489-2626

- Ontario Massage Therapist Association (416) 979-2010

- Prince Edward Island Massage Therapy Association
  (902) 368-8140

- Massage Therapist Association of Saskatchewan
  (306) 384-7077

- Fédération Québécoise des Massothérapeutes (FQM)
  (514) 597-0505 or 1-800-363-9609

Visit: www.massage.ca

Naturopaths

If your parents are more comfortable with idea of using natural treatments, you'll probably want to continue their treatments or get in touch with a naturopath or doctor of naturopathic medicine.

Naturopaths focus on the prevention of illness and disease in the body. In their efforts for both prevention and treatment, they rely upon natural substances and methods and try to make the best of the body's own natural healing processes.

Under the guidance of a naturopath, clients can expect customized treatment plans that focus on all aspects of their lives, from the nutritional to the environmental, physical, and emotional.

In Canada, registered naturopathic practitioners must complete a full-time four-year program at an accredited medical college. Naturopathic practice is not regulated in all provinces, but in the provinces where it is, you may want to look to naturopathic doctors belonging to the Canadian Naturopathic Association (these doctors must pass a rigorous licensing examination in order to gain membership into the association).

Be sure to ask for your physician's advice if you have any concerns at all about combining traditional and naturopathic medicine!

Where to Find

Visit the Canadian Naturopathic Association's Web site for more information about naturopathic medicine and listings of their member practitioners across the country.

Canadian Naturopathic Association
1255 Sheppard Ave. East
North York, ON M2K 1E2
Phone: (416) 496-8633 or 1-800-551-4381
Fax: (416) 496-8634
E-mail: info@naturopathicassoc.ca
Visit: www.naturopathicassoc.ca

Occupational Therapists

Expect a practical, no-nonsense approach to planning and coping with the needs of older adults and their caregivers with these folks. Occupational therapists are all about providing and measuring improvements in what they call "skills for the job of living." Their mission: to ambitiously search out ways for people to lead more productive, satisfying, and independent lives. Timely recovery, optimum function, safe, ergonomically friendly living spaces, and the increased enjoyment of free time are high on their "to do" list.

Occupational therapists work in a wide variety of settings in the home and also in the community with organizations such as home-care programs, health boards, community health centres, hospitals, clinics, nursing homes, insurance companies, and long-term care and rehabilitation or treatment facilities. In recent years, a growing number of occupational therapists have become self-employed and offer service in both private and publicly funded areas of health care.

For families in the eldercare world, an occupational therapist is an invaluable team member. Not only will he or she assist in the management of mental health concerns (read stress, depression, loss of cognition), but will give straightforward advice and support for daily physical tasks like dressing, eating, mobility, and energy management and will be able to prescribe appropriate assistive devices. Occupational therapists will teach adaptations for activities of daily living, such as how to prepare a meal, make a bed, and get dressed.

A qualified occupational therapist should be registered with a provincial regulatory body.

Ask an occupational therapist to recommend appropriate resources for care and potential funding sources.

Where to Find

Your family doctor can refer you to an occupational therapist. A number of insurance companies offer occupational therapy as an extended health-care benefit and with a referral, occupational therapy is offered under Worker's Compensation.

Canadian Association of Occupational Therapists
CTTC Building, Suite 3400
1125 Colonel By Dr.
Ottawa, ON K1S 5R1
Phone: (613) 523-2268 or 1-800-434-2268
Fax: (613) 523-2552
Visit: www.caot.ca

Orthotists and Prosthetists

These health pros are the people your parents will see if they require devices to either support or replace certain body parts.

Orthotists set patients up with braces or splints—orthoses—in order to treat deformities or protect painful parts of the body. Orthotists also specialize in preparing custom arch supports, or orthotics for achy feet. Prosthetists, on the other hand, design and fit patients with artificial limbs, or prostheses.

The work of both orthotists and prosthetists is extremely detailed and patient-focused. All aids are custom designed and uniquely fitted to the patient. Both specialists will almost certainly work as part of a team with a patient's physician. The physician will write up a prescription for the needed device. A clinician will take measurements, and once the device has been made, the orthotist or prosthetist will carefully fit the device to the patient and make any necessary adjustments.

Where to Find

Referrals to an orthotist or prosthetist will come through a clinic or the physician. The Canadian Association of Prosthetists and Orthotists also has a listing of practicing members available on its Web site.

Canadian Association of Prosthetists and Orthotists
267 Edmonton St., Suite 303
Winnipeg, MB R3C 1S2
Phone: (204) 949-4972
Fax: (204) 947-3627
E-mail: capo@mb.sympatico.ca
Visit: www.pando.ca/capo.htm

Pharmacists

Given that Canadians over the age of 65 take an average of 10 prescription medications, there is no doubt that a pharmacist will form a crucial part of your caregiving team.

The most accessible health-care providers, pharmacists work in every community and are always available without an appointment. Pharmacists are medication experts with a unique knowledge of drugs, their side effects, and potential interactions. They are licensed health-care professionals with years of university training and practical experience. They often advise physicians and other medical practitioners regarding the selection, dosage, and side effects of prescription drugs. Pharmacists practice in community pharmacies (drug stores), hospitals, universities, pharmaceutical companies, and government.

Caregiver Hint: Choosing a pharmacist is as important as choosing your doctor. Always visit the same pharmacy. Take responsibility by learning as much as you can about your elder's conditions and stay informed as to how he or she should take medications properly.

Whether you are filling a prescription or choosing over-the-counter medicine to treat an illness, never leave the pharmacy before you know the answers to all your questions. According to the Canadian Pharmacists Association, these are some of the questions you might want to ask:

- Why is my parent taking this medication?

- What side effects might he/she experience and what should I do?

- If a dose is missed, what should we do?

- Where should we store medicine?

- How do you suggest they remember to take the medicine?

- Can we get medicine in a container that's easier to open?

- Is there another medicine that might be easier to swallow?

- Is it okay to take this with other medications?

- What should I do if my parent refuses to take any of the prescribed medicine?

- Who keeps my parent's medication records?

- What foods, alcohol, or other drugs should be avoided while taking this prescription?

Expenses: A dispensing fee is added to the cost of prescriptions to cover the pharmacist's services. In some cases, drugs may be covered by insurance, provincial health plans (called formularies), or Veterans Affairs (See Appendix 1). Check costs before ordering medication. You may wish to save money by requesting generic equivalents (i.e., non-name brand drugs).

Pharmacists can also recommend non-prescription, or over-the-counter, medications and health products. A number of pharmacies have expanded to offer a range of home health-care products and assistive devices.

Where to Find

While you're probably already familiar with the pharmacies in your area, you may want to take a look at the Canadian Pharmacists Association Web site for a wealth of information about pharmacists and what they can do for you.

Canadian Pharmacists Association
1785 Alta Vista Dr.
Ottawa, ON K1G 3Y6
Phone: 1-800-917-9489 or (613) 523-7877
Fax: (613) 523-0445
E-mail: info@pharmacists.ca
Visit: www.pharmacists.ca

Physiotherapists

If Mom suffers a fall and needs some help recuperating, or if she could simply use some help in moving about more freely and less painfully, a physiotherapist could be a key resource!

Physiotherapy, or physical therapy, concerns itself with the assessment, maintenance, and restoration of the physical function and performance of the body. Depending on the issue, physiotherapy may be performed in isolation or in conjunction with other types of medical management and surgical techniques. Physiotherapy helps to provide a speedy and complication-free return to normal activity levels.

Using a variety of different techniques, physiotherapists treat a wide range of injuries and ailments. Often, the causes of pain and dysfunction are obvious, but sometimes things are not so black and white. For example, a stroke patient may be discharged from the hospital and need many services. Physical therapists will help with strengthening exercises, especially for the muscles on the affected side, and also to improve balance and walking.

At your parent's first physio appointment, expect the physiotherapist to test to identify the source of the problem. Treatment strategies will most often involve various exercises and programs to encourage movement. Also expect to be introduced to all sorts of fitness gizmos along with other types of equipment such as walking aids and splints.

Where to Find

Check out the Canadian Physiotherapy Association's Web site for a searchable database of physiotherapists across the country.

Canadian Physiotherapy Association
2345 Yonge St., Suite 410
Toronto, ON M4P 2E5
Phone: (416) 932-1888 or 1-800-387-8679
Fax: (416) 932-9708
E-mail: information@physiotherapy.ca
Visit: www.physiotherapy.ca

Psychiatrists

Depression, dementia, Alzheimer's disease, and late-life schizophrenia are just a few of the conditions related to mental health that may cause concern for older adults. A psychiatrist, a doctor who specializes in the diagnosis and treatment of mental and emotional disorders, will play a key role in the provision of care for an elderly person.

Geriatric psychiatrists are especially focused on the mental health needs of the elderly and recognize their special circumstances and unique needs. They are often involved with counselling family members who are concerned or worried about their parent's unusual or declining behaviour patterns.

Psychiatrists aim to treat mental health issues by way of identifying the possible causes of disorders and tailoring treatments to an individual patient's needs. They provide treatment primarily by way of prescription medications and psychotherapy. Psychiatrists often work in consultation with psychologists, social workers, and family doctors in order to coordinate the best treatment for their patients.

Where to Find

Contact your family doctor or local hospital for a referral to a psychiatrist in your area.

Real Estate Agents (With Services for Seniors)

Smart real estate agents are beginning to recognize the value of providing services that recognize the needs of families with aging parents. More counsellor-driven than sales focused, these innovators know how to assemble a team of advisers—financial planners, lawyers, accountants, etc.—to meet an older client's particular needs. These agents will be able to help you answer questions like these: How do we deal with inheritance tax on the sale of a house or rental properties? Should we take a reverse mortgage to pay for short-run care? How do we find or create a house that is accessible and safe? Can someone help us to clear up and move out prior to selling the house?

Many of today's agents are on the hunt for accessible homes with granny flats or in-law apartments and senior-friendly layouts.

A new breed of corporate-move adviser will also take your eldercare needs into account if your company transfers you. Check Royal LePage—their eldercare service program may allow you to access a variety of eldercare services and support from your company's moving benefits program.

Where to Find

Canadian Real Estate Association
344 Slater St., Suite 1600
Ottawa, ON K1R 7Y3
Phone: (613) 237-7111
Fax: (613) 234-2567
Visit: www.crea.ca

Note: www.mls.ca has house listings and a realtor search sponsored by the Canadian Real Estate Association

Royal LePage
Visit: www.royallepage.ca

Registered Nurses and Registered Nursing Assistants

Registered nurses are well prepared to play a major role in the provision of health care for any elderly person. Nurses have a positive impact, working in a number of environments from hospitals and health clinics to doctors' offices and home-care settings. They are integral team players in the current shift from facility-based to home care.

These days, the education and qualification level of nurses varies depending on their specific functions and areas of specialization. These include health promotion and prevention and clinical treatment, as well as identification of need, rehabilitation, and palliative care. In the past, you may have encountered a nurse only if your parents needed to visit the hospital, whereas today you may come to rely on a home-care nurse if your parents' needs are complex or palliative. Nurses will also be on hand to educate the patient and family on the medication regime.

Highly skilled nurses closely monitor not only the treatment during this time, but also watch for any complications that may occur in those patients who are often very ill and at risk for complications.

Nurses draw samples of the patient's blood to check the therapeutic antibiotic levels and communicate results to the physician. Also, teaching patients and caregivers to manage IV antibiotic therapy while the nurse closely monitors the patient is an additional nursing responsibility.

Home Care Services provide not only physical but also emotional and social support for homebound patients.

Where to Find

Finding a nurse to work with your family can be done through home-care programs and in facilities across the country (Of note: There is an increasing shortage of nurses, particularly outside urban centres.) Nurses can be found through provincial health-care programs, nursing agencies, family practice clinics, and long-term care facilities.

Respiratory Therapists

Heart attack and stroke can significantly affect older people's ability to breathe. Smoking, as well as ongoing conditions such as asthma and emphysema, are also concerns for many elderly people. If your parents are having trouble with their breathing, they will likely require the help of a respiratory therapist.

Respiratory therapists are health-care professionals who provide assistance to physicians in the assessment, diagnosis, treatment, and care of patients with lung and breathing disorders. Respiratory therapists are concerned with most medical and technical treatment involving breathing health, from administering drugs requiring inhalation, to assisting in CPR, to the provision of breathing aids and life support to those who can no longer breathe on their own.

While most respiratory therapists work in hospitals, many are now involved in home care for those with chronic lung diseases and other respiratory ailments.

Where to Find

While you'll probably be placed in touch with a respiratory therapist through your doctor or a hospital, you can find out more about what they do from their professional association:

The Canadian Society of Respiratory Therapists
102-1785 Alta Vista Dr.
Ottawa, ON K1G 3Y6
Phone: (613) 731-3164 or 1-800-267-3422
Fax: (613) 521-4314
E-mail: info@csrt.com
Visit: www.csrt.com

Social Workers

If there are times when you feel that you or your family could use some solid support and guidance, consider enlisting the help of a social worker. Social workers can provide you with more than counselling and advice; they are in tune with the needs of community members and are also experts at facilitating access to a wide range of convenient, helpful resources.

Social work recognizes the multiple, complex transactions between people and their environments. Its mission is to enable all people to fully develop their potential, enrich their lives, and prevent dysfunction. Often in solidarity with those who are disadvantaged, social work strives to promote social inclusion while recognizing the capacity of people to both be affected by and alter the many influences upon them. These health-care veterans looks at the barriers, inequity, and injustices in society and are trained to respond to crises and emergencies as well as to everyday personal and social problems.

When you engage the help of a social worker, expect counselling, family treatment, and holistic therapy. Social workers' ability and comfort level in making concerted interventions to arrange community support are key. In a time of crisis or difficult transition, call a social worker for assistance with coping skills. They'll listen, resolve, and connect families with the right local services and support.

Where to Find

Social workers work in a wide variety of public settings, though an increasing number of social workers also work in private practice. You should easily be able to access a social worker through your family doctor, local hospital, or Ministry of Health Office. For more information about the profession, contact the Canadian Association of Social Workers.

Canadian Association of Social Workers
383 Parkdale Ave., Suite 402
Ottawa, ON K1Y 4R4
Phone: (613) 729-6668
Fax: (613) 729-9608
E-mail: casw@casw-acts.ca
Visit: www.casw-acts.ca

Speech-Language Pathologists

Speech, language, and swallowing problems often accompany medical disorders associated with aging such as stroke, aphasia, and dysphagia. Sudden or even gradual loss of speaking and verbal ability can be devastating. However, in some cases, speech-language pathologists may be able to help your elderly loved ones improve or maintain their communication skills.

Speech-language pathologists assess and treat persons with speech, language, voice, swallowing, and fluency disorders. Depending on the patient's condition, a speech-language pathologist may select an alternative communication system that the patient and caregivers learn and use.

Because coping with decreased communication ability can be extremely difficult both for the people affected and their loved ones, speech-language pathologists also focus on helping caregivers and relatives become better, more effective communication partners.

Where to Find

While you will probably want to ask your family doctor or nurse for a referral to a qualified speech-language pathologist in your area, you may also want to visit the Web site of the Canadian Association of Speech-Language Pathologists and Audiologists, which has a coast-to-coast listing of practitioners.

Canadian Association of Speech-Language Pathologists and Audiologists
401-200 Elgin St.
Ottawa, ON K2P 1L5
Phone: (613) 567-9968 or 1-800-259-8519
Fax: (613) 567-2859
E-mail: caslpa@caslpa.ca <mailto:caslpa@caslpa.ca>
Visit: www.caslpa.ca/english/index.asp

Recreation Programmers/Therapists

Recreational therapists focus on the emotional, physical, and mental well-being of patients and provide treatment by way of various recreational activities. When working with the elderly, depending on the person's ability, recreational therapists may suggest treatment through sports, dance, and other movement as well as drama and music. Recreational therapists may also employ arts and crafts, animals, and games in their work.

Recreational therapists often work with patients with particular illnesses or disabilities in helping to improve their well-being and integration into society. Recreational therapy is not just about organizing fun and games; the key idea here is treatment through recreation.

Recreational therapists generally have a bachelor's degree in recreation with a specialty in therapeutic recreation. You're most likely to find a recreational therapist working in organized settings for older adults such as nursing homes or adult day centres.

Where to Find

Depending on where you live, it may be easier to join a local program at the community centre. Contact your doctor or local community centre for information on locations where recreational therapy services are available.

Further Reading

Making the Case for Care Managers

Jocelyn M. Jones, RN

Need help in getting proper care? Case managers may be the answer.

Navigating your way through the health-care system and accessing the support services you need at home or in the community isn't always easy. Your family has enough to deal with, helping someone recover from a major illness or cope with a long-term chronic disease. You don't need the added stress. Where do you find help or get the services you need?

Getting proper care for yourself or someone you love should be as easy as picking up the telephone. People tell us that it involves numerous phone calls, often getting too much or too little information. Quite simply, they say, the system is not user friendly.

There are answers, however. Many health/social service agencies or organizations working with disease or trauma-related situations provide case management services. In Ontario, the most familiar of these agencies are the Community Care Access Centres, or CCACs, in your area. Others include the Workers Safety and Insurance Bureau, home support agencies, insurance companies, and not-for-profit agencies working with specific illnesses (e.g., the MS Society).

Developed initially in the social and mental health community, case management is an approach to providing the care and service for people in a way that recognizes the client's preferences and makes the most efficient use of fiscal resources. People receive services in their home in a manner that meets their needs, preferences, values, and priorities.

Who are case managers?
The case manager is frequently a nurse, a therapist, a social worker, or other health-care professional who has done a great deal of community work and is knowledgeable not only about people, disease, and families, but also about systems, funding, eligibility, and the dynamics between key members of the care plan. The case manager is primarily responsible for organizing health and social services in the home.

As a resource for consumers and their families, physicians, and health and social service professionals, the case manager has skills in assessment, facilitation, collaboration, and problem solving to assist in planning and activating the services people require.

The case manager can effect an earlier discharge, find resources that are required (supplies, equipment, and specialized services), and encourage family-supported day-to-day care.

Also called a care co-ordinator or care manager, this individual is a health/social service professional.

The cost of case management is part of the service provided by applicable funding sources such as provincial governments. Insurance companies also provide case management services as part of their service, particularly when catastrophic illnesses or trauma occurs. In addition, private case management companies are developing throughout Canada. Clients are billed an agreed hourly rate and pay independently for these services.

How do you connect with a case manager?

Case management has been an almost invisible component of Canada's home care for many years. Families seeking out these services should ensure that the case manager belongs to their professional association (such as the Ontario Case Managers Association) and follows the guiding principles of their profession.

A knowledgeable, caring case manager will provide the support, links, and resources for families in need. To find a qualified case manager:

- Contact your family physician or health-care professional.

- Contact the local CCAC, Regional Health Authority, or relevant community service organization.

- In Ontario, call the Ontario Case Managers Association at (905) 727-3932 or (905) 727-9011.

Jocelyn M. Jones, RN, is past president of the Ontario Case Managers Association.

Source: Solutions Magazine

How Can Case Management Help?

Your 84-year-old mother is living alone in a seniors building. She accidentally burns dinner, setting off the building smoke alarms, resulting in a 911 call. This is the second incident. To top it off, on your last visit Mom just didn't seem as sharp as usual.

Contacting the local CCAC, you are referred to a case manager. The case manager will ensure that your mother and the family have all the information required to initiate services. Questions will be answered related to costs, funding, etc. The case manager will assist you and your mother every step of the way, or provide the information to allow you to access the resources. The case manager will also assist in locating and arranging for special services, supplies, and equipment when needed. Each client and situation will be assessed individually with the appropriate resources and service plan recommended.

Room
by Room

*Here's my heads-up guide to six key areas of the house where
there are usually issues of accessibility and/or safety*

1. Getting Inside

Problem: Steps are difficult to climb.

Solution: • Rebuild or replace steps if too narrow or too steep.
Add non-slip surfaces.

• Repair broken or loose steps.

• Build a ramp to create an alternative route.

• Add sturdy handrails on both sides (should extend
beyond the first and last step).

Problem: Ramp is unsafe or slippery.

Solution: • Install handrails on both sides and extend porch to
provide weather protection.

• Reduce the slope of the ramp.

• Add level platforms for landing spots at top and bottom of ramp.

• Add edge protection to keep wheelchair, crutches,
cane, or walker from slipping off edge.

2. Kitchen

Problem: Counters are too high to be able to work comfortably
from a seated position.

Solution:
- Use pull-out cutting board as lowered work surface.
- Place board across top of open drawer.
- Use lap tray for food preparation area.
- Pull kitchen table or card table near existing kitchen to create seated work area.
- Remove base cabinet(s) and install lower counter or table for seated work area; lower upper cabinet(s) above work area to create reachable storage.
- Install cabinets and counters that can be raised or lowered electrically.

Problem: Sink faucets are hard to reach from wheelchair.

Solution:
- Replace separate hot and cold faucets with single-lever control.
- Add extension arm to single-lever faucet.
- Remove floor of sink cabinet and centre doorstop to create knee access (attach doorstop to back side of door to keep cabinet appearance) and insulate pipes to prevent burns.

Problem: Can't reach items stored in refrigerator or freezer.

Solution:
- Use lazy susan to make items accessible.
- Use a reacher.
- Purchase a side-by-side refrigerator/freezer for easier access.
- Select a refrigerator that has a water and ice dispenser in the door.
- Purchase a small refrigerator for supplementary storage next to the seated work area.
- Ask someone else to transfer items from a chest freezer to the freezer section of refrigerator once a week.

Problem: The existing kitchen is too large for the wheelchair user.

Solution: • Create "mini-kitchen" that allows the wheelchair user to reach everything from one spot.

• Include in the mini-kitchen a microwave oven, portable appliances, and essential supplies and utensils; store small items on countertop shelf unit or rolling cart.

3. Living Areas

Problem: Windows and window coverings are hard to open and operate.

Solution: • Clear floor space in front of window so controls are easier to reach.

• Install auxiliary handle on bottom sash of double-hung windows.

• Replace double-hung windows with casement-style windows.

• Install mini-blinds with long wand.

• Install power-operated windows and draperies.

Problem: Your elder has trouble getting out of a chair or sofa.

Solution: • Place a pneumatic seat lifter in chair.

• Use chair that has sturdy arms.

• Raise chair or sofa on wood blocks.

Problem: Good furniture, walls, and woodwork are becoming damaged by the wheelchair.

Solution: • Move fragile or valuable furniture to protected location.

• Staple carpet remnants around doorframes.

• Make sleeves from carpet remnants to protect chair legs.

• Install more durable furniture.

• Use corner guards, carpet (wainscotting), and Plexiglass sheets to protect walls.

• Add rubber bumpers to footplates.

4. Bedrooms

Problem: Bedroom on the upper floor is not accessible.

Solution: • Relocate the bedroom on an accessible floor.

• Place the bed in one end of large room on accessible floor and use bookcases or screens to create privacy.

• Use a daybed in the living room to create a sofa by day and a bed by night.

• Install a stairlift to another floor (requires a transfer to and from the lift).

• Install a chair lift to another floor (lifts both wheelchair and person).

• Install residential elevator; elevator shaft can be located outside house by converting windows to access doors.

5. Bathrooms

Problem: You or your elder are worried about the prospect of falling in the bathroom, especially when taking a bath or shower.

Solution: • Install grab bars near the tub and shower (be sure grab bars are securely fastened into wall studs).

• Replace existing shower head with a hand-held shower to bathe while seated.

• Purchase bath bench that straddles tub (two legs inside, two legs outside).

• Use hydraulic seat or boom lift to transfer in and out of tub.

• Install transfer shower with built-in seat.

• Install roll-in shower (requires transfer to shower chair).

• Build combination shower/toilet compartment so toilet can be used as shower seat.

6. Laundry

Problem: Your parent or friend can't use stairs to reach laundry area in basement.

Solution: • Move existing laundry equipment to accessible floor.

  • Replace existing equipment with stacked washer-dryer unit located on accessible floor.

Problem: Can't reach controls on laundry equipment.

Solution: • Use reacher to operate controls.

  • Purchase laundry equipment that has touch controls or front controls.

  • Purchase front-loading washer and dryer for easier access.

  • Raise laundry machines on platforms.

Index

The author (right) with her mother

About the Author

Caroline Tapp–McDougall is the publisher of *Solutions* magazine, a Canadian publication dedicated to the wellness of seniors, their caregivers and family. The author has a background in health care communications and extensive editorial experience in the areas of health, wellness, and medical writing. She is also a respected speaker at conferences and events across Canada and hosts a daily radio health segment. Caroline and her brother provide care for her mother, who is stroke-disabled and living in a long-term care facility. Ms Tapp-McDougall is also the mother of three and resides with her family in Toronto, Ontario.